FEEL THE SPIRIT

FEEL THE SPIRIT

STUDIES IN NINETEENTH-CENTURY AFRO-AMERICAN MUSIC

EDITED BY
GEORGE R. KECK
AND
SHERRILL V. MARTIN

CONTRIBUTIONS IN AFRO-AMERICAN
AND AFRICAN STUDIES,
NUMBER 119

GREENWOOD PRESS
NEW YORK • WESTPORT, CONNECTICUT • LONDON

Library of Congress Cataloging-in-Publication Data

Feel the Spirit : studies in nineteenth-century Afro-American music /
   edited by George R. Keck and Sherrill V. Martin.
      p. cm. — (Contributions in Afro-American and African
studies, ISSN 0069-9624 ; no. 119)
   Bibliography: p.
   Includes index.
   ISBN 0-313-26234-9 (lib. bdg. : alk. paper)
   1. Afro-Americans—Music—19th century—History and criticism—
Congresses. 2. Music—United States—History and criticism—
Congresses. 3. Afro-American musicians—Congresses. I. Keck,
George Russell. II. Martin, Sherrill V. III. Series.
ML3556.F43 1988
781.7'296073—dc 19   88-15485

British Library Cataloguing in Publication Data is available.

Library of Congress Catalog Card Number: 88-15485
ISBN: 0-313-26234-9
ISSN: 0069-9624

First published in 1988

Greenwood Press, Inc.
88 Post Road West, Westport, Connecticut 06881

Printed in the United States of America

The paper used in this book complies with the
Permanent Paper Standard issued by the National
Information Standards Organization (Z39.48-1984).

10 9 8 7 6 5 4 3 2 1

Contents

Preface

This volume is an outgrowth of two seminars sponsored by
The National Endowment for the Humanities at Harvard University in the summers of 1982 and 1986. The seminars,
entitled "Afro-American Musicians in the Nineteenth
Century," were the conception of Dr. Eileen Southern, Professor of Music and of Afro-American Studies at Harvard
University. Dr. Southern fulfilled the role of seminar
director, mentor, and friend.

The seminars provided a unique opportunity for scholars
from different disciplines united by a common bond of
interest in the history of Afro-American music to meet
together for an eight-week period to study and to conduct
original research. The first seminar brought together
eleven scholars and the second twelve scholars. Utilizing
the vast collections of the Harvard University libraries
and of other libraries and archives in the Boston area,
participants pursued research covering many different
aspects of the seminar topic. Ten of the papers resulting
from the seminar work were revised for publication in this
volume.

Dr. Southern and participants in the seminars believe
that these papers are in the forefront of scholarship in
nineteenth-century Afro-American music and contain new
facts and insights which deserve wider dissemination. Dr.
Southern, therefore, asked us, two participants from the
second seminar with some editorial experience, to investi-
gate the possibility of publishing a volume of selected
papers. We approached Marilyn Brownstein, Humanities
Editor of Greenwood Press, with the idea for such a publication, and she encouraged us to pursue an anthology
utilizing papers from both seminars covering a wide range
of topics. The essays chosen for inclusion illustrate the
broad scope of activity of Afro-American musicians in the
second half of the nineteenth century.

Many persons contributed suggestions that are reflected
in the final draft of this book. The editors are especially grateful to Dr. Eileen Southern for guidance and
advice in all stages of the research; to Sandra Merkey of
Ouachita Baptist University for her help in typing and

proofreading; to the staffs of the Computer Centers at the University of North Carolina, Wilmington, and Ouachita Baptist University for help with computer printing of the many drafts of the essays and the final manuscript; and to Emma Jean Turner, Professor of Office Administration at Ouachita Baptist University for her constant help and advice at every stage in the development and preparation of the computer-generated manuscript of this book.

We wish to thank all the contributors, who patiently answered pleas for help, answered questions, and read with such care the drafts of their essays. It was a constant source of pleasure to work with such willing scholars and, through our many telephone conversations, to become personal friends with our colleagues.

Introduction

The papers in this anthology are about the experiences of
Afro-American musicians during the last four decades of the
nineteenth century. While each paper individually ex-
plores one facet of that experience, the papers collec-
tively reveal much about the cultural and musical changes
that took place for black musicians during this era.
Building on the foundations of the fertile black culture
established before the Civil War, musicians after the war
entered upon a period of activity filled with confidence in
their abilities, pride in their accomplishments, and the
determination to make significant contributions to the
cultural order in a new land of freedom and opportunity.

Although Afro-Americans were proud of their heritage,
views about blacks held by many white Americans around 1860
were based on two types of slave impersonations developed
in Ethiopian Minstrelsy. One stereotype was that of the
plantation slave, referred to as Jim Crow, with his ragged
clothes and thick dialect. The other portrayed the
strutting urban dandy, dressed in fine clothes and
identified as Zip Coon. Minstrelsy exploited the music and
dancing of slaves and caricatured slave life through jokes
and skits.

There are, however, several factors that reveal a
different picture of black culture before the war. While
the Civil War brought an end to bondage for four million
people, approximately one-half million blacks were already
free before the war. Some of these people formed middle and
upper classes which developed a substantial culture of a
high level. The early efforts of black cultural leaders in
such cities as New Orleans, Boston, New York, Charleston,
and Philadelphia were especially important in establishing
a foundation for developments after the war. In addition,
the influence of black churches and the success of several
talented individuals in achieving careers in music were
important parts of pre-Civil War musical activity for
blacks.

Beginning in the late seventeenth century, slaves
and free black musicians performed for military and
social occasions for blacks and whites. Frank Johnson

(1792-1844) was a celebrity in both communities in
Philadelphia. He established a reputation as a conductor
of military and dance bands and was the first black to
publish sheet music in America. In 1837 he took his band
to England for a tour. During the 1840s, Johnson conducted
concerts in Philadelphia in which both white and black
musicians participated as performers.(1)

Many performers, including those associated with Frank
Johnson, were active as composers. Aaron J. R. Connor,
James Hemmenway, Isaac Hazzard, and William Appo were well
known in Philadelphia. Joseph William Postlewaite was
active in St. Louis; Thomas J. Martin worked in New
Orleans; and the Lambert brothers, Lucien and Sydney, born
in New Orleans, studied and published works in Paris.

Some musicians achieved fame and established professional careers as concert artists. Elizabeth Taylor
Greenfield (ca1824-1876) was the first noted black concert
singer. She began her career in 1851 and remained active
throughout the 1860s. Greenfield's student, Thomas Bowers
(ca1826-1885), also achieved an outstanding career as a
singer, as did his sister, Sarah Sedgewick Bowers.

The most important centers for black culture before
1860 were the black churches, which were not only centers
of worship but also centers for amusement, relaxation, and
instruction. According to Eileen Southern, the black
church "is to be credited with laying the foundation for
black musical activity in the United States--secular as
well as sacred."(2) The black churches provided musical
training at Sabbath Schools, especially instruction in
reading music; singing schools were held there; periodic
lectures on sacred music were given there. And, perhaps
most important of all, churches often organized schools for
the children of black communities.

The churches also sponsored concerts. As early as 1827
these concerts were already common; programs were often
published in the newspapers of both the white and black
communities. Such concerts offered black musicians the
opportunity to perform the serious concert repertory of the
day and enabled audiences to hear the best musicians of
their own race performing the finest music literature.

With these black cultural foundations in place before
the war, combined with the new awareness of the richness of
their legacy and the promise of their future that developed
during the war, black musicians entered an unprecedented
era of optimism and activity when the war ended.

Black Americans had actively contributed to the dramatic events leading to emancipation. During the war, they
acted as soldiers and sailors, in addition to their service
in military bands. Northern soldiers, journalists, and
missionaries who came to the South during and immediately
after the war discovered and recorded the rich musical and
religious heritage of Southern blacks in newspapers,
journals, and letters. The first publication of slave
songs appeared in 1861; by 1867 collections of these songs
were published. In their music the slaves documented their
culture and consciousness, often including references to
the war itself.

While the publication of the songs brought attention to

this previously unknown repertory, singing tours by groups such as the Fisk Jubilee Singers further helped in the public recognition and acceptance of the slave songs. Beginning in 1871, the Fisk Jubilee Singers embarked on a series of tours to raise money to aid Fisk University. The beauty of the music and the sincerity of the performances led to wide acceptance by whites of this rich body of music and the black singers who performed it. In addition, the concert world began to draw on the spirituals as a source of repertory. It became standard practice to end concert programs with "folk" music.

The spirituals served as a source for collections such as that by Marshall W. Taylor entitled *A Collection of Revival Hymns and Plantation Melodies*. Taylor did not publish his work to preserve the musical authenticity of the songs as sung in black congregations of the time or to provide a repertory for concert singers--he published his collection as a surviving memorial of the history of the blacks.   Spirituals continued to unite the experiences of black Americans in the twentieth century with those of preceding generations.   After World War II gospel singers revived the spirituals because of the textual content. The spiritual texts that spoke of the hardships and struggles of slavery were a source of strength and encouragement during the turmoil of the civil rights movement.   These texts provided a source for borrowing for modern gospel songs.

Performances of the music of the black oral tradition provided only one outlet for public appearances by black performers.   They also embarked in greater numbers on careers as solo concert artists. The World Peace Jubilee organized by Patrick S. Gilmore in 1872 in Boston was an important turning point in the acceptance of black performers. According to Eileen Southern this was a decisive event, because for the first time black musicians were put on the concert stage as equals with white musicians.(3) Gilmore featured black artists as soloists and as members of the choir and orchestra, giving them exposure in several different musical roles.

Other great public events, such as the Centennial of American Independence at Philadelphia and the World's Colombian Exposition at Chicago in 1893, also provided black entertainers opportunities to appear before the American public. Black churches continued to sponsor concerts, but opportunities for black singers in opera performances and lieder recitals were limited.

During this period concert managers began to notice talented black performers and to include them as clients in professional concert management bureaus. James Redpath, founder of the Redpath Lyceum Bureau in Boston in 1869, was one of the first to include black entertainers among those whose careers he managed. In addition, he managed the lecture career of Henry Ward Beecher and the concert career of Patrick S. Gilmore, both of whom recommended outstanding black performers to the Bureau.

James G. Bergen built his entire career on the management of black concert artists. He conceived the original idea of the "star concert" in which he presented a famous

prima donna on a program with artists of local reputation.
Several blacks were also successful in the management business, notably William Dupree and James Trotter. Ednorah
Nahar successfully managed her own career as an elocutionist and later managed the careers of others.

In the last decades of the century five black female
prima donnas gained international fame and several more had
successful careers of lesser stature. Nellie Brown
Mitchell and Marie Selika Williams, both formally trained,
were among the first to achieve international renown. Each
began her career performing in local churches.

Equally important were the Hyers sisters, Anna Madah
and Emma Louise. The Hyers appeared successfully on both
the concert and minstrel stage and toured with their own
companies which at various times included the Luca
brothers, John and Alexander, Wallace King, and Sam Lucas.
They also sang for Gilmore's World Peace Jubilee and
appeared on the lyceum circuit for the Redpath Lyceum
Bureau. In many ways the Hyers sisters were pioneers,
because they were able to tour with their own concert
company, to sing the traditional nineteenth-century concert
repertory, and to accomplish both successfully.

Black male concert singers found it more difficult to
succeed on the concert stage than did the prima donnas.
They were more likely to find acceptance in minstrel shows,
traveling concert troupes, and musico-dramatic productions.
Sidney Woodward and Thomas J. Bowers are notable exceptions. Bowers began his career before the war and achieved
fame throughout the East and Midwest before his death in
1885. Woodward studied in both the United States and in
Europe and sustained an international reputation as a performer.

All-black minstrel shows were one of the most important
avenues for success for performers after the war. While
troupes of black entertainers were in existence before the
war, it was in 1865 that the first permanent black minstrel
troupe was formed.(4) These black minstrels included the
singing of spirituals in their shows, providing a link with
one of the most important legacies of black music. In
addition, black minstrel shows provided a training ground
for many young performers who started their careers as
minstrels and developed into stage performers with national
reputations.

Sam Lucas was probably the most famed performer of this
type. Known for his good looks and abilities as a singer
and actor, he moved easily back-and-forth between the
worlds of the minstrel show and the stage. As noted above,
he performed with the Hyers sisters and appeared in their
dramatic productions for the Redpath Lyceum Bureau. He
also achieved a reputation as a song-writer and capped his
career with a production of *Uncle Tom's Cabin* for World
Films in 1914.

The minstrel show also offered opportunities for the
development of instrumental music. The minstrel band was
one of the favorite attractions of the shows. Important
performers and conductors such as P. G. Lowery and W. C.
Handy began their careers playing for these bands and
achieved fame for the virtuosity of their performances and

for the excellence of the bands they organized.

The period from 1860 to 1900 was one of great optimism, hope, pride, and accomplishment for black musicians. In spite of obstacles to success there were unprecedented opportunities. When one avenue to success was closed to them, these resourceful and determined musicians found another outlet for their considerable talents. By the time the century ended, blacks had contributed more and accomplished more in the field of music than in any other. The papers in this anthology document the significance of their achievement.

NOTES

1. Eileen Southern, *The Music of Black Americans: A History*, 2d ed. (New York: Norton, 1983), 110.

2. Eileen Southern, "Musical Practices in Black Churches of Philadelphia and New York, ca. 1800-1844," *Journal of the American Musicological Society*, 1977, 298.

3. Stated in a conversation with George Keck, April 17, 1988.

4. Southern, *Music of Black Americans*, 229.

Music of Black Americans During the War Years, 1861-1865

SHERRILL V. MARTIN

On March 7, 1864, the *New York Times* published the following editorial:

> There has been no more striking manifestation of the marvelous times that are upon us than the scene in our streets at the departure of the first of our colored regiments. . . . Eight months ago the African race in this City [New York] were literally hunted down like wild beasts. When caught, they were shot down in cold blood, or stoned to death, or hung to the trees or the lamp-posts.
>
> How astonishingly has all this been changed! The same men who could not have shown themselves in the most obscure street in the city without peril of instant death, now march in solid platoons to the pealing strains of martial music. . . .
>
> It is only by such occasions that we can at all realize the prodigious revolution which the public mind everywhere is experiencing.(1)

Few events in American history match the drama of this "prodigious revolution" for the four million blacks in the United States. The active participation of black Americans in the Civil War not only won for them the right to fight as soldiers and sailors, but also enabled them to enlist in military bands and to pursue successful careers as concert and stage artists. In addition, when Northern soldiers, journalists, and missionaries came to the South, they discovered the black man's rich musical and religious heritage. In numerous newspapers, journals, letters, and other wartime documents, they recorded the music of the freedmen. These reports, and the songs themselves, constitute a valuable chronicle of black Americans during the Civil War: their joys and sorrows, their thoughts and reactions during their struggle for freedom.

When the Confederates fired on Fort Sumter, Lincoln called for seventy-five thousand volunteers "to put down combinations too powerful to be suppressed by the ordinary judicial proceedings." Numerous blacks in Boston, Providence, New York, Philadelphia, Cleveland, and Detroit, including the members of a superior band, immediately sought to enlist; they were rejected.(2)

Denied the opportunity to serve as soldiers, blacks sought other means to aid the war effort. In their music they had already expressed their struggle for freedom. Harriet Tubman, "the Moses of her people" and perhaps the most famous conductor of the Underground Railroad, used spirituals as signal songs while leading more than three hundred slaves to freedom. Sojourner Truth, who served as a spy for many Union regiments, raised money and solicited gifts for distribution in Union camps by singing and lecturing in various Northern states. And William Wells Brown, a noted lecturer and vocalist, published *The Anti-Slavery Harp*, a collection of forty-eight anti-slavery songs used at abolitionist meetings.(3)

Southern blacks were not spared from war service. Many officers took their body servants with them into battle. In the regiment of General John B. Gordon, Josephus Blake and two other servants provided the fife-and-drum marching music. Blake, a snare drummer, had acquired his skill by imitating the white drummer of a regiment which had once drilled near his master's plantation.(4)

Other Southern slaves and freedmen served as cooks, hospital attendants, stretcher bearers, and railroad workers. As they erected artillery foundations, built forts, and dug entrenchments, they reflected their wartime activities in their music. When General Pierre G. T. Beauregard took the slaves from the South Carolina islands to build the fortifications at Hilton Head and Bay Point, their song, *Many Thousand Go*, was heard for the first time.(5)

One of the first steps towards the permanent abolition of slavery occurred on May 24, 1861, when Major-General Benjamin F. Butler extended protection to three slaves who crossed the Union lines at Fortress Monroe, declaring them "contraband of war."(6) As news of his decision circulated, many slaves gained freedom by flocking into Fortress Monroe and Hampton, Virginia, the area where African slaves had first been brought to America in August 1619.(7)

The contrabands were put to work on the fortifications and given food, but were in dire need of other forms of assistance. In September 1861 the Reverend Lewis C. Lockwood, an employee of the Young Men's Christian Association (YMCA), was sent by the American Missionary Association to Fortress Monroe.(8) One of his immediate accomplishments was to transcribe Tubman's signal song, *Go Down Moses*. He published the first stanza in the *National Anti-Slavery Standard* on October 12.(9) By December 2 he sent the complete text, some twenty stanzas, to the YMCA secretary in New York, who forwarded it to the New York *Tribune*. *Go Down Moses*, printed in its entirety in the *Tribune*, was the first published spiritual;(10) a sheet-music edition, offered by the *National Anti-Slavery Standard* on December 14, 1861, was the first black spiritual published with music.(11)

On February 7, 1862, the Education Commission for Freedmen was formed in Boston to recruit teachers, missionaries, and superintendents for the contrabands. In its first year ninety-seven teachers and superintendents were sent to Port Royal, South Carolina, which had fallen to Union forces. One of these teachers was Charles P. Ware, the largest contributor to *Slave Songs of the United States* (1867), the first publication of a collection of spirituals and plantation songs. Other contributors included Ware's cousin, William Francis Allen; Lucy McKim; Laura Towne; and Charlotte Forten, a young black teacher from a free, upper-class Philadelphia family. Another Sea Islands teacher, Elizabeth Botume, wrote *First Days Amongst the Contrabands* (1893), which also contains much useful information about the music of the ex-slaves.

There was one abortive effort by northerners to recruit these freedmen for service. On May 7, 1862, Sergeant C. T. Trowbridge of the New York Volunteer Engineers was detailed to recruit South Carolina blacks for the Hunter Regiment. After four months in camp at Hilton Head, the regiment, plagued by lack of pay and desertions, was forced to disband.(12) Nevertheless, one black soldier wept in song about losing the detachment:(13)

> O Lord, I want some valiant soldier,
> I want some valiant soldier,
> I want some valiant soldier,
> To help me bear de cross.
>
> For I weep, I weep,
> I can't hold out;
> If any mercy, Lord,
> O pity poor me.(14)

A major step towards freedom occurred on July 17, 1862, when Congress passed the Confiscation and Militia Acts, allowing blacks to enlist as soldiers. On November 7, 1862, the First South Carolina Volunteers, commanded by Colonel Thomas Wentworth Higginson, became the first slave regiment mustered into the service of the United States. Colonel Higginson, a Harvard graduate, minister, and noted abolitionist, wrote one of the most valuable source books about the musical activities of black soldiers during the war, *Army Life in a Black Regiment*.

The First South Carolina Regiment was musically adept and versatile. On April 1, 1863, Colonel Higginson described his troops on picket:

> talking and singing are allowed, and of this privilege
> . . . they eagerly availed themselves. . . . Grave
> little boys, blacker than ink, shook hands with our
> laughing and utterly unmanageable drummers, who

greeted them with this sure word of prophecy, "Dem's de
drummers for de nex' war!" . . . Meantime the singing
was brisk along the whole column. . . . Such an odd
mixture of things, military and missionary, as the
successive waves of song drifted by. First,   *John
Brown*, of course; then, *What make old Satan for follow
me so*? then, *Marching Along*; then, *Hold your light on
Canaan's shore*; then, *When this   cruel war is   over* (a
new favorite, sung by a few).(15)

The soldiers learned *Marching Along* from Quartermaster
Bingham, and when the song's first words, "Gird on the
armor," became stumbling blocks, "some ingenious ear
substituted 'Guide on de army,' which was at once
accepted."(16) Colonel Higginson, himself, may have
introduced *John Brown* to his soldiers. He had been Brown's
friend, as attested by Brown's farewell note to him on
November 22, 1859;(17) only a month after Higginson's
arrival his regiment was singing about Brown with the added
verse, "We'll beat Beauregard on de clare battlefield."(18)
On the eve of the anticipated Emancipation
Proclamation, December 31, 1862, thousands of slaves and
freedmen gathered for prayer meetings and song services.
According to William Wells Brown, *Go Down Moses* was sung
several times at a District of Columbia contraband camp.
Afterwards, a woman on her knees loudly sang:

> If de Debble do not ketch
> Jeff Davis, dat infernal retch,
> An roast and frigazee dat rebble,
> Wat is de use ob any Debble?

Then one contraband began the following strain:

> The first of January next, eighteen sixty-three,--
> So says the Proclamation,--the slaves will all be free!
> To every kindly heart 'twill be the day of jubilee;
> For the bond shall all go free!

Next a small black man, "with a cracking voice, appearing by
his gestures to be inwardly on fire," began jumping and
singing:

> Massa gone, missy too;
> Cry! niggers, cry!
> Tink I'll see de bressed Norf,
> Fore de day I die.
> Hi! hi! Yankee shot 'im;
> Now I tink de debbil's got 'im.

The whole company then proclaimed:

> Oh! we all longed for freedom,
> Ah! we prayed to be free;
> Though the day was long in coming,
> That we so longed to see.

We'll strive to learn our duty,
That all our friends may see,
Though so long oppressed in bondage,
We were worthy to be free.

When the clock announced the New Year, Dr. Nichols broke an almost deadly silence with the announcement: "Men and women (for you are this day to be declared free, and I can address you as men and women), I wish you a happy new year!" According to the *Liberator*, "every heart seemed to leap for joy . . . the Day of Jubilee had come."(19)
Late on the next day, as crowds waited patiently at the nation's telegraph offices, news of Lincoln's Emancipation Proclamation was finally received:

WASHINGTON, Jan. 1, 1863.--I, Abraham Lincoln, President of the United States of America, do issue this my Proclamation: . . . That, on the first day of January, in the year of our Lord one thousand eight hundred and sixty-three, all persons held as slaves within any State or any designated part of a State, the people whereof shall then be in rebellion against the United States, shall be then, henceforward, and forever, free.

That evening Colonel Higginson recorded in his diary:

About ten o'clock the people began to collect. . . . The services began at half past eleven o'clock, with prayer. . . . Then the colors were presented. . . . All this was according to the programme. Then followed an incident so simple, so touching, so utterly unexpected and startling, that I can scarcely believe it on recalling. . . . The very moment the speaker had ceased, and just as I took and waved the flag, which now for the first time meant anything to these poor people, there suddenly arose . . . a strong male voice . . . into which two women's voices instantly blended, singing, . . .

My Country, 'tis of thee,
Sweet land of liberty,
Of thee I sing!

. . . Firmly and irrepressibly the quavering voices sang on, verse after verse; others of the colored people joined in; some whites on the platform began, but I motioned them to silence. I never saw anything so electric; it made all other words cheap; it seemed the choked voice of a race at last unloosed.(20)

A new classification of music, regimental battle songs, emerged with the formation of additional black regiments. On February 9, 1863, the first black regiment was raised in a Northern state, the Fifty-fourth Massachusetts Volunteer

Infantry. Commanded by Colonel Robert Gould Shaw, a New
England aristocrat and Harvard graduate, it included the two
sons of Frederick Douglass, Lewis and Charles, who were the
first New York blacks to enlist.(21) The Fifty-fourth's
regimental song was written by an anonymous black member of
Company A:

> Fremont told them when the war it first begun,
> How to save the Union, and the way it should be done;
> But Kentucky swore so hard, and Old Abe he had
>   his fears,
> Till every hope was lost but the colored volunteers.
>
> CHORUS:
> O, give us a flag, all free without a slave;
> We'll fight to defend it as our fathers did so brave;
> The gallant Comp'ny "A" will make the Rebels dance,
> And we'll stand by the Union if we only have a chance.

After dealing with McClellan's opposition to black
troops in the second verse and the fear of being executed if
captured in the third, the fourth continues:

> So rally, boys, rally, let us never mind the past.
> We had a hard road to travel, but our day is coming fast,
> For God is for the Right, and we have no need to fear;
> The Union must be saved by the colored volunteer.(22)

On May 28 at 12:15 P.M. the regiment, marching down
Boston's State Street to the tune of *John Brown*, was cheered
by a vast crowd that covered the sidewalks and filled the
windows. But, according to the *Boston Traveller*, the
regiment's black band did not perform, "being still under
practice." A musician of the Forty-eighth New York was
subsequently hired to instruct the band when the Fifty-
fourth was dispatched to Hilton Head.(23)

When the recruitment of black soldiers for the
Massachusetts Fifty-fourth proved so successful, efforts
began immediately to create a Massachusetts Fifty-fifth. A
band of seventeen members was organized from the enlisted
men, placed under the instruction of Professor Bond of
Boston, and provided with instruments "by interested
friends."(24) This ensemble improved rapidly, made a
creditable appearance on dress parades, and played
effectively on the march through Boston on June 21, 1863.
The band's manager was William H. Dupree of Ohio, a brass
musician, concert promoter, and impresario. Among the
Fifty-fifth's officers was James M. Trotter, who later wrote
Music and Some Highly Musical People, the first survey of
black concert musicians in the nineteenth century. While
the Fifty-fifth rapidly perfected its battalion drill and
military duties, a drum corp of twenty, mostly boys from
twelve to fifteen years of age, made progress under an
unnamed but "competent" instructor.(25)

In July 1863 the Massachusetts Fifty-fourth became the
first black troop to lead Union forces into combat at Fort

Wagner, South Carolina. Half the officers and men of the regiment were killed, wounded, or captured during the evening's fighting, but the blacks performed heroically. After this battle, a new stanza extolling the bravery and courage of the soldiers of the Fifty-fourth, led into battle by Colonel Shaw, was added to the regimental song.(26)

While the Massachusetts Fifty-fourth was braving enemy fire, the Fifty-fifth, its sister regiment, was digging trenches on the Union-held portion of Morris Island, South Carolina. Yet, simmering resentment over pay inequity was boiling over.(27) Blacks in the army received ten dollars a month, but were required to pay three dollars for their clothing; white soldiers received thirteen dollars plus clothing--a difference of six dollars per month. The pay of black soldiers was based on the Militia Act of July 17, 1862, which stipulated that blacks were to be paid as military laborers and not as soldiers.(28)

Instead of accepting such discriminatory terms many black soldiers refused any pay whatsoever, including all the men in the Massachusetts Fifty-fourth and Fifty-fifth Regiments and one-third of the men in Colonel Higginson's First South Carolina Regiment. "We'se gib our sogerin' to de Guv'ment, Cunnel," they said, "but we won't 'spise ourselves so much fo to take de seben dollar." They also expressed their frustration in song:

> Ten dollar a month!
> Tree ob dat for clothin'!
> Go to Washington
> Fight for Linkum's darter!(29)

Finally, after almost a year of turmoil, Attorney General Edward Bates ruled that blacks who were free men at the outset of the war would receive the same pay as white soldiers; but those slaves who had enlisted as contrabands, approximately two-thirds of the black soldiers, still received only ten dollars and continued to pay the clothing allowance. The second verse of *Hangman Johnny*, beginning "De buckra list for money," apparently referred to the pay inequity and to the more mercenary aims attributed to white soldiers.(30)

Despite these serious problems, thousands of blacks enlisted during the summer of 1863, many of them musicians. On July 20 Joseph G. Anderson, the famous conductor of the Johnson Band, became one of the two Principal Musicians for the Third United States Colored Regiment stationed at Camp William Penn. Approximately two hundred bandsmen from ten different black regiments were eventually trained at this military base.(31)

On October 25, 1863, Michigan Governor Blair authorized the calling of the First Michigan Colored Regiment.(32) Sojourner Truth wrote the regiment's song, *The Valiant Soldiers*, and sang it in Detroit and in Washington:

We are valiant soldiers who've enlisted for the war;
We are fighting for the Union, we are fighting for
     the law;
We can shoot a rebel farther than a white man ever saw,
As we go marching on.

CHORUS:
Glory, glory, hallelujah! Glory, glory, hallelujah!
Glory, glory, hallelujah, as we go marching on.

We are done with hoeing cotton, we are done with
     hoeing corn;
We are colored Yankee soldiers as sure as you are born;
When massa hears us shouting he will think 'tis
     Gabriel's horn,
As we go marching on.

Father Abraham has spoken, and the message has been
     sent;
The prison doors have opened, and out the prisoners
     went,
To join the sable army of African descent,
As we go marching on.(33)

Later a white officer of the First Arkansas Colored
Regiment, Captain Lindley Miller, notated the song in
dialect with a new first line. In this version it became
known as the *Marching Song of the First Arkansas Colored
Regiment*:

Oh! we're de bully soldiers ob de "First ob Arkansas,"
We are fightin' for de Union, we are fightin' for
     de law,
We can hit a Rebel furder den a white man eber saw,
As we go marchin' on.(34)

According to General Samuel C. Armstrong, the founder
of Hampton Institute, his regiment also contributed a
significant battle song:

While recruiting and drilling the 9th Regiment U. S.
Colored Troops at Benedict, Maryland, in the winter of
1863-4 the men gathered around the camp fires would
sing by the hour the melodies of the plantation slave
life that they had just left--not always very
melodious; but late one evening I was startled by a
magnificent chorus from nearly a thousand black
soldiers, that called me from my tent to listen to
its most inspiring strains, and I caught the following
words which I called the *Negro Battle Hymn*:

Hark! listen to the trumpeters,
They call for volunteers;
On Zion's bright and flow'ry mount
Behold the officers.

CHORUS:
They look like men,
They look like men,
They look like men of war,
All armed and dressed in uniform,
They look like men of war.

The trumpets sound, the armies shout,
They drive the hosts of hell;
How dreadful is our God to adore,
The great Emmanuel!(35)

Many songs, including *John Brown*, show continuous
textual improvisations as the war efforts escalated. In one
of the most severe conflicts of the war, the Battle of
Poison Springs, Arkansas, on April 19, 1864, one thousand
Union soldiers faced eight thousand Confederate troops. Six
hundred of the Union forces were blacks from Kansas, some of
whom had served under John Brown during the bloody struggles
in the territory. They went into battle singing this version
of the song:

Old John Brown's body lies a-mouldering in the grave,
While weep the sons of bondage, whom he ventured
     to save;
But though he lost his life in struggling for the slave,
His soul is marching on.

Ye soldiers of freedom then strike, while strike ye may,
The death-blow of oppression in a better time and way;
For the dawn of old John Brown has brightened into day,
And his soul is marching on.(36)

There were other forms of wartime musical expression.
When 3,500 men, women, and children assembled at Beaufort,
South Carolina, on January 2, 1865, to mark the second
anniversary of the Emancipation Proclamation, the *National
Anti-Slavery Standard* reported the festivities:

First came the Colored Band of the 102d U.S.C.T.,
formerly the 1st Michigan Colored Regiment. Their good
music added not a little to the enjoyment of the day
for all. . . . At the close of Gen. Saxton's speech
the Goddess of Liberty struck up *In That New Jerusalem*,
which to the colored people is like . . . *The Star-
Spangled Banner* to all Americans. . . . The words are
simple enough, but the effect is thrilling when they
are chanted by 3,000 people. The way they rolled out,
"We must fight for liberty," was grand; then in a
softer tone came, "We are not afraid to die;" after
which is the hope revived, "We shall wear a starry
crown." Can a song ever be like a symphony? . . . Later
in the program, the band played "one of their best
pieces."(37)

A milestone in this "fight for liberty" was reached on February 12, 1865, when the famous orator, Henry Highland Garnet, appeared before the House of Representatives to mark the anniversary of Lincoln's Proclamation; he was the first black to speak to the Congress of the United States. John Luca, of the Luca Family Singers, also participated in this service.(38)

Black regiments fought in many of the strategic battles in the closing months of the war. When Charleston fell on February 22, 1865, the *Tribune* reported that "prolonged and hearty cheering" greeted the Massachusetts Fifty-fifth as they marched into the city with a new second verse to *John Brown*:

> We'll hang Jeff Davis on a crab apple-tree,
> As we go marching on!(39)

The Fifty-fifth's regimental history continued the chronicle of its triumph:

> On through the streets of the rebel city passed the column, on through the chief seat of that slave power, tottering to its fall. Its walls rung to the chorus of manly voices singing *John Brown, Babylon Is Falling,* and the *Battle-Cry of Freedom*: . . . the national airs, unheard there, were played by the regimental band. The glory and the triumph of this hour may be imagined, but can never be described. It was one of those occasions which happen but once in a lifetime, to be lived over in memory for ever.(40)

Obviously the band played very well on this occasion, for new instruments were ordered for them and delivered on March 17.(41)

Shortly after the Confederate troops abandoned Richmond on April 2, 1865, the Fifth Massachusetts Calvalry, a black regiment commanded by Colonel Charles Quincy Adams, grandson of President Adams, entered the burning city singing:

> De massa run, ha! ha!
> De darkey stay, ho! ho!
> It must be now de kingdom comin',
> An' de yar ob Jubilo.(42)

Within hours a large number of residents and black soldiers gathered outside Lumpkin's Jail, located in Richmond's slave market, where imprisoned slaves could be heard proclaiming their eminent freedom:

> Slavery's chain done broke at las'!
> Broke at las'! Broke at las'!
> Most done waiting for de mornin' star!
> Gonna praise God till I die!(43)

The crowd outside joined in the song as the soldiers opened the slave cells of the jubilant prisoners.(44)

Four days later, blacks assembled for a Jubilee Meeting at the historical African Church on Broad Street. The *New York Times* correspondent described the memorable scene:

By the time services had commenced the building was crammed with a black mass of humanity, and among them were many of our colored soldiers. When we entered the audience was singing Watts' hymn, beginning "Jesus, my all, to heaven is gone," and after each line repeating three times the following, with great emphasis: "I'm going to join in this army; I'm going to join in this army of my Lord." When they came to the verse commencing, "This is the way I long have sought," the emphasis was so significant that the smiles of the spectators could hardly be repressed.(45)

On April 13, 1865, the Massachusetts Fifty-fifth Regiment was in bivouac at Rickersville, resting after a hard week of marching. At midnight a mounted orderly brought a dispatch from General Hartwell, announcing the fall of Richmond and Lee's surrender. The band was ordered out, and the camp awoke to the sounds of *Hail Columbia*, *The Star-Spangled Banner*, *Yankee Doodle*, *John Brown*, and *Babylon Is Falling*. Officers and men hurriedly appeared, many in less than regulation dress; cheers were heard as the news passed from company to company.(46)

One day later, on April 14, Abraham Lincoln was shot by an assassin; within hours he was dead. After impressive services at the White House, his coffin was carried to a funeral car, and the vast procession moved to the Capitol. The black hearse was followed by cavalry, artillery, naval and marine detachments, in addition to military bands, marching to muffled drums and dirge-tolling bells. Pacing the head of the column was the Twenty-second United States Colored Regiment, selected for this honor because of its outstanding participation in the Battle of Richmond.

When the war ended, more than 186,000 black men had served as soldiers in the 166 regiments of the United States Colored Troops. Approximately another 20,000 had participated as sailors, almost a fourth of the entire navy. Total casualties reached nearly 70,000; approximately 30,000, or one in six, had been killed. Although estimates vary, some authorities state that in the two years that they had been allowed to serve as Union soldiers, black regiments had fought in as many as 250 battles and had played a major role in as many as 60. The enlistment of black soldiers, therefore, was a key element in the war.

The black American had not only proven his abilities as a soldier but also had demonstrated his competency as a military bandsman as well. Approximately one thousand men had served as musicians in the United States Colored Troops, many under the direction of black Principal Musicians. Black military bandsmen had become a permanent part of the armed forces. Moreover, the nation became aware of the musical heritage of Afro-Americans when, during the war,

literally hundreds of their songs were published. Two years
later major collections of these songs began to be issued.
    Black Americans, thus, sang well and fought well.
Linking the military struggle with their belief in a
beneficent, liberating God, the soldiers strove for a
victory that would make them free men. In December 1862
Colonel Higginson recorded this black soldier's prayer:

> I hab lef' my wife in de land o' bondage; my little
> ones dey say eb'ry night, Whar is my fader? But when I
> die, when de bressed mornin' rises, when I shall stan'
> in de glory, wid one foot on de water an' one foot on
> de land, den, O Lord, I shall see my wife an' my little
> chil'en once more.(47)

    Three years later, on New Year's Day 1866, more than
ten thousand blacks attended the Emancipation Jubilee on the
race course in Charleston. One observer noted a happy
people who, having "fought for liberty," had found the "New
Jerusalem" of which they had often sung. Even the poorest
looked as if they "walked that golden street" and felt "that
starry crown" upon their heads. Colonel Trowbridge, the
commander of the First South Carolina Regiment from 1864
until 1866, took this occasion to bid his soldiers farewell.
When he ceased speaking, a freedman began to sing:

> Blow ye the trumpet, blow! . . .

    The vast assemblage joined in the singing, with the
final words of the chorus rolling out with tremendous force
and magnetic effect:

> The year of jubilee has come.(48)

NOTES

    1. "The Ovation to the Black Regiment," *New   York
Times*, March 7, 1864.
    2. William Wells Brown, *The Negro in the American
Rebellion* (Boston: Lee & Shepherd, 1867), 54.
    3. William Edward Farrison, *William   Wells Brown,
Author and Reformer* (Chicago: University of Chicago
Press, 1969), 10; William Wells Brown, *The Anti-Slavery Harp*
(Boston: Bela March, No. 25 Cornhill, 1848).
    4. Irvin Bell Wiley, *Southern Negroes, 1861-1865* (New
York, 1938), 136-37.
    5. William Allen, Charles Ware, and Lucy Garrison,
Slave Songs of the United States (New York: A. Simpson,
1867), 48.
    6. Benjamin F. Butler, *Autobiography and Personal
Reminiscenses of Major-General Benj. F. Butler* (Boston,
1892), 256-64.
    7. Mary Alice Ford Armstrong and Helen Ludlow.
Hampton and Its Students. By Two of its Teachers. . . .

With Fifty Cabin and Plantation Songs, Arranged by Thomas P. Fenner (New York: G. P. Putnam's Sons, 1874), 13.

8.   *American Missionary* 5 (October 1861), 241.

9.   *National Anti-Slavery Standard* (October 12, 1861), 3.

10.   Reprinted   in   *National Anti-Slavery Standard* (December 21, 1861), 4.

11.   *National Anti-Slavery Standard* (December 14, 1861), 3; Dena Epstein, *Sinful Tunes and Spirituals: Black Folk Music to the Civil War* (Urbana: University of Illinois Press, 1977), 247.

12.   Elizabeth Ware Pearson, ed., *Letters from Port Royal, Written at the Time of the Civil War* (Boston: W. B. Clarke, 1906), 29, 38, 42, 96; Thomas Wentworth Higginson, *Army Life in a Black Regiment* (Boston: Fields, Osgood & Co., 1870), 1, 272-274.

13.   Miles Mark Fisher, *Negro Slave Songs in the United States* (Ithaca, N.Y.: Cornell University Press, 1953), 148.

14.   Allen, Ware, and Garrison, 50.

15.   Higginson, 133.

16.   Ibid., 221.

17.   Mary Potter (Thacker) Higginson, *Thomas Wentworth Higginson* (Boston, 1914), 196; Fisher, 158.

18.   Surprisingly, the John Brown named in the *John Brown* song was not the militant antislavery crusader, but a Sergeant John Brown stationed at Fort Warren, Massachusetts, in the spring of 1861. Sergeant Brown was second tenor in his regiment's chorus. Begun by his comrades as a light-hearted spoof, the song's popularity soon began to spread spontaneously. Boyd B. Stutler, "John Brown's Body," *Civil War History* 4 (September 1958), 251-60.

19.   Brown,   111-17; *Liberator*, January 16, 1863.

20.   Higginson, 39-41.

21.   *New York Times*, May 29, 1863.

22.   Frank Moore, *Songs of the Soldiers* (New York: George P. Putnam, 1864), 234-35.

23.   Charles B. Fox, *Record of the Service of the 55th Regiment of Massachusetts Volunteer Infantry* (Boston, 1868), 1.

24.   James L. Bowen, *Massachusetts in the War, 1861-1865* (Springfield, Mass.: Clark W. Bryan, 1889), 683.

25.   Fox, 3-4.

26.   Charles H. Wesley and Patricia W. Romero, *Negro Americans in the Civil War* (New York: Publishers Company, 1969), 157.

27.   Bernard C. Nalty, *Strength for the Fight* (New York: Free Press, 1986), 39.

28.   Published accounts of the pay struggle include: Higginson, 280-92; Joseph T. Williams, *A History of the Negro Troops in the War of the Rebellion, 1861-1865* (New York, 1888), 151-60; Dudley Taylor Cornish, *The Sable Arm: Army Troops in the Union Army, 1861-1865* (New York, 1956), 181-96; James M. McPherson, *The Negro's Civil War: How American Negroes Felt and Acted During the War for the Union* (New York, 1965), 193-203.

29.   Higginson, 252.

30. Ibid., 221.
31. Compiled Military Service Records, United States Colored Troops, National Archives, Washington, D.C.
32. J. Willis Underwood, *Pacific Appeal* (October 25, 1863).
33. L. A. Scruggs, *Women of Distinction* (Raleigh, N.C.: L. A. Scruggs, 1892), 51.
34. Broadside published by the Supervisory Committee for Recruiting Colored Regiments, n.d.; Moore, 206-08.
35. *Southern Workman* 18 (April 1889), 47.
36. Brown, 225-26.
37. *National Anti-Slavery Standard* (February 4, 1865), 4.
38. *Indianapolis Freeman*, November 27, 1909.
39. "Scenes in Charleston," *National Anti-Slavery Standard* (March 11, 1865), 1.
40. Fox, 57.
41. Ibid., 65.
42. "Song of the Colored Soldiers," *National Anti-Slavery Standard* (April 15, 1865), 3.
43. Isabel B. Eustis, "Second Historical Meeting of the Armstrong League: Reminiscences," *Southern Workman* 23 (May 1894), 77.
44. *Christian Recorder*, April 22, 1865; *Black Republican*, May 20, 1865.
45. "The New Times in Richmond," *National Anti-Slavery Standard* (April 15, 1865), 2.
46. Fox, 74.
47. Higginson, 26.
48. Elizabeth Botume, *First Days Amongst the Contrabands* (Boston: Lee and Shepard, 1893), 204-05.

REFERENCES

Allen, William, Charles Ware, and Lucy Garrison. *Slave Songs of the United States*. New York: A. Simpson, 1867.
Armstrong, Mary Alice Ford, and Helen Ludlow. *Hampton and Its Students. By Two of Its Teachers. . . . With Fifty Cabin and Plantation Songs, Arranged by Thomas P. Fenner*. New York: G. P. Putnam's Sons, 1874.
Botume, Elizabeth. *First Days Amongst the Contrabands*. Boston: Lee & Shepard, 1893.
Bowen, James L. *Massachusetts in the War, 1861-1865*. Springfield, Mass.: Clark W. Bryan, 1889.
Brown, William Wells. *The Anti-Slavery Harp: A Collection of Songs for Anti-Slavery Meetings. Compiled by William W. Brown, a Fugitive Slave*. Boston: Bela Marsh, 1848.
____. *My Southern Home: Or the South and Its People*. Boston: A. G. Brown, 1880.
____. *The Negro in the American Rebellion*. Boston: Lee & Shepard, 1867. Reprint. New York: The Citadel Press, 1971.

Butler, Benjamin F. *Autobiography and Personal Reminiscences of Major-General Benj. F. Butler.* Boston, 1892.

Cornish, Dudley Taylor. *The Sable Arm: Army Troops in the Union Army, 1861-1865.* New York, 1956. Reprint. New York: W. W. Norton, 1966.

Emilio, Luis F. *History of the Fifty-fourth Regiment of Massachusetts Volunteer Infantry, 1863-1865.* 2d ed. Boston, 1894.

Epstein, Dena. *Sinful Tunes and Spirituals: Black Folk Music to the Civil War.* Urbana: University of Illinois Press, 1977.

Farrison, William Edward. *William Wells Brown. Author and Reformer.* Chicago: University of Chicago Press, 1969.

Fisher, Miles Mark. *Negro Slave Songs in the United States.* Ithaca, N.Y.: Cornell University Press, 1953.

Fox, Charles B. *Record of the Service of the 55th Regiment of Massachusetts Volunteer Infantry.* Boston, 1868.

Higginson, Mary Potter (Thacker). *Thomas Wentworth Higginson.* Boston, 1914.

Higginson, Thomas Wentworth. *Army Life in a Black Regiment.* Boston: Fields, Osgood, 1870.

Litwack, Leon F. *Been in the Storm So Long: The Aftermath of Slavery.* New York: Random House, 1979.

McPherson, James M. *The Negro's Civil War: How American Negroes Felt and Acted during the War for the Union.* New York, 1965. Reprint. Urbana: University of Illinois Press, 1982.

Moore, Frank. *Songs of the Soldiers.* New York: George P. Putnam, 1864.

Nalty, Bernard C. *Strength for the Fight.* New York: Free Press, 1986.

Pearson, Elizabeth Ware, ed. *Letters from Port Royal (1862-1868) Written at the Time of the Civil War.* Boston: W. B. Clarke, 1906.

Perdue, Charles L., Jr., Thomas E. Barden, and Robert K. Phillips, eds. *Weevils in the Wheat: Interviews with Virginia Ex-Slaves.* Charlottesville: University Press of Virginia, 1976.

Quarles, Benjamin. *The Negro in the Civil War.* New York: Russell & Russell, 1953.

Scruggs, Lawson A. *Women of Distinction.* Raleigh, N. C.: L. A. Scruggs, 1892.

Stutler, Boyd B. "John Brown's Body," *Civil War History* 4 (September 1958), 251-60.

Taylor, Susie King. *Reminiscences of My Life in Camp with the 33d United States Colored Troops, Late 1st S. C. Volunteers.* Boston: the author, 1902.

Towne, Laura M. *Letters and Diary of Laura M. Towne: Written from the Sea Islands of South Carolina, 1862-1884,* edited by Robert S. Holland. Cambridge, Mass.: Riverside Press, 1912.

Trotter, James M. *Music and Some Highly Musical People; with Sketches of the Lives of Remarkable Musicians of the Colored Race: with Portraits, and an Appendix*

Containing Copies of Music Composed by Colored Men.
   Boston: Lee and Shepherd, 1880, c1878.
Wesley, Charles H., and Patricia W. Romero. *Afro-Americans
   in the Civil War: From Slavery to Citizenship.* New
   York: Publishers Company, 1967.
Wiley, Irvin Bell. *Southern Negroes, 1861-1865.* New York,
   1938.
Williams, George Washington. *A History of the Negro Troops
   in the War of the Rebellion, 1861-1865.* New York,
   1888. Reprint. New York: Bergman Publishers, 1968.

Newspapers and Journals

American Missionary
Atlantic Monthly
Christian Recorder
Continental Monthly
Douglass Monthly
Dwight's Journal of Music
Indianapolis Freeman
Liberator
Nation
National Anti-Slavery Standard
New Orleans *Black Republican*
New Orleans Tribune
New Orleans *L'Union*
New York Times
New York *Tribune*
San Francisco *Pacific Appeal*
Southern Workman
Wilmington, N.C., Newspapers:
      People's Press and Wilmington Advertiser
      Wilmington Daily Journal
      Wilmington Herald
      Wilmington Chronicle

Choirs of Angels Armed for War: Reverend Marshall W. Taylor's *A Collection of Revival Hymms and Plantation Melodies*

ROBIN HOUGH

Reverend Marshall W. Taylor (1846-1887) was born in Lexington, Kentucky, to Samuel Taylor and Nancy Ann Boyd, the latter of whom "was set free . . . just before the time of her son's birth."(1) Taylor was licensed to preach in 1868 by the Lexington Conference of the Methodist Episcopal Church and by 1882 was the "presiding elder on the Ohio District of the Lexington Conference."(2) Taylor appears to have relocated to New Orleans in 1884, as he became the editor of the *Southwestern Christian Advocate*, beginning with the edition of June 5, 1884. After Taylor's death in 1887, A. E. P. Albert assumed the editorship of that New Orleans-based weekly journal, beginning with the edition of September 29, 1887.(3)

The first edition of Taylor's hymnal (1882), entitled *A Collection of Revival Hymns and Plantation Melodies*, was apparently successful, for as Taylor informed his readers on the endpage of the second edition, "within the first month after the issue our first edition has been sold."(4) This first edition included the words and music for 150 songs and the words only for an additional seven. The second edition added six songs with words and music (all arranged by the otherwise unidentified "L. A. D.") and another eleven songs with words only.(5) Both editions were published by Marshall W. Taylor and W. C. Echols in Cincinnati, and by the time of the second edition, the volume was also being distributed by Phillips and Hunt in New Orleans and by Walden and Stowe in Chicago and St. Louis. Taylor, in the second edition, announced that the book was available in "Music and Book Stores everywhere" for 50 cents and gave his own home address as well as that of W. C. Echols for those prospective buyers who could not purchase the volume locally.(6)

What Taylor accomplished in publishing his hymnal was the production of a text that is as interesting for its political and religious agenda as it is for its musical content.(7) Taylor had a clear purpose in publishing his text, and he was explicit about at least part of that purpose. In the preface he said, "The best history of a nation is often found in its poetry when that is fairly and

fully interpreted. I propose to preserve the history, but
the interpretation I leave to another time and possibly to
other and more skilled hands."(8)   Thus, Taylor disclaimed
the ability to interpret the songs, though he makes several
provocative points in his preface that suggest his sense of
the meaning and value of the songs.   For instance, he
considered the slave songs as

> the only surviving memorial of those days agone.   A
> vivid recollection of those times, red and fiery with
> their record of suffering, will serve well to chasten
> and keep us pure. While these songs remain the colored
> people, like the Jews of old, will remember that "they
> were once bondsmen in Egypt;" and then will they go
> their way with memory on the alert, lest a worse thing
> come unto them.(9)

For Taylor, memory of the songs should provide a course
corrective for black people in the future, since only
through those songs would they be able to recapture that
past time when their fate paralleled that of the ancient
Jews.   There is also here an explicit warning that should
memory of these songs lapse, dire consequences would
follow.
     Taylor wished to keep the memory of the "plantation
melodies" alive, and he certainly wanted the songs to be
sung rather than read, but for him the words were the real
jewels. He gave to Miss Josephine Robinson the full
responsibility for the musical compositions prepared "for
use only in this book," and took for himself the task of
organizing the words into their present form.(10) As Irene
Jackson-Brown points out in her analysis of the music:

> Because many of the melodies were apparently notated
> during actual performance, variants were inevitable.
> In terms of actual performance, adjustment (i.e., fit-
> ting syllables or text to music) must have been diffi-
> cult for the text is not indicated on the score. . . .
> We can only make educated guesses about performance
> practice in relation to Taylor's hymnal.   More than
> likely the melodies were sung as written, and probably
> the practice of lining out was employed.(11)

Taylor seemed to have been aware of some of the difficulties experienced by those who attempted to sing the songs
(especially the whites) as seen in his note to the second
edition:

> Should there at first appear difficulties in producing
> the desired effect with any piece, perseverance will
> bring it out.   Almost any colored person can sing the
> pieces, and such would cheerfully aid in the way de-
> sired; then, with a little imagination applied, all
> will be well.(12)

Taylor's suggestion that it might require the aid of a
colored person to help the whites with the songs points
towards the larger purpose underlying the publication of

his hymnal.   Taylor's book was designed to help heal the
scars of the war by showing how, through mutual understanding,   blacks and whites could lay claim to a common
religious heritage and thus create a common political
future.   He intended to combine the best of the religious
songs of the slaves with a sampling of the white revival
hymns most popular among blacks at the time. Thus, ideally,
the freedmen and religiously sensitive whites could view
through music their recent, common past as a time in which
God intervened directly in history to free the slaves
through the agency of the Civil War.   It is possible to
discern part of Taylor's agenda when he says, "If you would
know the colored people, learn their songs."(13) His political purpose is clear when he adds, "Whoever will learn
and sing these melodies, drinking from the same spring
whence they flow, will of necessity grow warmer in feeling
for those whose fathers sang them first."(14) Singing the
songs would help the whites empathize with the freedmen
more easily, while the publication of the text would enable
the blacks to retain the powerful songs which helped them
survive slavery.
     These ideals, both religious and political in nature,
led Taylor to make some textual decisions that could be
questioned by modern scholars, for, as he said, "Verses
apparently meaning-less have been given an interpretation
which renders them no less beautiful, but far more useful.
The syntax has occasionally been corrected."(15) In addition, F. S. Hoyt, in the introduction to Taylor's text,
indicated something of the nature of Taylor's method of
compilation thusly:

     Some were written down as he heard them sung in reli-
     gious meetings; others from dictation; others were
     found in "balladbooks;" and a few have been composed by
     Dr. Taylor when he found no appropriate words--that is,
     no words appropriate for his book.(16)

It is certainly true that Taylor's purpose in publishing
his text was something other than the attempt at an exact
rendition of the songs as they were sung in performance, as
was *Slave Songs of the United States* (1867), compiled by
Allen, Ware, and Garrison. However, Taylor's method would
appear to have much in common with that of Bishop Richard
Allen, inasmuch as the earlier Afro-American minister and
hymn compiler also seems to have selected songs from available printed sources, drawn from the oral tradition of his
parishioners, and written a few himself.(17)
     One facet of Taylor's uniqueness is the manner in which
he blended the specific religious significance of the songs
with his political agenda.   The religious songs of the
slaves were, for Taylor, not simply songs of praise or
hope. As he stated concerning the slaves:

     They have been sustained by the instrumentality of
     these songs, under God.   Indeed, these songs were ac-
     cepted of God, and he seemed to use these simple
     ditties, as some of our modern ministers and people
     have chosen to call them, as his means of communication

with his people from whom the oppressor had denied and
taken his Holy Book away. "What God has cleansed, call
thou not common or unclean."(18)

Taylor was likely responding to a growing feeling within
the black congregations that the old slave songs should no
longer be sung, as they spoke of a time of great suffering
which had passed, and the work of the songs had already
been accomplished, that is, they had sustained the slaves
until emancipation. In combating the tendency to neglect
these songs, Taylor exhorted the faithful to understand
their true nature; they are channels where two-way communication between God and the singing community took place.
What Taylor suggested was not simply that in the absence of
the Bible the songs would have to suffice as a pale reflec-
tion of the sacred texts, rather he was saying as a
believer and religious leader, that the songs operated as a
direct line of communication with the divine, allowing
sacred communication to flow in both directions. Not only
were the songs heard as prayer by the divine, but the
singers were also directly instructed and inspired in their
singing by God, who taught the slaves through the songs.
Thus, for Taylor the songs of the slaves were truly sacred,
since they were the occasion for a hierophany, a direct
manifestation of the divine presence. The power of the
songs clearly pointed towards emancipation, but, in
addition, they contained untapped potential for the future,
since they were more-than-human songs. In a prescient
passage, considering the frequent re-emergence of the slave
songs in a variety of contexts, notably during the civil
rights movement, Taylor said:

> My work is to rescue them, lest after all these good
> fruits they themselves perish from the minds of men.
> Their influence is not done. The race is free, an era
> of light and culture has dawned, but ere all the fruits
> of freedom be gathered these melodies have many a
> mighty task to perform, in lifting up bowed hearts to
> Jesus and overturning the prejudices against color,
> which are so ruinously widespread.(19)

Taylor did not divide his hymnal into separate sections
reserved for "revival hymns" and "plantation melodies," but
it is still possible to discern the different types of
songs upon which he drew. Using George Pullen Jackson's
categories, it is clear that Taylor chose some religious
ballads, such as *Wayfaring Stranger*, which appears in
Taylor as *I'm Just A-Going Over Home*. He also used, as
would be fitting for a Methodist Episcopal minister, some
folk hymns such as *Drooping Souls No Longer Grieve* and *How
Tedious and Tasteless the Hours*, both found in John
Wesley's *Methodist Hymns*. There are also a number of
revival spirituals that follow the rule of the simplifica-
tion of a standard text of Wesley's or Isaac Watts' in four
lines followed by a four-line chorus.
Taylor's hymnal included variations on many of the
standard black "spirituals" also found in the Fisk
publication *The Jubilee Singers and Their Campaign for*

Twenty Thousand Dollars, written by Reverend G. D. Pike
(1873), the Hampton publication *Hampton and Its Students*,
by M. F. Armstrong and Helen Ludlow (1874), and *Slave Songs
of the United States*. There is an indication in the introduction that Taylor might have been aware of the Hampton
and Fisk collections,(20) but he himself maintained that
"This collection is no competitor with other books of song;
it fills a place and supplies a want wholly its own."(21)
Precisely how Taylor's text differs from the other early
collections can most readily be seen by a comparison of
Taylor's version of songs also found in the Hampton and
Fisk collections.

Taylor's version of *Go Down Moses*, for instance, is
quite similar to that found in the Fisk collection. The
only word changes are incidental; the melodies, though
differing, cohere on the phrase "Let my people go," and,
though Taylor arranged the verses into four-line stanzas
instead of two, he did not deviate from the sequence found
in the Fisk version. Taylor's version included but ten of
the twenty-five verses found in Fisk, and he named F.
Minter as his source for the song.

Taylor lists his grandfather as the source for *Lis'ning
all the Night*, and here his text differs significantly from
that found in either Hampton or Fisk. Both of the latter
include the following as the first verse in the text:

> Some say that John the Baptist was nothing but a Jew
> But the Holy Bible tells us he was a preacher too.

This verse is entirely absent from Taylor, though he used
as his first verse that found as the second in both Hampton
and Fisk:

> Go read the third of Matthew
> And read the chapter through
> It is a guide to Christians
> To tell them what to do.(22)

At that point the Fisk version is complete, and the Hampton
version includes one further stanza concerning John the
Baptist's search for the Savior. Taylor, on the other
hand, concluded his text with five additional stanzas which
tell a progressive story of John's prophetic career culmi-
nating in the meeting between John and Jesus and a synopsis
of the religious meaning of the song. The last two stanzas
are:

> When John was preaching Jesus,
> The all-atoning Lamb,
> He saw the blessed Savior,
> And said: "Behold the man."
>
> Appointed to the Father
> To take away your sin,
> When you believe in Jesus,
> And own him for your king.(23)

Taylor certainly did not simply reprint his text from other

sources, and he seemed interested in having the song develop into a coherent story complete with homily at the end.   Since Taylor intended his hymnal for religious services, this didacticism serves his purpose well.

The Fisk version of *Nobody Knows the Trouble I See, Lord* and the Hampton version *Nobody Knows the Trouble I've Seen*, with their very different tunes, both stand as recognizable songs with their own integrity built around a familiar chorus.   In Taylor the chorus is found in *Hunting My Redeemer*, attributed by Taylor to M. Macoomer.   The seven stanzas, once again, show a development of theme, this time towards finding the Redeemer: (In this hymn and in all succeeding texts, repetitive phrases are omitted.)

> Come all the world and you shall know
> Hunting my Redeemer;
> How I was saved from endless woe,
> Hunting my Redeemer.
>
> CHORUS:
> Nobody knows the trouble I see, the trouble I see,
>   the trouble I see,--
> Nobody knows the trouble I see, Hunting my Redeemer.
>
> I strove indeed, but could not tell
> How to shun the gates of hell.
>
> What to do I did not know,
> I thought to hell I'd surely go.
>
> I looked this way and that, to fly
> I tried salvation for to buy.
>
> I prayed in the east and prayed in the west
> Seeking for eternal rest.
>
> At last I looked to Calvary,
> And saw my Jesus on the tree.
>
> I felt the pardon, heard the voice
> My soul was happy, and I rejoiced.(24)

Taylor's use of the chorus from *Nobody Knows the Trouble I See* in this new context may be idiosyncratic, or it may represent evidence of a real fluidity in the performance practices of the black congregations of his day. Probably the carefully structured sequence of stanzas with their clear didactic intent indicate Taylor's own idea of what the song should mean.

The song *Walk in Jerusalem Just Like John*, which continues to be popular among modern gospel singers, is found in the Fisk collection under the title *I Want to Be Ready*. Here the song speaks of John the Evangelist's vision of the New Jerusalem in the New Testament book *The Revelation of John*.(25)   Taylor attributed his version to Edward Nathan, and the song is entitled *Walk Jerusalem Just Like Job* and refers to Old Testament texts.   The song, unlike those

discussed above, appears to be a collection of traditional
couplets and a rather odd reference to Joshua, which serves
to keep the Old Testament focus:

> Mary wears a golden chain,
> We'll walk Jerusalem just like Job.
>
> Every link bears Jesus' name,
> We'll walk Jerusalem just like Job.
>
> CHORUS:
> When I come to die I want to be ready,
> When I come to die
> We'll walk Jerusalem just like Job.
>
> Joshua was the son of Nun
> Prayed to the Lord to stop the sun.
>
> When I came out I wrote my name
> Never to return again.
>
> As we go round the shores of time
> We will leave this sinful world behind.(26)

Taylor often used traditional couplets to fill out a song,
and these formulaic phrases, he left little doubt, could
easily be transferred from song to song since they are not
identified with any particular text. In this case there is
no thematic progression in the stanzas, for almost any
couplet with the right rhythm would apparently fit; the
discreteness of the song would seem to rest only in the
repetition of the title line, *Walk Jerusalem Just Like Job.*

Taylor's version of *My God Delivered Daniel* repays
close attention, since it exhibits clearly a number of his
central themes. In the Fisk version *Didn't My Lord Deliver
Daniel* the four verses are as follows:

> He delivered Daniel from the lion's den
> Jonah from the belly of the whale
> And the Hebrew children from the fiery furnace
> And why not every man?
>
> The moon runs down in a purple stream
> The sun forbear to shine
> And every star disappear
> King Jesus will be mine.
>
> The wind blows East and the wind blows West
> It blows like the judgment day
> And every poor soul that never did pray
> Will be glad to pray that day.
>
> I set my foot on the Gospel ship
> And the ship it began to sail
> It landed me over on Canaan's shore
> And I'll never come back any more.(27)

The song is a general statement of the parallel that exists

between every believer and the believers of old whose
stories are found in the Bible. It is possible to see a
veiled reference to an escape from slavery in the last
stanza, though most white Protestants of the time could
have sung the stanza without any thought that it referred
to anything other than the Gospel ship of faith. The version found in Hampton, *My Lord Delivered Daniel*, likewise
offers participation to all believers as these verses
unique to Hampton indicate:

> I met a pilgrim on de way
> And I ask him whar he's a gwine
> I'm bound for Canaan's happy land
> An' dis is de shouting band.
>
> De richest man dat eber I saw
> Was de one dat beg de most
> His soul was filled wid Jesus
> And wid de Holy Ghost.(28)

Once again, it is easy to infer a double meaning from the
reference to the pilgrim bound for Cannaan, but escape from
slavery is not an overt theme in the song.
     Taylor, by comparison, made the defeat and escape from
slavery explicit as his major theme in *My God Delivered
Daniel*. He named Georgia Thornton as his source, but
clearly he endorsed the contents himself:

> Ye servants of the living God
> From Afric's sunny shore
> Your deliverer praise with all your soul,
> And to Egypt return no more.
> We want no cowards in our band
> Who will their colors fly;
> We call for valiant-hearted men,
> Who're not afraid to die.
>
> Hold up your heads with courage bold
> And do not be afraid
> For God has delivered Daniel,
> And why not every man?
>
> Three Hebrew children in the fiery furnace,
> Daniel in the lion's den--
> My God delivered each of them,
> And why not you and me?
>
> Behold this army dressed in white;
> How brave they do appear,
> All dressed and armed in uniform,
> They must be men of war.

O when you hear my heart-strings break,
How sweet my moments roll;
With a mortal paleness on my cheek
And glory in my soul.(29)

The second, fourth, and fifth stanzas are traditional, but within the context set by the first, they take on a new meaning. The spiritual battle is here merged with the military contest against the slaveholders. Apparently, Taylor was more interested in the defeat of slavery than in the escape from it. Even the last stanza with its general statement of the glory of the soul of one who is dying, would not seem out of place if viewed as a battlefield death scene, especially in conjunction with the preceding stanza.

Taylor, like other religious leaders of his day, saw the essence of human life as a spiritual battle between cosmic forces that were invisible but ubiquitous. This constant spiritual struggle is shown in *The Mourner's Race*, attributed by Taylor to D. Tucker:

There's trouble here, there's trouble there
I really do believe there is trouble everywhere.

There are devils here, there are devils there
I really do believe there are devils everywhere.

My Jesus is here, my Jesus is there,
I really do believe my Jesus is everywhere.(30)

For the slave, according to Taylor, there were constant companions who helped to give spiritual aid on the side of Jesus in this battle. The angels for Taylor had a number of traditional functions: they would offer succor to the sorrowing slave, they would guide the souls of the dead home to God, and they would operate as mediators between the divine world and the human. In addition to these familiar angelic functions, Taylor saw the angels as having had a unique place among the devout slaves:

These melodies have sweetened the bitter pang of cruel mockings and lashing, and turned the gall into honey for the praying, singing slave. Oftimes in the field amid the cane, the corn, the cotton, the rice, the hemp, or the tobacco, has God met and blessed them. Almost visible choirs of angels have at times seemed to join them in these strains of praise to the Father of lights.(31)

Taylor included numerous references in his hymnal to "joining the angel band" or the angels "swinging down" to take up the dead. These are, of course, among the most common phrases in all early collections of the slave songs. However, Taylor viewed the angels in a way that goes beyond the traditional phrases. One of the songs that Taylor selected from one of his unidentified sources, presumably white, was particularly useful for his purpose. In this song, which Taylor identified by the generic title *The*

Dying Christian, the relationship with the angels depicted
herein recalls the "almost visible choirs of angels":

> Methinks they're descending to hear while I sing
> Well pleased to hear mortals a-praising their king.
>
> O angels, O angels, my soul's in a flame;
> I faint in sweet rapture at Jesus' name.
>
> Sweet spirits attend me, till Jesus shall come;
> Protect and defend me, till I am called home.(32)

Angels appear in nearly half of Taylor's songs, and in
addition to their traditional functions, there is a sense
of immediate angelic presence that is a distinct mark of
Taylor's collection as a whole. This is seen most clearly
in the unusually direct military role which the angels
often play in Taylor's hymnal. In *Make Ready*, attributed
by Taylor to Hattie Hill, some stanzas similar to those
found in *My God Delivered Daniel* are added to new stanzas
to create a martial hymn:

> Hark! listen to the trumpeters;
> They sound for volunteers,
> O'er Zion's bright and flowery mount,
> Behold the officers.
>
> Their horses white, their garments bright,
> With crowns and bows in hand;
> Enlisting soldiers for the king
> To march for Canaan's land.
>
> The army now is on parade,
> How martial they appear;
> All dressed and armed in uniform,
> They look like men of war.
>
> They follow their great General,
> The great eternal lamb;
> His garments stained in his own blood--
> King Jesus is his name.(33)

Here, the angel officers who enlist soldiers for the king
are preparing a cosmic battle, certainly on one level the
final apocalyptic battle between the forces of good and
evil. It has long been an accepted metaphor in Protestant
hymnody to see the angels preparing for a spiritual conflict as though for a military battle, and it might appear
that Taylor is simply following this pious conceit. The
angel army has performed acts of aiding believers trapped
by evil forces in the biblical past, and these angels now
appear in military guise to help fight the cosmic battle.
Taylor was certainly interested in this spiritual battle
between good and evil waged by the angels, but, in a
remarkable song attributed to B. J. Carter, *Slavery Is
Dead*, Taylor made it clear that the spiritual battle had a
very real human parallel in direct military combat:

Our glorious flag is floating
Triumphantly at last
Our nation is exulting,
The rebels' die is cast.
Rebellion now is conquered,
No more to lift its head,
And best of all we now can sing
Old slavery is dead.

We are a happy nation,
Because our country's free
From war and desolation,
And from bold tyranny.
The tyrant's arm is broken
No more to hold a slave.
This is the year of Jubilee,
So let our banner wave.

We stood and fought like demons
Upon the battlefield,
Both slave and northern freeman
Have faced the glowing steel.
Our blood beneath this banner
Has mingled with the whites,
And 'neath its folds we now demand
Our just and equal rights.

The world has seen our valor,
And nations now confess,
That man is not in color,
In fashion nor in dress.
In Charleston and old Richmond,
In spite of Lee and Bragg,
We dropped the rebs in wild dismay,
And planted there our flag.

We've fed the Union soldiers
When fleeing from the foe;
And led them through the mountains,
Where white men dare not go.
Our hoecake and our cabbage,
And pork we freely gave,
That this old flag might be sustained--
Now let it proudly wave.(34)

Taylor's use of this song makes quite clear a number of
allusions which might otherwise be interpreted as simply
referring to the spiritualized battle between good and
evil. The specificity of this song, even to the point of
naming Confederate generals, makes it clear that, for
Taylor, the Civil War was a foreshadowing of the final
apocalypse; indeed it was the sacred battle of the age.
Just as the slaves were the double of the ancient Hebrews,
the battle that freed them was the double of the apocalypse
to come. Certainly the songs in his collection reflect
Taylor's assertion that "every line contained in these
melodies breathes a prayer for liberty, physical and spiritual."(35) One thing that makes Taylor truly unique is his

direct reference to the Civil War as an occasion for sacral
warfare.   To Taylor's way of thinking, God worked directly
in history, and the divine intention was for the rebels and
slaveholders to be defeated, since the fate of the slaves
was to duplicate the biblical story of the deliverance of
the Hebrews. By the same token, the angels who visited the
devout slaves in the fields as they sang the sacred songs
could later be seen as the same angels who fought alongside
the Union army and led it to victory. A kind of angelic
continuity could be seen by believers as constituting one
proof that the slaves had been faithful to their religious
duty and the songs they sang were truly sacred, since they
were in harmony with the divine will.
     The idea that the problem of slavery was "finally
solved by God himself, in his own time and his own way"(36)
was common among the early compilers of the slave songs as
this quote from *Hampton and Its Students* indicates. In the
edition of the Fisk volume *The Story of the Jubilee Singers*
written by J. B. T. Marsh (1883), the   author   stated   that
the Civil War

     was really a war, on one side to perpetuate slavery,
     and on the other to abolish it. The South understood
     this from the start. So did those at the North who were
     wise to read the signs of the times, and especially
     those who had the spiritual instinct to interpret the
     meaning of God's providences.(37)

Despite the unanimity on this point, only Taylor drew the
explicit conclusion that the slave songs were an integral
part of the physical and spiritual warfare of the age and
insisted on including the insight directly into his hymnal.
     In *Slavery Is Dead*, which seems secular and political
in tone, Taylor connected the needs of the contemporary
freedmen with the awareness of new religious obligations.
He employed the traditional form for hymnals of his day by
including a scriptural passage at the top of the page of
each song. For *Slavery Is Dead*, he used Deuteronomy 15:12-
14 (King James version), which reads in part:

     And if thy brother, a Hebrew man or a Hebrew woman, be
     sold unto thee, and shall serve thee six years, then in
     the seventh year thou shalt let him go free from thee.

     And when thou sendest him out free from thee, thou
     shalt not let him go away empty. Thou shalt furnish
     him liberally out of thy flock and out of thy floor and
     out of thy winepress.

     Thus, Taylor utilized the jubilee scriptural passage to
suggest that righteous treatment of the freedmen is not
mere benevolence but a religious duty, and to the whites he
clearly proposed that to be in harmony with the divine
will, as known through the Bible, they must aid in the
economic and political needs of the freedmen. Since the
Civil War was, for Taylor, a divinely inspired war, the
central result of which was the freeing of the slaves, the
freedmen could see how their political emancipation was, in

fact, of divine origin. The whites could see that the war
had been a holy war and that the work yet to be done in
race relations was a part of the religious requirement. The
blacks could see the sacrality of the songs and the importance of remembering them, and the whites could see their
new religious obligations in the context of a hymnal that
included many of their own familiar sacred songs interwoven
with the black sacred songs.

For Taylor it was crucial that the slave songs not be
forgotten since they contain articulate messages from the
deity and hence have a divine power capable of re-emerging
when needed. It is possible upon examination of the hymnal
as a whole to isolate themes seen by believers as divine
messages embedded in the songs. The first of these is "God
is the true source of power," as the world order represented by the slaveholders is provisional, not eternal, and
is identified with Babylon. The power of the slaveholders
is nothing compared to the power of God, and human time,
therefore, is subsumed under divine time. The oppressive
world order does not reflect the divine will but is an
arrogant and finally doomed usurpation of power; it is a
rebellion against God to be righted by God in God's own
time. The way to touch the true source of power is through
prayer, particularly prayer in song. That is, through
religiously and musically altered speech, one communicates
directly to the God who is the source of power behind the
world of apparent but illusory power, and one receives
direct communication from God in return through the song.

The second theme that can be identified is that "the
slaves were in an especially close relationship with the
divine." The signs of this close relationship are the
sacred state of receptivity of mind when the angels seemed
to join the slaves in the singing, the two-way communication between the divine and the slave community that is
experienced in song, and the disclosure of the secret that
the slaves could hear the Bible stories communicated to
them through song (and sometimes by unwitting slavemasters)
and see in those stories their own fate, since they would
identify with the ancient Hebrews.

The third major theme that can be seen in these songs
is the prophecy "that a change is going to come." That
change is multiform and could be the apocalypse anticipated
in the Bible or its equivalent, that is, the process of
being freed from slavery by divine action and military
conflict. The promise of change is inherent in many songs
in the early collections of religious slave songs, and this
hope could both sustain those who had to endure misery and
encourage those who could to participate actively in the
creation of that change. The change to come is announced
in the songs as divinely initiated, but often, at the same
time, as requiring active human participation for the pro-
phesied culmination. Several of the more directly militant
hymns in Taylor's collection stress this active participation unusually strongly.

In addition to being a source of themes, which are
often found to parallel those in other early collections,
Taylor's hymnal is a rich source for traditional rhymed
couplets, several of which are not found in the other early

sources. Taylor primarily relies on traditional couplets,
though it is possible that he may have originated some
himself.   These couplets are often so concise and so
striking that they become memorable and are capable of
wandering from song to song, of becoming the basis for a
chorus, or of becoming the title of a new song. In this
regard, Taylor's work is interesting because there are a
number of recurring couplets that stress his religious and
political agenda.

Each of the following couplets appears up to half a
dozen times in Taylor's work, indicating their significance
for him.   They are all clearly traditional, and because
they hint of the divinely aided overcoming of slavery, they
must have appealed to Taylor:

> The very time I thought I was lost
> My dungeon shook, my chains fell off.
>
> I'll put on my breast plate, sword and shield
> Boldly I'll march through Satan's field.
>
> You can hinder me here but you cannot there
> He sits in heaven and he answers prayer.(38)

The following couplets also appear several times in Taylor,
and they have parallels in the other early collections.
Many of these have continued to operate vitally within the
modern gospel tradition:

> Should I get to the mountain top
> I'll praise the Lord and never stop.
>
> Old Satan thought he had me fast
> I broke his chain, I'm free at last.
>
> The prettiest thing that ever I've done
> Was seeking of religion when I was young.
>
> Religion's like a blooming rose
> It's none but those who feel that knows.
>
> My head was wet with the midnight dew
> The morning star was a witness too.
>
> It was just about the break of day
> I thought my soul would fly away.(39)

Among the couplets that appear originally in Taylor are two
that have partial parallels in the Fisk collection, where
the phrases "Oh, the rocks and mountains shall all flee
away" and "Gonna chatter with the angels sooner in the
morning" both appear.(40) The more vivid versions recorded
by Taylor reappear in records by the Heavenly Gospel
Singers and Blind Willie Johnson recorded in the 1930s.
This does not mean that those singers were influenced
directly by Taylor, but it does mean that Taylor was in
touch with an otherwise unrecorded oral tradition that
survived into the twentieth century:

Rocks and mountains skip like lambs
All must come at God's command.

I'll argue with the Father, chatter with the Son
And talk about the world I've just come from.(41)

Other couplets that appear first in Taylor and do not have
parallels in the Fisk, Hampton, or Allen collections include the following:

My mother has broke the ice and gone
And now she sings the morning song.

I'll leave this world like a shooting star
Look in heaven, you'll find me there.

I'll tell you as a matter of fact
If you've left the devil, don't never turn back.

No use waiting for the blowing of the horn
No use hollowing when the train's done gone.

Run mourners run for low is the Bible
Run mourners run for low is the way.(42)

Taylor used his couplets as though weaving a tapestry.
They reappear with enough regularity to make the reader of
the hymnal aware of their constant presence, but they do
not arise often enough to be obtrusive. They help to make
the songs seem familiar on first hearing, and they give a
coherence to the work, as though one song blends into
another to form a whole. It would appear that Taylor's
purpose is well served by these reappearing couplets, since
a number of them reinforce the role played by the divine in
the struggle against slavery, and their singing serves
powerfully to evoke that past time once more.
     The overall uniqueness of Taylor's work arises from his
purpose in compiling the hymnal. It was not meant to
provide standard texts to be presented in concert by
trained singers, nor was it intended as a scholarly edition
of the songs as they were sung in black congregations of
the time. Taylor's purpose was primarily religious in
nature, and his primary concentration was on the texts, in
which one can see Taylor's guiding hand in nearly every
song. The ideal, for Taylor, would have been for the
hymnal to help provide a new common ground for mutual
understanding between the races in the generation following
the Civil War.

NOTES

     1. F. S. Hoyt, introduction to *A Collection of Revival
Hymns and Plantation Melodies*, by Reverend Marshall W.
Taylor, (Cincinnati: Taylor and Echols, 1882), 11.
     2. Hoyt, 1.
     3. OCLC printout of Taylor's written works. This is

the source of the personal information on Taylor that
updates the work of Irene Jackson-Brown, cited below.

4.   Rev. Marshall W. Taylor, endpage of second edition
(1883) of his *Collection*.

5.   The only song in the first edition dropped from the
second is a version of *The Prodigal Son*.

6.   Taylor, endpage of second edition.

7.   I wish to thank Bernadette Ellsworth for the insight that the political and religious agendas presented by
Taylor were so tightly interwoven as to be almost indistin-
guishable. Conversations with Ms. Ellsworth concerning
Taylor have influenced a number of sections of this text in
subtle ways, and I wish to express my sincerest thanks for
her valuable aid.

8.   Taylor, 3.

9.   Taylor, 4.

10.   Taylor, 6.

11.   Irene Jackson-Brown, "Afro-American Song in the
Nineteenth Century: A Neglected Source," *Black Perspective
in Music*, Spring 1976, 26.

12.   Taylor, endpage of second edition.

13.   Taylor, 3.

14.   Taylor, 5.

15.   Taylor, 4-5.

16.   Hoyt, iii.

17.   Eileen Southern, *The Music of Black Americans: A
History*, 2d ed. (New York: W. W. Norton, 1983), 26.

18.   Taylor, 3.

19.   Taylor, 5.

20.   Hoyt, iii.

21.   Taylor, 5.

22.   Taylor, 152.

23.   Ibid.

24.   Taylor, 105.

25.   J. B. T. Marsh, *The Story of the Jubilee Singers:
With Their Songs* (New York: S. W. Green's Sons, 1883),
259.

26.   Taylor, 120.

27.   Marsh, 134.

28.   Mrs. M. F. Armstrong and Helen Ludlow, *Hampton and
Its Students* (New York: G. P. Putnam's Sons, 1874), 193.

29.   Taylor, 38.

30.   Taylor, 152.

31.   Taylor, 4.

32.   Taylor, 84.

33.   Taylor, 70.

34.   Taylor, 114.

35.   Taylor, 3.

36.   Armstrong and Ludlow, 7.

37.   Marsh, 2.

38.   Taylor, 186, 20, 27.

39.   Taylor, 27, 226, 28, 98, 25, 25.

40.   Marsh, 139, 141.

41.   Taylor, 80, 207.

42.   Taylor, 64, 119, 106, 132, 153.

REFERENCES

Armstrong, Mary Alice Ford and Helen Ludlow. *Hampton and Its Students*. New York: G. P. Putnam's Sons, 1874.
Jackson-Brown, Irene. "Afro-American Song in the Nineteenth Century: A Neglected Source," *Black Perspective in Music* (Spring 1976), 26.
Marsh, J. B. T. *The Story of the Jubilee Singers: With Their Songs*. New York: S. W. Green's Sons, 1883.
Taylor, Marshall W. *A Collection of Revival Hymns and Plantation Melodies*. Cincinnati: Taylor and Echols, 1882. 2d ed. 1883.

Black Female Concert Singers of the Nineteenth Century: Nellie Brown Mitchell and Marie Selika Williams

Carolyne Lamar Jordan

The late nineteenth century was a golden era for the development of a new political, social, and artistic culture in America. The rise of the black prima donna in the years between 1820 and 1920 was one of the manifestations of the ever-changing profile of black society throughout the country.

The age was heralded by the birth of Elizabeth Taylor Greenfield (ca1824-1876), known as "The Black Swan," in Natchez, Mississippi. She was followed by the renowned church soloist and concert singer, Nellie Brown Mitchell (1845-1924); the operatic soloist, Marie Selika Williams (1849-1937), called the "Queen of Staccato;" and two sisters, Anna Madah Hyers (1853-1934) and Emma Louise Hyers (1855-1890). In the next decade were born Flora Batson Bergen (1864-1904), the "Double-Voiced Queen of Song," and M. Sissieretta Jones (1869-1933), who became internationally famed as the "Black Patti." While the musical careers of these seven highly accomplished women flourished during the last half of the nineteenth century, only five of them were deemed operatic "prima donnas;" Anna and Emma Hyers, lauded for their superb voices, primarily achieved theatrical fame. Other notable contemporary musicians included Adelaide G. Smith (Terry), Edna Brown (Bagnell), and Edith Lew (Mrs. Frederick P. White), all of Boston.

Most of these black concert singers acquired professional training. Several studied and concertized in Europe, while others reached similar attainments in this country. Elizabeth Taylor Greenfield was the first black American concert singer to receive acclaim in England; she studied with George Smart, organist of Queen Victoria's Chapel Royal in London in 1853-54.(1) Nellie Brown and the Hyers Sisters were trained by various teachers using the "Guilmette method," originated by C. A. Guilmette.(2) Marie Selika, a coloratura soprano, studied with Signor G. Bianchi(3) and Farini(4) in America, and Mazzoni in Europe.(5) Flora Batson, whose vocal range extended from the clearest coloratura to baritone, studied at the New England Conservatory in Boston. Sissieretta Jones was professionally trained in Providence and in Boston by conservatory teachers.(6)

In her article, "Black Women in Song: Some Socio-Cultural Images," Georgia A. Ryder traces the genesis of the black singer to Harriet Tubman's singing of chants on the Freedom Trail. Other sociological beginnings may be hypothesized; nonetheless, a remarkable ascendancy of musical culture occurred throughout the country during this period. Afro-Americans, newly freed from bondage and exhibiting growing aspirations and accomplishments, participated broadly in this new musical cultural thrust. The "star" concert developed, in which audiences heard virtuoso performers. These concerts drew large audiences in Boston, New York, Philadelphia, Washington, and other major cities. Among the first to be represented in this phenomenon were Nellie E. Brown and Marie Selika. Both women were called "prima donnas:" Brown in her "star" billings and Selika in the press, initially during her Eastern tour of Washington and Philadelphia in 1878-79.

Nellie E. Brown, the daughter of Charles J. and Martha A. Runnels Brown, was born in Dover, New Hampshire, in 1845. She had a brother, Eugene L. Brown, and sister, Edna Brown (Bagnell), also of musical note. Her father had moved to Dover from Boston during the year of her birth. After serving an apprenticeship, he successfully established his own business, as a hair dresser and maker of wigs.(7)

As a young woman Nellie studied at the Franklin Academy in Dover, a private school, during the fall and winter terms of 1864-65. In that year she was reportedly "discovered" by Miss C. A. Brackett, a local voice teacher, who encouraged her to pursue a professional career. Miss Brackett, a member of the 1872 World Peace Jubilee chorus, remained her teacher and mentor for several years; a "Soirée Musicale" program of Miss Brackett's students in 1874 lists Nellie Brown as one of the soloists.(8)

Nellie began her professional career in 1865 when she became soloist for the Free Will Baptist Church in Dover.(9) She served this congregation until 1872, when she accepted a similar post at the Grace Methodist Episcopal Church of Haverhill, Massachusetts. In December 1873 the *Dover Democrat* announced, "Miss Nellie Brown will give a grand Vocal and Instrumental Concert in City Hall, this Friday Evening the 19th. ... There is no question that this musical entertainment will be one of rare merit and excellence, and we hope it will be liberally patronized."(10) The reviewer reported in the next day's paper:

> Miss Brown was very warmly greeted, and surprised all with the ease and grace of her appearance, the richness of her voice and the fine rendering of her music. She was encored, and acquitted herself in all respects faithfully and well. . . . The whole entertainment was very fine indeed, and may be said to have been a complete success.(11)

In the 1874 season Miss Brown gave many notable

performances and received wide critical acclaim in Boston, New York, and Washington. One of her first reviews printed in the *Boston Globe* was of a concert at the North Russell Street Church, Boston, in commemoration of the ratification of the fifteenth amendment to the Constitution:

> The program consisted of choruses from the *Creation* and *Judas Maccabaeus*, interspersed with solos by three sopranos, Miss Nellie Brown of Dover, N.H., Miss E. J. Fisher of New York, and Miss Georgia Smith. . . . The audience was enthusiastic and vociferous in their applause, nearly every number on the program being encored. Miss Nellie Brown showed a particularly well modulated voice and trained study and appreciation of method, which served her well in the pleasant rendering given by her so gracefully and unaffectedly.(12)

A month later she participated in a benefit concert at the Melonaon in Boston for Rachel Washington:

> All the artists taking part acquitted themselves with marked acceptance, and their efforts were loudly applauded. Besides the beneficiary, Miss Nellie E. Brown of Dover, N.H., Miss Fannie A. Washington, Mr. B. F. Janey, Mr. T. M. Fisher of Portland, Me., Mr. S[amuel] Jamieson, and Mr. F[redrick] E[lliot] Lewis, violinist, took part.(13)

This particular concert was significant because it included some of the pioneer artists of New England. Fannie A. Washington, a contralto, studied at the New England Conservatory; T. M. Fisher of Portland, Maine, a baritone, sang frequently in Boston and Portland; B. F. Janey, a tenor and flutist, also studied with a New England Conservatory professor. Frederick E. Lewis, a violinist and composer, was a member of the World Peace Jubilee Orchestra in 1872 and was active in Boston musical circles. Samuel Jamieson had achieved success during tenure at the Boston Conservatory when he was a student of James M. Tracy. Frequently these and other individuals assembled for benefits and performed solos, duets, and chamber music by such composers as Verdi, Rossini, and Thomas.

In November 1874 Nellie Brown made her debut at Steinway Hall: "Miss Nellie Brown . . . possesses a voice of rare power and beauty which she has diligently labored to cultivate and improve. . . . She has also a rare charm of manner, which, united with her exquisite singing, won for her an enthusiastic reception."(14)

In addition to presenting concerts, Miss Brown successfully organized and conducted a group of fifty young girls in the juvenile operetta, *Laila, The Fairy Queen*, in May 1876: "The Misses, ranging from five to fifteen years, possess very sweet voices; and the music was given with much taste, and a degree of artistic excellence reflecting great credit on Miss Brown's efforts. . . . The audience were greatly pleased with the rendering of the music."(15)

Miss Brown later presented the same operetta in Haverhill, Massachusetts, using students from the high

school. That performance was also favorably reviewed:
"The presentation of the operetta of *Laila* at City Hall,
on Wednesday was a gratifying success. . . . The musical
and dramatic talent displayed by them are certainly very
creditable both to her [Miss Brown's] superintendence and
their co-operation."(16)

An important milestone of Nellie's life was her
marriage in 1876 to Lieutenant Charles L. Mitchell of the
Fifty-fifth Army Regiment. Lieutenant Mitchell had served
in the Union army during the Civil War. Following their
marriage, Nellie moved to join him in Boston where he was
attached to the Naval Office.(17) Nellie's concert tours
became less frequent after her marriage, but she continued
as soprano soloist at the Bloomfield Street Methodist
Episcopal Church and pursued further studies at the
Guilmette School of Vocal Art.(18) Upon completion of
these studies, she resumed her concert engagements, including a successful Chicago debut in 1880.(19)

In 1883 numerous reviews attested that Madame Mitchell
had reached the pinnacle of her concert career. She was an
acknowledged "prima donna,"(20) "the greatest stage artist
among our people."(21) She enjoyed wide popularity in New
York City, appearing as the lead artist in a number of
Bergen Star Concerts. A concert on October 30, 1883, for
the benefit of the Bethel Church in New York elicited the
following review in the *New York Globe* of November 3:

> Tuesday evening last was . . . one of the greatest
> musical events that has ever transpired in this city.
> The greatest artists in the country were congregated to
> give us a treat in music unequalled in the annals of
> N.Y. Colored Society. . . . Mme Nellie Brown Mitchell,
> the great Boston cancatrice [sic], upon her entrance
> received a perfect ovation. It was evident that much
> was expected of her, nor did she disappoint her ad-
> mirers; and her flute-like notes resounded clearly
> and distinctly through the hall, her voice, whose
> velvet-like softness added an indescribable charm to
> her singing, together with her grand stage presence,
> stamped upon her beyond a doubt the greatest stage
> artist among our people.

In the last section of the same newspaper, Madame Brown
advertised that she was a "Teacher of the Guilmette Method
of Vocal Technique and Respiratory exercises, 16 Mills St.,
Boston, Mass.," with "Terms for concert engagements and
lessons."(22) In November 1883 Madame Mitchell gave a
Thanksgiving Day concert at Lincoln Hall, Washington,
D.C.(23) A series of concerts followed in 1884 with continued favorable reviews; in January from twenty-five
hundred to three thousand persons attended a Bergen Concert
at the Academy of Music, Brooklyn, featuring Nellie. In
March Bergen presented her in a concert at Steinway Hall:

> Mme Nellie Brown Mitchell--who has ever been a warm
> favorite with our New York audiences, on this occasion
> received an ovation upon her rendition of the beautiful
> song *Far Away*, which was given tenderness and a pathos

almost indescribable and so impressed was every
listener that as if with one accord, as the last note
died so "far, far away" and its sweetness lingered all
around, even after the singer had left the stage, they
burst into thunders of applause and her re-appearance
was demanded. This scene was repeated until the fair
songstress had been three times before the foot-
lights.(24)

In the summer and fall of 1886 Madame Mitchell toured
the South and Midwest, where she was warmly received:

Nashville has rarely been favored with a visit by so
talented a vocalist as Mme. Mitchell. Each appearance
of the singer elicited a burst of thundering applause.
With breathless delight the audience hung upon every
note. . . . The range and magnificence of Mme.
Mitchell's voice was marvellous, and frequent passages
possessed a wonderful mellowness and sweetness. . . .
No musician or lover of the beautiful in the human
voice should forego the pleasure of hearing her.(25)

Similarly in 1887 the Nellie Brown Mitchell Concert
Company "won unstinted praise" in Eastern Canada:

Every number of the program was enthusiastically
encored, and then the audience was not satisfied. Miss
Nellie Brown-Mitchell has a fine, powerful voice, which
was heard to particular advantage in . . . *Bright Star
of Love*. . . . She responded to one of her encores with
Coming Thro' the Rye, which was given in a very
pleasing manner.(26)

From 1888 until 1890, Mme. Brown taught in the Vocal
Music Department of Hedding Chautauqua at East Epping, New
Hampshire,(27) made another tour of the South, and
performed in the Grand Musical and Literary Jubilee with
Selika and Edna Brown. In 1892 she performed in Brooklyn
with Edna Brown, and in Washington, D.C., under the
auspices of the YWCA. After 1895 she conducted the Women's
Relief Corp, taught, and performed occasionally.
Nellie Brown Mitchell remained in Boston throughout
most of her career. She became an important figure in the
community because of her musical programs and her talent as
a director. She died in Boston in 1924.
A soprano often compared with Madame Mitchell was her
contemporary, Madame Marie Selika (née Smith). Although
she was listed in Scruggs, Trotter, and Majors, as well as
in the biographies of performers such as Ike Simond and Tom
Fletcher, little is known of her life before 1875 except
that she was born in Natchez, Mississippi, and moved to
Cincinnati shortly after her birth. She lived there until
about 1874 or 1875 when she moved to San Francisco.
The press and other sources suggest that Marie Selika
was a student of Signor Bianchi in California for about
three years.(28) From there she moved to Chicago and
presumably at this juncture met her husband, Sampson
Williams. They were both students of Antonio Farini, who

lived in Chicago and later at 149 Tremont Street, Boston. Farini, who listed his specialty as "operatic and operatic stage studies," taught the "Italian Method." He charged $40 for twenty half-hour lessons.(29)

Marie Selika was noted as early as 1877 for her ability to sing trills and staccato passages. In a composition written for her by Frederick G. Carnes, a variety of advanced vocal techniques were indicated. This piece, entitled *Selika-Grand Vocal Waltz of Magic*, demanded a vocal range of more than two octaves. The last portion of the composition included staccato passages and trills with a chromatic passage and a vocal cadenza just before the ending.

Her voice quality and technique were extolled early in her career:

> Madame Selike [sic], the colored prima donna from the West, is now in Washington. She sang before a number of musical critics in the parlors of the 1st Congregational Church last Wednesday night and was at once endorsed by them. In such selections of difficult character as *Polka Staccato* from Mulder and "Cavatina" from *Lucrezia Borgia* she is said to show a remarkable quality of voice.(30)

A month later a Philadelphia correspondent to the *Musical Record* related:

> We have heard recently at the Academy, Madame Selika, a colored prima donna, who created a genuine sensation in Washington and came to us with all the halo of her successes there still about her. Her voice is of remarkable compass and possesses that peculiar timbre often found in the race to which she belongs. Her first selection Mulder's *Staccato Polka* showed at once its richness and pathos, and a triple encore was accorded her to which she responded with operatic selections. With Madame Selika as a future prima donna . . . who can say the "color line" is not gradually fading away.(31)

On the next page, the *Musical Record* announced that "Madame Selika, the famous colored prima donna, has arrived in Boston."

The success of Selika's Eastern tour continued in 1879:

> a recent concert in Washington, given at Lincoln Hall, in aid of St. Luke's (Colored) Episcopal Church, was attended by an unusually fashionable audience . . . Madame Selika's performance there was received with special enthusiasm, and gained for her pleasant words of praise from the "first lady of the land." Mrs. Hayes is well known as always ready to recognize any musical talent and encourage it by graceful and hearty encomium.(32)

As early as 1877 Madame Marie Selika Williams chose to use "Selika" as her professional name. An article in 1879

made reference to her interest in the role of Selika, the
leading female character in Meyerbeer's popular opera,
L'Africaine, written in 1865:

> Mrs. S. W. Williams professionally known as Madame
> Selika has been singing again in Philadelphia, and this
> time in aid of charity. Her magnificent voice was
> heard Thursday evening at a concert given in aid of the
> First Presbyterian Church at Concert Hall. She was
> accompanied by Prof. F. W. Jamieson of Boston. Her
> selections "Caro Nome" by Verdi and "Robert toi que
> j'aime" by Meyerbeer were effectively rendered. She
> also sung [sic] several duets with her husband S. W.
> Williams, which were heartily applauded. We learn that
> Madame Selika is desirous of making an operatic debut
> as Selika in *L'Africaine*. . . . Her voice is vibrating,
> of great compass and with intonations rich, sweet, and
> pathetic, but her method is faulty, and her taste in
> some respects uncultivated. To make a successful ap-
> pearance on the operatic stage much is required, and
> years may be counted well spent, if the reward of
> standing before the world as an acknowledged prima
> donna is at last gained.(33)

Surprisingly, Selika may already have sung the
Meyerbeer role. According to the black press she was
invited to Boston in 1878 to replace Etelka Gerster in a
concert; because of this opportunity, she was later invited
to sing the role of Selika in a stage production of
Meyerbeer's *L'Africaine* at the Academy of Music in
Philadelphia.(34) Although this report has not yet been
verified, it may have some validity. Historical records do
indicate that Gerster was in Boston on tour in 1878 and
that during that time Marie Selika was receiving favorable
press reviews in the same location.(35)

Selika made her New York debut at Steinway Hall on May
7, 1879. The reviewer for the *New York Times* stated:

> Mme. Selika, who has come to New York from the West
> with the favorable notices of several prominent jour-
> nals and Messrs. Max and Maurice Straskosch, made her
> debut last evening at Steinway Hall. . . . The perform-
> ance was generally creditable, and was received with
> enthusiasm by a good-sized audience. Mme. Selika has a
> voice of considerable power and of musical quality and
> showed in her performance last evening that she has
> given study and attention to the art of singing, in
> which she has every reason to expect to excell. Her
> rendering of the cabaletta from *Traviata* was her best
> performance to which she added in response to an encore
> *The Last Rose of Summer*, which was well sung and de-
> served the applause it received.(36)

The Strakosch brothers, Max and Maurice, Selika's men-
tors during this period, were well-known entrepreneurs of
operatic and concert ventures. Maurice was manager for his
sister-in-law, Adelina Patti. In speaking of the
"sweetness" of Selika's voice, he declared it "rarely to be

found outside of Italy."(37)   Later, the brothers were
managers of the Appollo Theatre in Rome, when Selika was on
the continent.(38)
     A playbill from this time advertised Selika as "The
Colored Prima Donna from Bianchi's Musical Conservatory,
San Francisco California in Operatic and Ballad Selec-
tions," and Mr. S. W. Williams, "late of Farini's Opera
College, Chicago . . . in operatic duets with Mme.
Selika."(39) In June 1882 Madame Selika sailed for Europe.
Correspondence from Marie and Sampson Williams to James M.
Trotter and others indicate that they spent the next year
in England. On October 14, 1882, she sang at Saint James
Hall in London. She also appeared with Carlotta Patti and
Signor Vergora in a London benefit concert for the Cuban
Slave Children under the patronage of Marquis de Cuna
L'Aiglesia.(40)
     Selika's European successes were recounted in the
American press:

     Madame Selika is doing well in her profession. She is
     making a tour of Europe and everywhere she has appeared
     she has won the plaudits of kings and queens, lords and
     dukes. Madame Selika is under the instruction of one
     of the greatest masters in music in Europe. . . .
     Besides appearing in Paris she will do Russia and
     Germany before she returns to London. She is attended
     by her husband Mr. S. Williams.(41)

Before her return to the United States, she performed at
the Musée du Nord in Brussels, Belgium, sang Weber's *Der
Freischutz* in Germany, and toured Russia and Denmark.
     The Washington press heralded Selika's return in the
fall of 1885:

     While aborde [sic] the Madame was the recipient of
     great attention and social distinction by crowned heads
     and nobility of the old world; singing in St. James
     Hall, London, on the same stage with Madame Patti under
     the directorship of Sir Julius Benedict, world renowned
     Maester de Baton. It is now proposed to make occasion
     of her visit here a memorable one in the musical
     circle.(42)

The laudatory review of the concert in the *New York Freeman*
indicated that both Selika and Sampson Williams had
profitted from their European experiences:

     Madam [sic] Selika was most warmly received and
     exhibited great improvement in her manner, and methods.
     Each of her selections--a cavalina [sic] from Rossini
     and another from Donizetti--were encored.   Mr.
     Williams, of the two, shows the greatest improvement.
     His voice is now a robust bass, which he uses in a
     manly and artistic manner, and possesses a breezy style
     that is quite captivating.

The review continues, describing the poor caliber of the
accompanying personnel assisting Selika, and alluding to

her continuous problems with management:

> The singing of Mr. Benjamin was so sloven and inartis-
> tic as to be a positive infliction, while the four
> ladies who appeared under the name of the "Selika
> Quartet" were a great disappointment. . . . It is to be
> hoped that this will prove their last appearance (the
> quartet's) until a reorganization takes place and
> voices are collected which will at least show a dis-
> position to blend and make music. Their effort was
> simply a waste of mediocrity. Selika is to appear
> later in the season, when it is to be hoped her
> support will be more worthy of her great ability. Mr.
> C. A. Fleetwood was the director and Mr. Daniel Murray
> manager.(43)

Concurrent with this activity was the Grand Benefit Concert
for the Charles Street A.M.E. Church presented at Tremont
Temple on Wednesday evening, November 11, 1885. Madame
Marie Selika, hailed as "The Patti of the Colored Race,"
was assisted by Miss Carrie Melvin, violin and cornet
soloist; S. W. Williams, Primo-Baritone soloist; and Miss
Addie G. Smith. The Boston community, in "appreciation of
the Madame's brilliant success in her studies and of her
various achievements in Europe," planned to give special
honor by having the leading citizens, "including his
Excellency Gov. Robinson, his Hon. Mayor H. O'Brien, Hon.
Henry B. Piercy, Hon. Alex. H. Rice, Judge Geo. L. Ruffin,
. . . Lieut J. M. Trotter, W. H. Dupree, Esq. and others"
request the attendance of the community at the Boston
homecoming of Marie Selika.(44)
     Numerous notices appeared in the next months in Boston
and New York newspapers:

> Grand Testimonial Planned--Selika accepts invita-
> tion(45)

> Madame Marie Selika and S. W. Williams contemplate a
> Western trip in the later [sic] part of February.(46)

The following three notices appeared in the *Boston
Advocate*, February 6, 1886:

> Madame Selika, Mme Nellie Brown-Mitchell and Miss A. G.
> Smith three of our most noted prima donnas and Miss
> Carrie Melvin the phenomenal instrumentalist will ap-
> pear in a grand concert.

> Miss Edna E. Brown, of Dover, N.H. will make her first
> appearance in Boston at the Benefit Concert of the
> *Advocate* (along with Nellie Brown Mitchell and Marie
> Selika).

> Madame Selika and Mr. S. W. Williams are at present in
> Boston, and will render some of their excellent selec-
> tions at the *Advocate*'s benefit Monday evening at
> Charles Street Church.

A series of other benefit concerts were given in this
period. The review of the Paul Drayton Commandary Concert
is of special interest, for it verified that a rising star,
Miss Batson, shared the honors with Madame Selika:

> Mme. Marie Selika's rendition of her selections was
> grand.   Mme. Selika should always be greeted with
> crowded houses, as nothing so inspires. She will not
> sing again this season in this part of the State, but
> at her return in the Fall New York should take the lead
> in giving her a grand opening concert.   Miss Flora
> Batson, the queen of ballad singing, was fully up to
> her usual tone and articulation.   It seemed in her
> first selection that she felt the effect of the bril-
> liancy of Selika's *Ieda* [sic]; but on her encore she
> was fully at home and her admirers were as enthusiastic
> as those of the prima donna.(47)

The work Selika sang is presumably an aria from *Aida*, not
"Ieda" as the reviewer reported.
     Although Selika is mentioned in fewer and fewer adver-
tisements in the press, the March 12, 1887, edition of the
Cleveland Gazette cited Nellie Brown Mitchell as Selika's
only rival.   Later, the *New York Age* advertised a perform-
ance with "Blind Tom."(48)
     Madame Selika concertized in Cleveland at the Mt. Zion
Congregation Church in 1888.(49)   In 1889 she successfully
toured the South with Hallie Q. Brown, the elocutionist:
"The Selika Combination, Mme Selika, Sampson Williams and
Hallie Q. Brown take Savannah by storm."(50)   During the
following year, she performed in Chicago and in Brooklyn,
New York.(51)   On January 30, 1891 she appeared with B. F.
Lightfoot in Boston in a benefit concert for Livingston
College.(52)   The New York *Clipper* of April 25, 1891,
reported a second European tour:

> Manager William Foot, whose big scheme for a represen-
> tative Negro Organization has recently accomplished a
> "coup d'état" in the engagement for a term of three
> years of Maria Selinka [sic], the "Black Patti" and M.
> Velouski, Madame Selinka's husband, a tenor, in Foote
> and Co's enterprise April 25th, the steamship Vandern,
> chartered for the purpose will sail with the entire
> party of 40 or more for Hamburg, Germany where the
> European tour will open.   William Gottschalk of Hamburg
> is the foreign agent.   All performers are colored.

On July 18, 1891, the *Indianapolis Freeman* reported
that "Madame Selika the famous Afro-American now in Europe
with Foot's Dramatic Co receives $7,000 a year and
expenses."   And later, "Madame Marie Selika is touring
Europe with great success. Kolo Vilaska [sic], the basso
is making a tour through Europe with much success."(53)   By
the end of the month the following was reported:

> Last account of Mme. Marie Selika and her husband
> Signor Velasco (né Sampson Williams) found them in
> Germany at the head of an opera troupe numbering 50

people where a Negro opera is to be given. An English
writer makes this inquiry about them, "As Selika in
L'Africaine it will be all right but how about 'La
Dame Blanche'?"(54)

By the fall of 1891 the notices stated simply that "Madame
Selika will visit France soon."(55)

In the summer of 1892 newspaper reports cite Madame
Selika and her husband as being in Pittsburgh, Indianapolis, and other cities of the Midwest; on October 22, 1892,
a critic for the *Cleveland Gazette* compared her with
Sissieretta Jones:

> In the rendition of the staccato notes, Mme Selika has
> not been excelled, even by Patti, and her shading is so
> smooth and even that you cannot but commend it. Mrs.
> Jones is a great singer; Mme Selika is the greatest
> colored singer. You hear Mme Jones with pleasure; you
> hear Mme Selika with profit.(56)

In 1893 she sang at the World's Fair in Chicago and moved
to Ohio.

Her career declined during the late 1890s, and she
retired from the stage following her husband's death about
1911.   In 1916 she accepted a teaching position at the
Martin-Smith School in New York. She sang at a Testimonial
Concert given in her honor in New York in 1919, and she
remained active as a private teacher until shortly before
her death in 1937.(57)

In conclusion, the musical lives of the early black
prima donna, from Greenfield to Jones, span more than fifty
years. At the peak of their careers, Greenfield, Selika,
Jones, and Batson performed for Queen Victoria. Late in
their concert careers, Brown and Selika became teachers;
Jones, Batson, and the Hyers Sisters relied on stage entertainment for their livelihoods. Several factors may have
underlaid this decline in the demand for their talent as
operatic and concert artists.

By 1891 Nellie Brown Mitchell was programmed with the
De Wolf sisters, Sadie and Rosa. This pair engaged in a
vaudeville circuit before joining Sam Jack's Creole Co. As
vaudeville, minstrel shows, and other forms of entertainment became the rage, there were fewer musical and literary
programs; black audiences were not able to sustain and
support concert artists indefinitely.

Opera was in its youth in America and most of the
acknowledged opera stars, including Lind, Patti, Gerster,
and Nilsson, were foreigners when Nellie Brown Mitchell and
Selika began their careers. By the end of the century
opera promoters such as Strakosch, who had supported Selika
early in her career, had gone to Europe to work in the
opera centers there. In addition, by the 1890s there was a
trend away from the light soprano voice.

Most of the performance opportunities for black prima
donnas of the nineteenth century were on European operatic
stages. Although the Drury Opera Company provided a viable
vehicle for serious musical performers from 1889 to 1908,
Drury documents the American performance difficulties

encountered by even one of the finest opera singers, Selika:

> Madame Marie Selika, one of the first among the queens of song . . . as a singer she compares favorably with the great singers of the world. Such arias as "Shadow Song" from *Dinorah*, "Il Dolce Suono" (*Lucia*) and many others were always sung in Italian. Selika sings in German also. Her greatest point was her brilliant execution which was wonderful. She has sung before the late Queen Victoria of England, and most of the crowned heads of Europe. Owing to the conditions of race questions at present in America, Madam [sic] Selika spends most of her time abroad, where she meets with the greatest success.(58)

The lack of support that had developed by 1900 stands in stark contrast to the enthusiastic reception granted the black prima donnas in the 1880s. The legitimate operatic stage in America was denied them; their access to public audiences was primarily limited to traveling troupes and occasional church benefits; and the public did not support careers based solely on the concert stage. Despite the outstanding talent and training of the early black prima donnas, black opera stars were not accepted in America until well into the twentieth century.

NOTES

    1. James Monroe Trotter, *Music and Some Highly Musical People* (Boston: Lee and Shepard, 1878), 80-83.
    2. *Folio*, 1879, 1880.
    3. Playbill, Harvard University Theatre Collection. Also see Eileen Southern, *Biographical Dictionary of Afro-American and African Musicians* (Westport, Conn.: Greenwood Press, 1982), 334.
    4. *Folio*, 1882.
    5. Trotter, 1883.
    6. *Cleveland Gazette*, December 16, 1893.
    7. *Dover Enquirer*, March 22, 1895.
    8. Program, C. A. Brackett, 1875, Harvard University Theatre Collection.
    9. Trotter (1878), 195.
    10. *Dover Democrat*, December 19, 1873.
    11. *Dover Democrat*, December 20, 1873.
    12. *Boston Globe*, March 31, 1874.
    13. *Boston Daily Evening Traveller*, April 16, 1874.
    14. *New York Gazette*, November 4, 1874.
    15. *Boston Journal*, May 17, 1876.
    16. *Haverhill Bulletin*, December 14, 1876.
    17. *Foster's Weekly Democrat* (Dover, New Hampshire), April 19, 1912.
    18. *Cleveland Gazette*, March 12, 1887.
    19. *Folio*, 1880.
    20. *New York Freeman*, January 31, 1883.
    21. *New York Globe*, December 1, 1883.

22. *New York Globe*, November 3, 1883.
23. *Washington Bee*, November 17, 1883.
24. *New York Globe*, March 29, 1884.
25. *New York Freeman*, June 19, 1886. Reprinted from the Nashville *Daily Union*, June 4, 1886.
26. *New York Age*, December 10, 1887. Reprinted from the St. John, New Brunswick (Canada), *Daily Globe*.
27. Southern, 53.
28. Playbill, Harvard University Theatre Collection. Also see Southern, 334.
29. *Folio*, 1882, 196.
30. *Musical Record*, November 30, 1878, 30.
31. *Musical Record*, December 14, 1878, 163.
32. *Musical Record*, March 29, 1879, 404.
33. Ibid.
34. *Cleveland Gazette*, April 28, 1888.
35. Alexis Chitty, "Etelka Gerster," *Grove's Dictionary of Music and Musicians*, 9 vols. (New York: St. Martin's Press, 1959), 3:608.
36. *New York Times*, May 8, 1879, 4.
37. *New York Globe*, March 3, 1883.
38. "Maurice Strakosch," *Grove's Dictionary of Music and Musicians*, 5 vols. (London: Macmillan, 1945), 5:156.
39. Playbill, Harvard University Theatre Collection.
40. *Cleveland Gazette*, March 3, 1883; April 28, 1888.
41. *New York Globe*, March 3, 1883.
42. *Washington Bee*, October 10, 1885, 3.
43. *New York Freeman*, November 14, 1885.
44. *Boston Advocate*, February 6, 1886.
45. *Boston Advocate*, February 13, 1886.
46. *Boston Advocate*, January 30, 1886.
47. *New York Freeman*, May 29, 1886.
48. *New York Age*, November 5, 1887.
49. *Cleveland Gazette*, March 24, 1888.
50. *Indianapolis Freeman*, March 2, 1889.
51. *Indianapolis Freeman*, November 8, 1890.
52. *Indianapolis Freeman*, January 3, 1891.
53. *Indianapolis Freeman*, October 17, 1891.
54. *Indianapolis Freeman*, October 31, 1891.
55. *Indianapolis Freeman*, November 14, 1891.
56. *Cleveland Gazette*, October 22, 1892.
57. Southern, 335.
58. *Colored American*, 1902, 324-26.

REFERENCES

Fletcher, Tom. *100 Years of the Negro in Show Business.* New York: Burdge, 1954.
Hare, Maude Cuney. *Negro Musicians and Their Music.* Washington, D.C.: Associated Publishers, 1936.
James, Edward T., and Janet Wilson. *Notable American Women 1607-1950: A Biographical Dictionary.* 5 vols. Cambridge, Mass.: Belnap Press, 1971.
La Brew, Arthur. *Studies in Nineteenth-Century Afro-American Music.* Detroit: Privately printed by the author, 1976.

Majors, Monroe Alphus. *Noted Negro Women.* Chicago: Donohue and Henneberry, 1893.

Odell, George. *Annals of the New York Stage.* 15 vols. New York: Columbia University Press, 1927-49.

Ryder, Georgia A. "Black Women in Song: Some Sociocultural Images," *Negro History Bulletin* 39:601-03.

Scruggs, Lawson. *Women of Distinction.* Raleigh, N.C.: Published by the author, 1893.

Simond, Ike. *Old Slack's Reminiscence and Pocket History of the Colored Profession from 1865 to 1891.* 1891. Reprint, with preface by Francis Lee Utley and introduction by Robert C. Toll. Bowling Green, Oh.: Bowling Green University Press Popular Press, 1974.

Southern, Eileen. *Biographical Dictionary of Afro-American and African Musicians.* Westport, Conn.: Greenwood Press, 1982.

Trotter, James Monroe. *Music and Some Highly Musical People.* Boston: Lee and Shepard, 1878, 1883.

Newspapers and Journals

Boston Advocate
Boston Globe
Boston Traveller
Cleveland Gazette
Dover (N.H.) Enquirer
Folio
Foster's Daily Democrat
Indianapolis Freeman
Musical Record and Review
New York Age
New York *Clipper*
New York Times

The Nineteenth-Century Spiritual Text: A Source for Modern Gospel

Oral L. Moses

Black American spirituals provide one source for much of the textual content of today's gospel music. For more than a century, these Afro-American religious songs served as a dominant medium through which the black American expressed his dissatisfaction with his station in life, vented his longing desire to live as a free man, and humbly sought peace and salvation from God:

> The songs of the slave represent the sorrows, rather than the joys, of his heart; and he is relieved by them, only as an aching is relieved by its tears. Sorrow and desolation have their songs, as well as joy and peace. Slaves sing more to make themselves happy, than to express their happiness.(1)

As another observer wrote:

> They sang so that it was a pleasure to hear; with all their souls and with all their bodies in unison, for their bodies wagged, their heads nodded, their feet stomped, their knees shook, their elbows and their hands beat time to the tune and the words which they sang with evident delight. One must see these people singing if one is rightly to understand their life.
>
> I have seen their imitators . . . who travel about the country painted up as negroes, and singing negro songs in the negro manner, and with gestures, as it is said; but nothing can be more radically unlike, for the most essential part of the resemblence fails--namely, the life.(2)

The method of composition, style of performance, and sociological significance of black spirituals are vital parts of black life and are easily recognizable through the texts of spirituals. Strong evidence of dissatisfaction with this life can be observed in the spiritual *Nobody Knows the Trouble I See*. Additional examples of this discontent are expressed in such spirituals as *Didn't My*

Lord Deliver Daniel, in which blacks communicated directly
with a God whom they believed would deliver them from the
evils of slavery, and *I'm Going to Live with Jesus*, where
they tried to assuage their hardships and grasp some hope
for a better future.

Like the spiritual, gospel music is also firmly
grounded in its texts. Charles Albert Tindley (1856-1933),
the progenitor of gospel music,

> concentrated on texts that gave attention to such im-
> portant concerns of Black Christians as worldly
> sorrows, blessings, and woes, as well as the joys of
> the after-life. . . . He also allowed space for the
> inevitable improvisation of text, melody, harmony, and
> rhythm so characteristic of Black American folk and
> popular music.(3)

Thomas A. Dorsey (1899-   ) was greatly influenced by
C. A. Tindley. In defense of his "bluesy" songs, composed
in a style similar to that of Tindley, he stated:

> The message is not in the music but in the words of the
> song. It matters not what kind of music or what kind of
> movement it has, if the words are Jesus, Heaven, Faith
> and Life then you have a song with which God is pleased
> regardless of what critics and some church folk say.(4)

Because of the importance of the textual content,
gospel singers started a revival of interest in the
spiritual during the World War II and Martin Luther King,
Jr. eras. In the midst of these periods of severe
hardships and struggles, the gospel song, like the
spiritual during slavery, was a source of strength and
encouragement. These spirituals and plantation songs provided twentieth-century gospel singers with words that were
strong in their spiritual convictions and carried a message
of the social pressures and frustrations that had burdened
black Americans since slavery. Such a revival of interest
serves to connect and preserve an oral tradition passed
down from the earliest existence of the spiritual that
continued through the 1940s.

Three sections of the spirituals' texts frequently
borrowed for the texts of gospel songs are the chorus, an
incipit, and part of an inner verse. In addition to these
direct borrowings, gospel texts often substitute or omit
some of the original words (see Appendix A).

Oh, Give Way, Jordan is found in the collection *Hampton
and Its Students*, 1874, 1875, 1878.(5) There are two parts,
the chorus:

> Oh, give way, Jordan, Oh, give way, Jordan
> Oh, give way, Jordan, I want to go across to see my
>   Lord.

and the stanza:

> Oh, I heard a sweet music up above
> I want to go across to see my Lord
> An' I wish dat music would come here,
> I want to go across to see my Lord.

A gospel song of the 1950s, *Oh, Get Away, Jordan*, borrows only the text of the chorus. It is sung in a call and response style:

CALL: Get away
RESPONSE: Get away Jordan
CALL: Get away
RESPONSE: Get away oh chilly Jordan
CALL: Get away
RESPONSE: Get away Jordan
ALL: I want to cross over to see my Lord.

Some of the words of the spiritual are omitted or substituted. The original text, "Oh, give way, Jordan, I want to go across to see my Lord," becomes in the gospel song, "Get away, Jordan, I want to cross over and see my Lord."

The second stanza appears as follows:

> Oh, stow back de powers of hell,
> I want to go across to see my Lord
> And let God's children take de field,
> I want to go across to see my Lord
> Now stan' back Satan, let me go by,
> I want to go across to see my Lord
> Gwine to serve my Jesus till I die,
> I want to go across to see my Lord.

"'Stow back' means to shout backward."(6) This term is used in reference to the religious dance that was an integral part of the early folk church worship. This shout ceremony took place after the main part of the service:

> After the sermon they formed a ring, and with coats off
> sung, clapped their hands and stomped their feet in a
> most ridiculous and heathenish way. I requested the
> pastor to go and stop their dancing. At his request,
> they stopped their dancing and clapping of hands, but
> remained singing and rocking their bodies to and fro.
> This they did for about fifteen minutes.(7)

The words "stow back" indicate that this spiritual was used specifically for the shout ceremony. As the term is passed down into gospel music, "stow back" becomes "stepback":

CALL: Oh, stepback
RESPONSE: Stepback Jordan
CALL: Step way back
RESPONSE: Stepback oh chilly Jordan.

When this stanza is currently sung, the gospel singer may make appropriate movements indicated in the text.

The spiritual, *Anybody Here*, from *Old Plantation Hymns* by William E. Barton (1899), is an example in which, again, only the chorus is borrowed:

> Is there anybody here that love my Jesus:
> Anybody here that love my Lord?
> Oh, I want to know if you love my Jesus?
> I want to know if you love my Lord.

With minor textual alterations, this chorus appears in the modern gospel version (ca1979) as:

> Anybody here love my Jesus
> Anybody here love my Lord
> I want to know if you love my Jesus
> I want to know if you love my Lord.

This custom of borrowing texts was already commonplace among black Americans during slavery:

> We have too, a growing evil, in the practice of singing in our places of public and society worship, merry airs, adapted from old songs, to hymns of our composing; often miserable as poetry, and senseless as matter, and most frequently composed and first sung by the illiterate blacks of the society.(8)

Similar borrowings are found in spirituals. William Barton stated:

> One song is satisfied to snatch a single line from any convenient hymn, and pair it with one of its own in the refrain, while borrowing couplets right and left for the stanzas.

> While the fitting together of couplets and refrains almost at random leads to some odd and incongruous combinations, upon the whole one is surprised to find with what good taste the mosaic is made, especially when the singing is led by an old-time leader with a wide range of couplets to choose from. Some of these men when confronted by an inquirer with notebook and pencil can hardly recall half a dozen of these stanzas; but in the fervor of their worship they not only remember them by the score but by a sort of instinct rather than taste or judgment fit together words from different sources without a second's reflection or hesitation.(9)

Three spirituals that exemplify these customary borrowings are *Keep Your Lamps Trimmed and Burning, Rise and Shine*, and *Jacob's Ladder* (see Appendix B).

Observe *Keep Your Lamps Trimmed and Burning* from the collection, *The Story of the Jubilee Singers with Their Songs* by J. B. Marsh (1887), as the parent spiritual. There are two parts, the chorus:

Keep your lamps trimmed and a-burning
Keep your lamps trimmed and a-burning
Keep your lamps trimmed and a-burning
For this work's almost done.

and the stanza:

Brothers, don't grow weary
Brothers, don't grow weary.

There are two additional sections that are repeats of the chorus. The second time the chorus is repeated, the text is changed. Of the three lines of text, two are borrowed from the spiritual, *We Are Climbing Jacob's Ladder*:

Tis religion makes us happy, [etc.]
We are climbing Jacob's ladder, [etc.]
Every round goes higher and higher, [etc.]
For this work's almost done.

Both spirituals, *We Are Climbing Jacob's Ladder* and *Rise and Shine*, draw on the text of the chorus and on the stanza of *Keep Your Lamps Trimmed and Burning*.
Rise and Shine, from *Jubilee and Plantation Songs* (1887), uses two inner stanzas from the spiritual, *Keep Your Lamps Trimmed and Burning*. The first phrase, "Keep your lamps trimmed and burning," appears as the second part of the second stanza:

You may keep your lamps trimmed and burning, burning
You may keep your lamps trimmed and burning, burning
You may keep your lamps trimmed and burning, burning
For the year of Jubilee.

The second inner stanza, substituting "children" for "Brothers," appears as the beginning of the third stanza:

Oh, come on children, don't be weary, weary
Oh, come on children, don't be weary, weary
Oh, come on children, don't be weary, weary
For the year of Jubilee.

Each of these spirituals is being used in the twentieth century as a gospel song or as a borrowed text for a gospel song.
The gospel arrangement of *Jacob's Ladder* uses the chorus of *Rise and Shine* as one of its stanzas. This is achieved by omitting the word "and" on the fourth beat of each measure in the chorus and substituting "Soldier of the cross" for "For the year of Jubilee" in the last four measures of the chorus:

Rise, shine give God the glory, glory
Rise, shine give God the glory, glory
Rise, shine give God the glory, glory
Soldier of the cross.

Keep Your Lamps Trimmed and Burning, the gospel song,

maintains the original character of the spiritual, but
incorporates many gospel features. The text, "Keep your
lamps trimmed and burning," is retained, but "For this
work's almost done" replaces "For the time is drawing
nigh." Also, "Brother don't get weary" becomes "Children
don't be weary." A new stanza is also added:

> Christian journey soon be over
> Christian journey soon be over
> Christian journey soon be over
> The time is drawing nigh.

An example of incipit borrowing occurs in the chorus of
the spiritual, *I Don't Feel Noways Tired*, found in the
collection, *Hampton and Its Students*, (1903). The first
phrase of the chorus of the spiritual:

> Lord, I don't feel noways tired
> Children oh glory hallelujah
> For I hope to shout glory when dis world is on fiah
> Children oh glory hallelujah.

appears as the first phrase of the chorus of the gospel
version:

> I don't feel noways tired
> I've come too far from where I started from
> Nobody told me the road would be easy
> I don't believe he brought me this far to leave me.

In conclusion, consideration will be given to the spiritual, *The Old Ship of Zion*. In examining nineteenth-
century sources for its relationship to gospel, it was
discovered that there are at least eight different versions
of this spiritual: *The Chorus* (1860)--1 version; *Homes
of the New World* (F. Bremer, 1851)--1 version; *Slave Songs
of the United States* (Allen, McKim, 1867)--2 versions;
Army Life in a Black Regiment (T. W. Higginson, 1870)--3
versions; and *Jubilee Singers* (1877)--1 version.
According to William Frances Allen in *Slave Songs*
(1867), this spiritual was sung approximately 150 years
ago:

> We have received two versions of the *Old Ship of Zion*,
> quite different from each other and from those given
> from Col. Higginson. The first was sung twenty-five
> years ago by the colored people of Ann Arundel Company,
> Maryland. The words may be found in *The Chorus*
> (Philadelphia: A. S. Jenks, 1860), p. 170.(10)

Based on the publication date of the preceding quote, it is
probable that this version dates back to approximately
1842.
This spiritual, popular among black Americans of the
nineteenth century, remains a favorite gospel song in the
twentieth century. The song, with textual variations,
appears in at least three gospel collections: *Wings Over
Jordan* (1940s)--1 version; Thomas A. Dorsey (1950)--1

version; and *Modern Gospel* (1985)--1 version.

Although some of the corresponding stanzas are not the same, there is a common thread that connects the different versions. The primary connection is the chorus:

Tis the old ship of Zion, hallelujah
Tis the old ship of Zion, hallelujah

which appears in all but two of the versions. The second connecting feature is the stanza:

King Jesus is the Captain
King Jesus is the Captain

which is borrowed from the spiritual for the gospel versions.

The longevity and popularity of *The Old Ship of Zion*, as both a spiritual and a gospel song, indicate the importance of the text: when the black man of the twentieth century needed to express his dissatisfaction with this world, he often used the words inherited from the rich oral tradition of the spirituals of the nineteenth century. Through the power of the texts of these songs, dealing with the struggle for survival, black Americans continue to find hope and affirmation, and, according to W. E. B. DuBois, "a faith in the ultimate justice of things."(11)

APPENDIX A

Texts of Spirituals Borrowed for Gospel Songs

Spiritual	Gospel Song
	I. Chorus Only Borrowed
Jesus Is a Rock	*Why My Jesus Is a Rock in a Weary Land*
Witness	*My Soul Is a Witness for My Lord*
I Want to Be Ready	*Walk in Jerusalem*
Good News, de Chariot's Comin'	SAME TITLE
Oh, Give Way Jordan	*Get Away Jordan*
O Redeemed	*Oh Redeemed, Redeemed, I'm Washed in the Blood of the Lamb*
We'll Stand the Storm	*Oh! Stand the Storm, It Won't Be Long*
Fix Me Jesus	*Fix Me Jesus, Fix Me Right*

The Lord Will Provide	SAME TITLE
Is There Anybody Here?	*Anybody Here*
I Shall Not Be Moved	SAME TITLE
Dust and Ashes	*He Arose, He Arose from the Dead*

II. Incipit Borrowed

We Are Out On the Ocean Sailing	SAME TITLE
I Don't Feel No-Ways Tired	SAME TITLE
What Ship Is That A-Sailin'?	*Tis the Old Ship of Zion*

III. Substitution of Words

Swing Low, Sweet Chariot	SAME TITLE
When I Lay My Burden Down	*Glory, Glory Hallelujah*
Let de Heaven Light Shine on Me	*Shine on Me*

IV. Chorus and Stanza Borrowed

When I Am Gone, Gone, Gone	SAME TITLE
Some o'Dese Moaning's	*Look Away in de Heaven*
Roll Jordan, Roll	*Roll, Jordan, Roll, I Want to Go to Heaven*
When Moses Smote the Water	SAME TITLE
Ever' Time I Think about Jesus	*Calvary*
Steal Away	SAME TITLE
In Dat Great Gettin-up Mornin'	SAME TITLE
A Great Camp Meeting in the Promise Land	SAME TITLE
O Lord, Remember Me	*Do Lord*
Be Ready When He Comes Again	SAME TITLE
O Mary, Don't You Weep	SAME TITLE
He Led My Mother All the Way	*Let Jesus Lead You*
The Blood Has Signed My Name	*Oh the Blood*

Hush, Hush, the Angels Calling Me   SAME AS TITLE

Didn't It Rain?   SAME AS TITLE

There Is a Balm in Gilead   SAME AS TITLE

APPENDIX B

RISE AND SHINE

Oh, rise and shine and give
  God the glory, glory
Rise and shine and give
  God the glory, glory
Rise and shine and give
  God the glory, glory
For the year of Jubilee

Jesus carry the young lambs
  in his bosom, bosom
Jesus carry the young lambs
  in his bosom, bosom
Jesus carry the young lambs
  in his bosom, bosom
For the year of Jubilee

Oh, come on mourners
  get you ready, ready
Come on mourners
  get you ready, ready
Come on mourners
  get you ready, ready   *KEEP YOUR LAMPS TRIMMED*
For the year of Jubilee

You may keep your lamps   Keep your lamps
  trimmed and burning, burning   trimmed and a-burning
You may keep your lamps   Keep your lamps
  trimmed and burning, burning   trimmed and a-burning
You may keep your lamps   Keep your lamps
  trimmed and burning, burning   trimmed and a-burning
For the year of Jubilee   For this work's almost done

Oh, come on, children   Brothers don't grow
  don't be weary, weary   weary
Come on children   Brothers don't grow
  don't be weary, weary   weary
Come on children   Brothers don't grow
don't be weary, weary   weary
For the year of Jubilee   For this work's almost done

Oh, don't you hear them   Preachers don't grow
  bells a-ringing, ringing   weary
Don't you hear them   Preachers don't grow
  bells a-ringing, ringing   weary
Don't you hear them   Preachers don't grow
  bells a-ringing, ringing   weary
For the year of Jubilee   For this work's almost done

WE ARE CLIMBING JACOB'S LADDER	*KEEP YOUR LAMPS TRIMMED* (continued)
We are climbing Jacob's ladder	We are climbing Jacob's ladder
We are climbing Jacob's ladder	We are climbing Jacob's ladder
We are climbing Jacob's ladder	We are climbing Jacob's ladder
Soldier of the cross	For this work's almost done
Every round goes higher, higher	Every round goes higher, higher
Every round goes higher, higher	Every round goes higher, higher
Every round goes higher, higher	Every round goes higher, higher
Soldier of the cross	For this work's almost done

Sinner do you love my Jesus

Sinner do you love my Jesus

Sinner do you love my Jesus

Soldier of the cross

If you love him why not serve him

If you love him why not serve him

If you love him why not serve him

Soldier of the cross

NOTES

1. Frederick Douglass, "My Bondage and My Freedom (1855)" in *Readings in Black American Music*, 2d ed. Eileen Southern, ed. (New York: W. W. Norton, 1983), 84.
2. Fredrika Bremer, *The Homes of the New World; Impressions of America*, Mary Howitt, trans. (New York: Harper & Brothers, 1853), 124-30.
3. Horace Clarence Boyer, "Charles Albert Tindley: Progenitor of Black-American Gospel Music," *Black Perspective in Music* (Fall 1983), 109.
4. Thomas A. Dorsey, a personal interview videotaped at the University of Michigan in 1981.
5. Mary Alice Ford Armstrong and Helen Ludlow, *Hampton and its Students. By Two of It Teachers . . . With Fifty Cabin and Plantation Songs, Arranged by Thomas P. Fenner* (New York: G. P. Putnam's Sons, 1874), 195.
6. "The Negro Dialect," *Nation*, December 14, 1865, 744-45.

7. Daniel Payne, "Recollections of Seventy Years (1888)," in Southern, *Readings in Black American Music,* 69.

8. John Fanning Watson, *Methodist Error; or, Friendly Christian Advice, to those Methodists, Who Indulge in Extravagant Religious Emotions and Bodily Exercise by a Wesleyan Methodist* (Trenton, N.J.: D & E Fenton. Reprint. Cincinnati: Philips & Speer, 1819), 15-16.

9. William Eleazer Barton, "Old Plantation Hymns," *New England Magazine* (December, 1898. Reprint. Katz, 1899), 23.

10. William Francis Allen, Charles Pickard Ware, and Lucy McKim Garrison, comps., *Slave Songs of the United States* (New York: A. Simpson, 1867), 102.

11. W. E. B. DuBois, *The Souls of Black Folk* (New York: Fawcett Publications, 1961), 189.

REFERENCES

Allen, William Francis, Charles Pickard Ware, and Lucy McKim Garrison, comps. *Slave Songs of the United States.* New York: A. Simpson, 1867. Reprint. New York, 1967.

Armstrong, Mary Alice Ford, and Helen Ludlow. *Hampton and Its Students. By Two of Its Teachers . . . With Fifty Cabin and Plantation Songs, Arranged by Thomas P. Fenner.* New York: G. P. Putnam's Sons, 1874.

Boyer, Horace Clarence. "Charles Albert Tindley: Progenitor of Black-American Gospel Music," *Black Perspective in Music* 11 (Fall 1983), 109.

Bremer, Fredrika. *The Homes of the New World: Impressions of America.* Translated by Mary Howitt. New York: Harper & Brothers, 1853.

Douglass, Frederick. "My Bondage and My Freedom (1855)," in *Readings in Black American Music,* 2d ed. Edited by Eileen Southern. New York: W. W. Norton, 1983.

Payne, Daniel. "Recollections of Seventy Years (1888)," in *Readings in Black American Music,* 2d ed. Edited by Eileen Southern. New York: W. W. Norton, 1983.

Watson, John Fanning. *Methodist Error; or, Friendly Christian Advice to those Methodists, Who Indulge in Extravagant Religious Emotions and Bodily Exercise by a Wesleyan Methodist.* Trenton, N.J.: D & E Fenton. Reprint. Cincinnati: Philips & Speer, 1819.

P. G. Lowery
and His Musical Enterprises:
The Formative Years

Clifford Edward Watkins

Perhaps the best-loved stories within our society are those
of the pull-up-by-your bootstrap, underdog-wins-despite-
the-odds genre. The story of Perry G. Lowery is precisely
of that nature. Born into a farming family that enjoyed
making music, Lowery and his older brothers were encouraged
at an early age to play musical instruments. Lowery first
learned to play a small drum, which enabled him to join
what he called his "family band." He then selected a
cornet, which was a bit more challenging: "After picking
the cornet, he appreciated that he had a long road to
travel, and with courage and confidence, he started out to
climb the ladder of fame."(1) Lowery did not become an
instant star in the highly competitive field of musical
entertainment; in time, however, he became the yardstick by
which bandmasters were measured.

The "show" bands of the mid-nineteenth century included circus, minstrel, concert, and military bands.
The quality of these bands depended on the calibre of the
musicians and leaders. An aspiring professional musician
often served an apprenticeship with lesser-quality bands
before progressing into a better situation; Lowery, in his
quiet, polite manner, diligently paid these "dues."
Gradually the established professionals discovered his
talent and ability:

> He struggled along for five years unnoticed with
> different minor bands, but at last the day came and the
> tie was broken and he found himself breathing a new
> atmosphere surrounded by a similar class of aspirants.
> This change of air was due to the untiring efforts of
> his talented friend and admirer Mr. George Baily,
> the great trombone soloist with [the] Darkest America
> Band. Mr. Bailey secured a position for him with the
> famous Mallory Brothers Minstrels.(2)

Lowery learned to listen, compare, study, and practice.
In 1898 W. C. Handy, the band director of Mahara's
Minstrels, noted Lowery's emerging personality and perform-
ance trademarks:

[He] followed along behind our band in Council
Bluffs, Iowa. He was a dark, handsome man, but
noticeably shy and bent on attracting as little attention as possible. I couldn't imagine what he was up
to. No words were exchanged. He simply followed,
watching and listening intently, as if he had been
employed to shadow me.

That night, I saw him again. He was at the Omaha
[Trans-Mississippi] Exhibition then [1898], blowing a
horn in such a manner as to suggest that he might have
been Gabriel's right-hand man.(3)

Handy's statement portended things to come. During his
career, Lowery was to take the measure of many performers,
including Handy:

That night we got together . . . like a pair of game-
cocks in a crowing match. I called for a number, and he
gave it to me with plenty of gravy and dressing. He
named his terms and I came back with my Sunday best.
From that day, my great ambition was to outplay P.
G.(4)

By the time Handy met Lowery and that phenomenal
"crowing match" ensued, Lowery was an outstanding
performer, but in an often-questioned field of music,
minstrelsy. Oakley stated that "minstrels were a
disreputable lot in the eyes of a large section of the
upper-crust Negroes . . . but it is also true that all the
best talent of that generation came down the same
drain."(5) These minstrel shows also did "provide the
first real employment for Negro entertainers."(6)
    From the beginning of his professional career with the
Mallory Brothers Minstrels, Lowery continued to climb the
ladder of success in such organizations as the Great
Wallace-Hagenbeck Circus, the Original Nashville Students,
the Forepaugh & Sells Brothers Circus, Richard and
Pringle's Minstrels, Cole Brothers, and Barnum and
Bailey.(7) His services as a businessman/manager and
talent scout were also sought by many others.
    P. G. Lowery's tours with these organizations were
divided into a summer tour that ran from mid-spring to late
fall, and a winter tour that consumed the rest of the year
except for occasional two- or three-week breaks. For
Lowery's winter tours the Original Nashville Students Concert Company combined with the P. G. Lowery Concert Band to
perform vaudeville acts but not minstrel shows.
    In January and February 1897 the *Indianapolis Freeman*
reported that the personnel for that winter tour included
P. G. Lowery (cornet/band leader), A. H. Montgomery (violin/
orchestra leader), Preston T. Wright (singer/owner/mana-
ger), as well as twelve other musicians, comedians, and
those in managerial positions.(8)
    A year later the band, with P. G. Lowery as leader, had
grown to include eleven musicians, four of whom were designated as soloists, plus six managerial positions. The
orchestra consisted of fourteen musicians, plus the new

leader, Dan Desdunes.   Most of the members in the company
were assigned two or more positions, such as band/orches-
tra, band/stage manager, or band/comedian. This practice
of "doubling" was not uncommon in show organizations, especially within small troupes.(9)
    Although the personnel of the show worked well as a
unit and met with repeated successes on the road, an unexpected alteration in the roster occurred on or about April
2, 1898, with the death of Preston T. Wright, the proprietor of the Nashville Students Company.   Despite the shock
of his death, the group continued the tour after his burial
in Paola, Kansas.   Mrs. Wright assumed management and
subsequently planned a larger company for the 1898-99
season.(10)
    According to E. O. Green, the Nashville Students Show
proved so successful that the company had not closed since
the tour began in August 1896.   In addition to his musical
duties, Green also served as the special representative of
the *Indianapolis Freeman*.
    In September 1898 Mrs. Wright added two song writers
and show designers to the show, plus a gun manipulator and
juggler.   S. H. Dudley became the stage manager, replacing
Harry Gilliam, and Dan Desdunes became the musical director.   Lowery, who had closed with the company in order to
perform at the Trans-Mississippi Exposition in Omaha,
Nebraska, was replaced as cornetist and bandmaster by Harry
Prampin.(11)
    Following the close of his performance series at the
Omaha Exhibition, Lowery became the director of the J. E.
George Concert Band.   Although the identity of George and
the roster of the organization has not been discovered at
this writing, Lowery did state that the band contained "a
lot of first-class musicians which will be ready to meet
any band of its size, regardless of color."(12) Only one
week after this statement was made, Lowery was reported to
be "scoring a big hit with his concert band with the
Georgia Up-To-Date [Minstrels]."(13) Apparently he took
the George band into that show.   He and three other
soloists were featured: Fountain Woods (trombone), Joe
Pleasant (tuba), and Henry Lane (clarionet [sic]).
    Lowery's bands were noted for their balance of instru-
mentation, technical expertise, and clarity of tone.   These
elements of performance were so striking, especially in
comparison to the quality of other bands, that his con-
ceptual approach was often labeled the "school of tone
culture."(14) By Christmas Eve 1898 his Concert Band's
instrument-to-instrument ratio represented an exact balance
formula for a brass band, and the same approximate ratio as
those of the later larger twentieth-century bands: one
clarinet, four cornets, two alto horns, one trombone, one
baritone euphonium, one tuba, and three percussions.(15)
    One frequently used method of attracting musical talent
during this period was via advertisement in "trade papers."
These papers carried notices concerning vacancies, persons
"at liberty" (having no job but desperately looking), and
calls for contracted persons to report at specific locations to begin the performance season. Performers who were
able to execute more varied tasks were the most employable.

In the January 28, 1899, edition of the *Indianapolis Freeman*, Lowery requested the following personnel:

> Lady cornetist or prima donna to feature in band concert; also good cook and waiter who can play in band. Reeds preferred. State full particulars and lowest salary in first letter. Address all communications to P. G. Lowery. . . . P. S.—would like to hear from the Morrisons.(16)

The post-scripted sentence either indicated his preference in personnel or alerted all applicants that their abilities should be at the level of the "Morrisons" or better.(17)

By April 1899 Lowery, with the assistance of his stage manager and drummer Julius Glenn, had selected his necessary replacements and had begun building his own vaudeville stage troupe. On April 8, 1899, the *Freeman* carried the call for all summer season members to report to Brooklyn, New York, no later than April 27. Apparently, Lowery's connection with the Nashville Students was not severed; when Lowery's Famous Concert Band opened with the Forepaugh-Sells Bros. Circus and Show on May 1, 1899, he had with him the personnel of the Nashville Students Company. The only exceptions were Harry Gilliam, who cancelled because of the death of his mother,(18) and Fountain B. Wood, who had been named band director of the Georgia Up-To-Date Company.(19)

At the close of the Forepaugh-Sells Bros. Circus season, Lowery wrote to the *Freeman* from Alexandria, Louisiana, that, with the help of his musicians and entertainers, his unique venture of combining circus and vaudeville shows had been such a success during the summer season that the management of the Forepaugh-Sells organization had decided the Lowery band would play a concert under the "big top" at each show during the next season.

At the onset of the winter season, Lowery was busy practicing his cornet, writing an educational article for the *Freeman*,(20) and making plans for the next summer tour with Forepaugh-Sells Bros. He also went on tour again with "The Original Nashville Students combined with Lowery and Greens [E. O.?] Improved Minstrels."(21) This group was comprised of twenty-five persons with Lowery managing and serving as cornet soloist. Also included were comedians, actresses, and a contortionist.(22) The remainder of the company were unnamed musicians who may have played on the summer tour with the Lowery Concert Band and Vaudeville Show.

The summer tour (1900) of the Concert Band and Vaudeville Show opened with Forepaugh-Sells Bros. on April 23 at Baltimore. Equipped with new uniforms and the largest bandwagon on parade at that time, Lowery amazed his audiences with an orchestra of eight persons and a "super" band of fourteen pieces. In addition to his musical duties, Lowery was also titled "contractor and manager" of Lowery's Vaudeville.(23)

The circus closed their successful season in Aberdeen,

Mississippi, on or about November 3. Of this event, Lowery
made this statement:

> the 22 members that constitute my band, orchestra, and
> Vaudeville show . . . are all here to shake hands and
> bid God's speed. This is one event nearly incomparable
> [as] a joyful yet a sad event. To the members of my
> band and company; you have my sincere wishes for
> health, wealth, and prosperity; may you ever prove
> yourselves ladies and gentlemen as you have under my
> management and build for your contractor a reputation
> of professional experience and good judgment as you
> have me. . . . As ever, P. G. Lowery.(24)

As a further testimony to his skills as a band leader and
manager, Lowery was given a twenty-four-month contract by
the Forepaugh-Sells organization to manage three shows with
a personnel of sixty people.(25)

By December 17, 1900, Lowery was again on the circuit
with what was now called W. I. Swain's Original Nashville
Students and P. G. Lowery's Colored Concert Band, which
opened at the Peoria (Illinois) Auditorium for a two-night
stand.(26) Again, the names of the sidemen were not provided, but it is assumed that the band/orchestra was
smaller, yet adequate to accompany the vaudeville
performers. While carrying out his musical duties, Lowery
also worked as the show's assistant manager and the
personal representative of W. I. Swain (now manager of the
Nashville Students); manager of the Forepaugh-Sells Bros.
Vaudeville Show; and also was "engaged by another large
tent show to secure twenty-five people for summer engagement."(27)

At the close of the winter season, Lowery began final
preparations for the commencement of the summer season, his
third with the Forepaugh-Sells organization. He was in New
York in early April 1901 with his veteran musicians:
Thomas Mays, Arthur Prince, William Mays, Henry Rawles,
George Hambright, Jeff J. Smith, James Morton, and James
Hall.(28)

After the opening of the show, Lowery, in Brooklyn, New
York, wrote:

> [The] vaudeville show and band are meeting with great
> favor and rendering some fine music. The company num-
> bers twenty-two people including a band of fourteen
> pieces, male quartet and female quartet.(29)

After the band began the concert, these musicians
changed uniforms and instruments and performed other
responsibilities within the vaudeville show performance:

> [The] minstrel bands generally were small and composed
> of versatile musicians . . . expected to play more than
> one instrument. . . . For the show concert . . . some
> players had to "double," exchanging their wind instru-
> ments for fiddles, guitars, banjos, mandolins, and
> percussion[s].(30)

The orchestra for the show was composed of seven players, including the leader Calvin Jackson. The other players from the band either had specific acts that they performed, such as A. L. Prince, the slack-wire artist, or were involved in supporting roles, such as participating in comedy sketches, and/or singing in the chorus.(31)

In reporting to the *Freeman* on the progress of his show, Lowery explained that

> I have the services of a New York quartette with the two well-known soloists W. S. Ball, baritone, and Chas. B. Foster, basso, whose lowest register is unknown. The female quartette is composed of Mrs. Beadley, Miss Ida Larkins, Miss Cara Scott and Miss Josie Sutton; they are professionals, and introduce some new and catchy songs with drilled movements, the first of the kind ever used under canvas. Our stage manager, Billy Bradley, has the show in splendid running order; he being well versed in that line of work.(32)

Lowery always tried to give recognition through the newspaper to all the people that directly or indirectly contributed to the success of the show. He even listed members of the train crew, including Elmer Mason, the headwaiter, and Charles Stewart, the head porter.(33)

When the company reached Indianapolis, they received a great welcome, complete with press coverage. Woodbine, "The Stage" editor for the *Freeman*, stated:

> The colored band and vaudeville show idea is the newest novelty in the circus line, and long may it live for no greater drawing card is before the American people today than a genuine troupe of colored minstrel performers accompanied by a good band and orchestra. Other shows will follow. The start was all that was necessary. And no cleverer set of gentlemen than Prof. Lowery and band members, and no better set of performers than his vaudevillians could have been endorsed by Mr. Connors [of Forepaugh-Sells Bros.] to make the maiden effort, which has proven a multiplicity of successes. May it ever prosper.(34)

Apparently the secret of Lowery's success with his bands was his careful selection of instrumental specialists who had studied with some of the better teachers of the day:

> Prof. [C. D.] Jackson class of 1900, New York City, G. P. Handright [sic] clarionettist from the Warren Conservatory, J. J. Smith, advanced pupil of P. G. Lowery, the May brothers, William and Thomas, also James Morton and Sam Elliott are of rare ability.(35)

Lowery's high standards for his musicians were well known throughout the entertainment circuit. In his advertisements for performers, he indicated the desired qualities in such phrases as: "first class performers," "up-to-date," "must be good," "can't use kickers, none need apply," and "amateurs save [your] stamps."(36)

This 1901 summer tour, described by Lowery as "the most successful of all, the band being stronger and the vaude- ville company much better having more workers and better singers," closed on November 2 at Clarksdale, Mississippi.(37) Lowery's show had remained intact through more than twenty-six weeks of consecutive performances.

While some of the company vacationed in St. Louis after the closing, Lowery began preparations for the winter tour. The *Freeman* carried a "Talent Attention" call on October 5 for persons interested in touring with "Swain's Original Nashville Students in Mighty Unison with P. G. Lowery's Concert Band" to make their contacts.

The success of the Original Nashville Students Company continued with W. I. Swain, who assumed ownership around 1900. "Swain's Nashville Students employs more business agents and has the strongest backing, and uses more paper than any other colored show of its kind on the road today."(38)

At least two factors contributed to this success. Dan Washington, the stage manager, said, "P. G. Lowery is the same old drawing card."(39) An additional drawing card, however, was the plush ten-thousand dollar "palace" rail- road car in which the company traveled. This car had been utilized since 1898, and people would often greet the train at the station to get a glimpse of this rolling palace. L. E. Gideon added, "We travel only in one car, but ask those who have seen it and they will tell you the rest."(40)

By the end of November 1901 the show was ready to begin the winter tour. The company included P. G. Lowery (cornet/assistant manager/band leader), C. D. Jackson (alto horn/orchestra leader), the members of the band and orches- tra, a vaudeville troupe, and Miss L. C. Haynes as the prima donna. Miss Haynes, a music graduate of Fisk Univer- sity, had performed with the London Jubilee Singers before joining the Students.(41)

On April 11, 1902, Lowery and his company deviated from their road circuit when they performed for a carnival sponsored by the Douglass Club at the Murray Hill Lyceum. Of that concert, Woodbine stated:

> [It] was excellent. The cornet solos of P. G. Lowery clearly proved to the audience that he is master of the instrument. . . . After the band concert, the hall was cleared and dancing followed until the hour of five.(42)

This first documented performance of a Lowery band playing for a dance is important, because it heralds the emergence of a new type of dance music:

> By the late 1890's the world of entertainment was beginning to absorb a new music . . . from the black culture . . . ragtime, and the dance craze that went with it, the "cakewalk." And that same period also saw the early glimmerings of jazz and blues, both of which had much to do with ragtime, and all of which had something to do with black folk culture--the world of

the unknown, untrained musician in "honky-tonks, barrel
houses, bawdy houses," and levee camps.(43)

Apparently Lowery's instrumental dance music consisted
of arrangements of piano ragtime compositions written by
Scott Joplin and possibly other lesser-known composers of
the style. Substantiating this concept of the dance-music
repertory is the presence of a new player in the band and
orchestra, Wilbur C. Sweatman, the clarinetist and violinist who had replaced C. D. Jackson:

The dance craze had hit the east . . . and musicians of
all kinds began flocking into New York. Among them was
Wilbur Sweatman, a clarinet player from Kansas City.
He came to New York in the early 1900's to join
Forepaugh and Sells Brothers Circus as a member of
Professor P. G. Lowery's Band.(44)

Sweatman's playing was uniquely exciting and infectious.
In the circus parades, "the crowds that lined the sidewalks
started following the band just to hear Sweatman playing
his clarinet."(45) Fletcher further stated:

When people talk or write about ragtime and jazz, they
invariably begin by saying that jazz was started in New
Orleans, Louisiana. Actually, Wilbur Sweatman, the
first musician to bring that style of playing to the
attention of the American public, was playing it and
making it popular way back when he joined P. G. Lowery,
before he joined W. C. Handy's band with the W. A.
Mahara's Minstrels. And even in the early part of 1910,
when he introduced his style of playing in the leading
vaudeville theaters, it was before some of the men now
given credit for introducing jazz were born or at least
when they were too young to know what a clarinet
was.(46)

The winter season closed shortly after this unusual
performance. The fourth summer season of Lowery's Concert
Band and Vaudeville Company opened with the Forepaugh-Sells
Bros. Circus in Philadelphia on April 21, 1902. The show
was larger: the band consisted of twelve returning Lowery
veterans, in addition to W. C. Sweatman; the vaudeville
company included the Four-In-Hand Quartette, Miss Sallie
Lee, Miss Essie Williams, and Miss Gracie Hoyt. The business staff consisted of "Lowery, manager and director of
the band; J. J. Smith, assistant band master; W. C.
Sweatman, leader of the orchestra; Ambrose Davis, stage
manager; James Martin, librarian; and Sallie Lee, authorized agent for the *Freeman*."(47)

The itinerary for this season took Lowery's company
from New York through Maryland, West Virginia, the District
of Columbia, Pennsylvania, New Jersey, the New England
states, and then into Canada (June 30-July 19). Lowery had
become ill while in Pittsburg, but he returned to the show
by May 31. During the three weeks in Canada many members
of the cast began studying French, and Henry Rawles and

Johnnie Jones decided to play French horns rather than alto horns.

Although only weeks into the summer season, Lowery was in the process of planning for the following winter season to "be much better than last season," indicating that he wanted an eighteen-piece band.(48) Lowery also continued to studiously avoid the image of the minstrel show by clearly stating in his advertisements: "Not a Minstrel Show, No Parade."(49) The parade was perceived as a staple of advertising when a minstrel show was in town:

> The day of a minstrel company typically began at 11:45 A.M. with the traditional parade through the principal streets of the town or city. The procession started off with the managers in their carriages. Then . . . followed the stars of the show. . . . Next in line was the "walking company" . . . the singers, comedians, acrobats, and dancers, and instrumentalists. . . . The bandsmen marched in pairs, maintaining a distance of from ten to twelve feet between pairs so that the parade might stretch out as long as possible.(50)

Perhaps a part of Lowery's professional notoriety came from his refusal to follow predetermined patterns set by other organizations. When his band participated in the circus parades, the members rode on a specially constructed band-wagon, reportedly the largest of its kind then in use.

During his Canadian tour, Lowery indicated that he would like to hear from Fountain B. Wood, one of his former bandsmen (1898-1899) and trombone soloists.(51) By August 23 the "Notes from P. G. Lowery's Company" in the *Freeman* included the statement: "We were glad indeed to welcome into our company F. B. Wood, H. I. Clark, and Albert Edwards."(52) Wood again became the featured trombone soloist. He also brought with him his music library, probably from the Georgia Up-To-Date Minstrels, which he led after Lowery's departure. This library, combined with Lowery's, created "the largest and most choice repretoi [sic] of music carried by any colored traveling musical organization on the road."(53)

The summer 1902 tour ended in the South, with Lowery's show still receiving accolades such as "people [are] wondering where we get so much music from."(54) Lowery had yet another bout with illness, but was on his feet and working. While reviewing the accomplishments of what Lowery had termed his best show, Lewis Sells, the manager of Forepaugh-Sells Circus wrote:

> P. G. Lowery, leader of our side show band has been in the service of the Forepaugh and Sells Bros. Circus for the past four seasons. We have found him reliable and a splendid musician. His band is without a doubt the best colored musical organization in America and his people are a credit to their race.(55)

Possibly because of his illnesses, Lowery did not make a 1902 winter tour, but instead, went home to Reece, Kansas, where he maintained a farm. Miss Sallie Lee,

Arthur L. Prince, H. I. Clark, and James Morton, all members of his company, went with him. He gave private cornet lessons to H. I. Clark, and, as he reported to the *Freeman*, was engaged to direct the twenty-piece white band at Reece, which "is quite an honor down here."(56)

During this working vacation, Lowery finalized plans for P. G. Lowery's "Progressive Musical Enterprise." This enterprise would consist of two complete vaudeville companies: "No. 1 will have twenty five under the full management of P. G. Lowery. Company No. 2 will have fifteen people, with H. Qualli Clark as musical director." This brief description, accompanied by a "Wanted" ad for "good reliable people in all branches," was carried in the February 14, 1903, edition of the *Freeman*.

The "call" was issued via the *Freeman* on April 4, 1903, for all contracted personnel to report to St. Louis, Missouri, on April 12. The No. 1 company, assigned to the Forepaugh-Sells Bros. Circus, was directed to 1306 Clark Avenue; the No. 2 company, assigned to the Luella Forepaugh Fish Wild West Show, was directed to Prairie Avenue and Second Street.

In order to furnish more competition for the rapidly growing Ringlings, James A. Bailey, of Barnum & Bailey Circus fame, created the Adam Forepaugh-Sells Bros. Circus by merging his Forepaugh Circus with that of the Sells Brothers in 1896. Bailey also bought the Buffalo Bill Show; and the Luella Forepaugh Fish Wild West Show may have been a spin-off of this acquisition.(57) These wild west shows, popular since the 1880s, stressed continuous action, including "trick riding, . . . roping, races, . . . sharpshooting, etc.,"(58) very much like the modern rodeo. Adam Forepaugh, the original owner of the Forepaugh Circus, added such a show to his circus around 1887, which quite possibly was the basis of the later Forepaugh Fish Show. Charles W. Fish was a highly skilled rider who retired in 1899.(59)

Lowery's Enterprise Show No. 2, under the direction of Clark, opened in St. Louis on April 18, 1903, for a one-week stand. The primary feature of this production was the popular "cakewalk," led by Fred [Ted] Morton.

The origins of the cakewalk are rooted in ballroom dancing:

> Just before the ball was declared finished a long procession of couples was formed, who walked in their very best manner round the room three times before the criticising [sic] eyes of a jury of a dozen old people, who selected the best turned-out pair and gravely presented them with a large plum cake.(60)

From these folk beginnings the cakewalk became both a popular dance and an integral part of minstrel/vaudeville programming. In the Enterprise Show No. 2 production, the winners of the vaudeville cakewalk received a prize of $5 per week instead of a plum cake.

The exact opening date of Enterprise No. 1 is not listed, but they did perform in Kansas City on or about May 9 of that year. During the early weeks of the show, Lowery

and the company were visited in Detroit by the noted actor
and comedian Sam Lucas.

Two of the most noteworthy musicians in this No. 1
company were Pearl Moppins, a trombone player, and George
McDade, a thirteen-year-old cornetist, violinist, and
orchestra director.(61) Lowery wrote of McDade:

> The boy wonder, Little George, was born in Knoxville,
> Tennessee, January 23, 1890. He commenced the study of
> music at the age of ten--the cornet was his first
> instrument--his advancement was so rapid he then took
> up the study of the violin and today he stands among
> the best leaders in the business regardless of his age.
> Beside his wonderful accomplishment on the two instru-
> ments, he possesses the most remarkable ear so accurate
> and true he can at any time tell the exact tone made on
> an instrument. He is justly honored the wonder of the
> 19th Century.

> I consider Master George McDade a cornetist of rare
> ability, a boy of wonderful good ideas, on both violin
> and cornet. With good teaching Little George will out
> rival any cornetist of his race before he leaves the
> ranks of boyhood. Keep your eye on the new star from
> Knoxville.(62)

The No. 2 Company initially met with great favor, and a
new set of uniforms was ordered for the band. While in
Wisconsin, the two branches of Lowery's enterprises
performed in adjacent towns, No. 1 in Lacross and No. 2 in
Osage.(63) However, a hint of some unnamed problems sur-
faced in a small item in "The Stage" column of the *Freeman*:

> J. E. Adams and son Steve, Al Hutt, Sallie Lee, Essie
> Williams and Daisy Lee, all of the P. G. Lowery No. 2
> Concert Company of the Luella Forepaugh Fish Wild West
> Show, can be reached at J. E. Adams, 105 North
> Thirteenth Street, St. Louis. We closed in Janesville,
> Wisc., July 27th.(64)

No further mention was made concerning either Company No. 2
or the Fish Show. One reason for the early demise of
Forepaugh-Fish in Wisconsin may have been the costly terri-
torial battles between the different circuses and shows,
especially between the Forepaugh forces and the Ringlings:

> Forepaugh-Sells provided formidable opposition for the
> Ringling [Bros. Circus] Enterprises at many stands.
> The battle continued all over Illinois, Wisconsin,
> Minnesota, the Dakotas, Nebraska, Iowa, and Missouri.
> The Ringlings made some money but Forepaugh-Sells
> didn't.(65)

Lowery also may have been experiencing problems within
his own organizational ranks. Lowery, in an attempt to
answer some of the questions that were being asked in the
trade papers, responded by divulging some of his organization's plans for the winter season:

1. The well-known actor and refined comedian Mr. Sam
    Lucas is my stage manager.
2. I consider Harry Gillam one of the strongest at-
    tractions I have.
3. Miss Pearl M. Crawford spent several seasons
    abroad . . . she is engaged as prima donna, and
    she is one of the finest colored vocalists now
    facing the footlights.
4. My band will number fourteen men, but will give
    concerts, no parades.
5. Master George McDade is the boy wonder from
    Knoxville. He will lead the orchestra. I will
    only feature his cornet solos on the state [sic].
    I will do all outside cornet solo work.
6. I will only carry seven women.
7. There are only four in the executive staf[f]. P.
    G. Lowery, owner; Carl Hathaway, general manager;
    A. Baker, business manager; Ed. Busey, advance
    representative.
8. Our vacation between the closing of my present
    engagement to the opening of my winter show will
    be about eight days. Hoping I have answered all
    questions properly, I sign . . . (66)

Despite obvious problems with show No. 2, Lowery
reported that his No. 1 Company was progressing "nicely."
As the show neared the close of its summer tour with the
Forepaugh-Sells Bros. Circus, there was still speculation
as to whether there would be a winter tour; Lowery continued his preparations.   A series of items in "The Stage"
documented his activities:

P. G. Lowery, Al Baker and Joseph Baker are now in St.
Louis, looking after the interest of the Nashville
Students, while Carl T. Hathaway and Mr. Harvey are in
Chicago looking after some business for the show.

Miss Sallie N. Lee and Miss Essie Williams will close
with the Sells & Downes' Circus and join P. G. Lowery's
Nashville Students November 6th.

Sam Lucas, stage manager for P. G. Lowery's Nashville
Students, will reach St. Louis November 6th to look
after the interest of the show.

Miss Pearl Crawford has refused three propositions to
go abroad to fill the position as prima donna with P.
G. Lowery's big attraction.

P. G. Lowery and his famous band is taking a two weeks
vacation in St. Louis before rehearsal starts for the
winter attraction.

Master George McDade is preparing some tasty cornet and
violin solos to feature in P. G. Lowery's Nashville
Students.(67)

The Forepaugh Circus, after playing as far South as

Southern Texas, in October began the homeward trek that closed the season near St. Louis, on or about November 6, 1903.

After ten days of rest and rehearsal, the Nashville Students and P. G. Lowery's celebrated Concert Band opened their winter season on November 6, 1903, at Mascoutah, Illinois, to a standing-room-only audience. Whatever the problems of the past summer, they were now gone, along with some of the Enterprise No. 2 personnel. The talent that Lowery had amassed, organized, and prepared became not just a show, but also a major "production."

Previously, the entire company had traveled in one "plush" railroad car, belonging to the Nashville Students. For this season, Lowery acquired a new coach called the "Pana" for the use of his band and orchestra. His company consisted of some twenty-five staff and performers, including: Sam Lucas ("The Prince of All Actors"), stage manager; Harry Crosby, asst. stage manager, stage director, writer, and principal comedian; Oliver Payne, programmer; Sam Elliott, chorus director and percussionist; George ("The Boy Wonder") McDade, orchestra director, cornetist and violinist; and P. G. Lowery, general superintendent, owner, band director and solo cornetist. Traveling ahead of the show to handle the bookings were advance representatives Joe Becker and Harvey Lipp. The business managers were Carl Hathaway and Al S. Baker.

The Nashville Students closed the 1903 winter tour in Illinois. The press, and perhaps also the show's promoters, built up an imaginary "rivalry" between Lowery and McDade, both of whom now were drawing cards: "Master George McDade, the boy wonder is without a doubt the coming rival of P. G. Lowery. Mr. Lowery wishes to state publicly he has the field without a struggle."[68] Although he was an excellent cornetist and violinist at an early age, McDade did not continue as a professional musician but eventually returned to his hometown of Knoxville, Tennessee, where he maintained a successful law practice until the time of his death.[69]

January 1904 found the show still intact and pleasing very large audiences throughout Southern Missouri and Arkansas, despite the winter weather. Although Harry Crosby was apparently still a part of the company, John W. Carson was appointed assistant stage manager.[70]

As the itinerary carried the show westward from Arkansas and Missouri into Kansas, Lowery received a most pleasant surprise:

The Nashville Students were awfully surprised on reaching Eureka, Kansas, the native home of P. G. Lowery, at the massive crowd to welcome Mr. Lowery home. Cheers rang up, after which the concert band of thirty pieces struck up a lively march while the Nashville Students were ushered to cabs and were led to the opera house, which was completely sold out before the company reached the little city. The show was greeted at night by the largest audience ever known to gather in the opera house. Wire reached Mr. Hathaway and Baker in Eureka, a special train was arranged to

greet P. G. Lowery and his excellent company at
Madison.   The manager of the opera house was the first
one to enter our car and quietly broke the news, "The
house is sold." In fact, the Nashville Students have
met every want of the theatrical going public. Nothing
succeeds like success.(71)

Lowery had returned to his hometown to receive a hero's
welcome.   Having established a reputation during these
formative years as the foremost black cornetist and bandmaster of his time, Lowery continued to be successful for
another three decades until his death in the 1930s in
Cleveland, Ohio.   The small-town boy who began his career
as a member of his family's band had indeed achieved the
American dream of success.

APPENDIX

Performers associated with the bands organized and
conducted by P. G. Lowery are here listed. Information is
taken from newspaper accounts which document the activities
of Lowery during this period.   The list of performers is
arranged chronologically by date of the source.   Headings
identify the sources and dates of references.   Performers
are listed by name with the roles each performed where
such information was found in the reference cited.   Names
and titles are given with the original spelling.

Indianapolis Freeman, January 16, 1897

W. A. Dean/E. O. Green-Trombone soloist/P. G. Hampton-
Comedy, Music director/C. P. Johnson-Comedy/P. G. Lowery-
Cornet, Band leader/A. H. Montgomery-Violin, Orchestra
leader/John A. Stewart-Tuba/Ida Lee Wright-Singer, Dancer,
Treasurer/Preston T. Wright-Singer, Owner, Manager.

Indianapolis Freeman, January 23, 1897

H.   Andrews/Moses H. McQuitty-Baritone euphonium/C. F.
Richardson-Clarionet/W. H. Rider/Anne Scott/Jesse Wilbur-
Business manager.

Indianapolis Freeman, January 8, 1898

Band Members

Gordon C. Collins-Snare drum/Dan F. Desdunes-Solo alto
horn/Lash E. Gideon-Cornet/Harry Gilliam-1st alto horn/E.
O. Green-Solo trombone/A. P. Harris-Bass drum/Perry G.
Lowery-Cornet, Band leader/Ed McGruder-2nd trombone/Moses
McQuitty-Baritone euphonium/Fred C. Richardson-Clarionet/
John A. Stewart-Tuba.

Soloists for the Season

McQuitty/Green/Gideon/Desdunes/Stewart

Managerial Positions

P. T. Wright-Manager (Wright died unexpectedly on or about April 2, 1898, and Mrs. Wright assumed management of the band)/Ida Lee Wright-Treasurer/Joe Becker-Advance man/Harry Gilliam-Stage manager/P. G. Lowery-Band director/Dan Desdunes-Orchestra leader.

Orchestra Members

Dudley/A. P. Harris-Bass drum/Gordon Collins-Snare drum/ Allie Gilliam/Moses H. McQuitty-Euphonium/Lash E. Gideon-Cornet/Clarence Kelly/E. O. Green-Trombone/Ed McGruder-Trombone/Fred Richardson-Clarionet/Harry Gilliam-Alto horn/ Bessie Gilliam.

Indianapolis Freeman, February 29, 1898

Dudley and Harris-"Jolly Jesters," Comedians/John and Anna Stewart-Sketch: "The Night Before the Circus"/Harry Gilliam-"The Acrobatic Comedian"/Bessie Gilliam-Soubrette/ Al F. and Cecil Smith-Watts-Song writers and show designers/Major John Pamplin-Gun manipulator and juggler/S. H. Dudley-Stage Manager/Dan Desdunes-Musical director/Harry Prampin-Cornet, Bandmaster.

Indianapolis Freeman, December 3, 1898

Tom J. Lewis-Cornet/William Malone/H. S. Lane-Clarionet/ Harry Gilliam-Alto horn/J. J. Smith/W. G. Bostwick/Jack M. Oliver/Fountain B. Wood-Trombone/James Marton-Trombone/J. D. West/R. O. Henderson/Joe Pleasant-Tuba.

Indianapolis Freeman, January 7, 1899

S. H. Lewis-Clarinet/J. T. Lewis-Cornet/P. G. Lowery-Cornet/William Malone-Cornet/Jeff Smith-Cornet/John Adams-Alto horn/Harry Gilliam-Alto horn/Fountain Wood-Trombone/R. O. Henderson-Bariton euphonium/Joe Pleasant-Tuba/Ben Benbry-Percussion/A. Gilliam-Percussion/Julius Glenn-Percussion.

Indianapolis Freeman, December 2, 1899

Robert Cooper-Trombone/Skip Farrell-Drums/Mrs. Farrell-Singer/A. T. Gillam-Stage manager, Cake Walk leader, Percussionist/C. W. Gossett-Trap drummer/Jones-Orchestra director/Tom J. Lewis-Cornet/Mrs. Lewis-Cornet, Singer/ William May-Tuba/Moses McQuitty-Baritone euphonium/James Marton-Trombone/Mr. and Mrs. Prentis Oliver-Singing duo/

James White-Comedian/Robert Wilson/James Taylor-Tenor
soloist.

Indianapolis Freeman, December 30, 1899

Lowery-Manager, Cornet soloist/Perkins and Chapman-
Comedians, Buck wing dancers/Harry L. Gilliam-Acrobatic
Hebrew comedian/Horn player/Mme. Hattie Lucas-Soprano/Allie
Gilliam and Tina Mazelle-"Up-to date" sketch/Arthur Prince-
Slack-wire and juggling artist/Miss Ella Dorsey-Extremely
clever female contortionist.

Indianapolis Freeman, April 23, 1900

Black-B flat clarionet/H. G. Brown-E flat clarionet/Charles
Clark-2nd alto horn/Bob Cooper-2nd trombone/Skip Farrell-
Snare drum/A. T. Gillam-Bass drum/Ed Heater-3rd trom-
bone/Tom J. Lewis-Cornet/P. G. Lowery-Cornet, Leader/James
Marton-1st trombone/William (Billy) May-Tuba/Moses H.
McQuitty-Euphonium/J. J. Smith-Solo cornet/Bob Wilson-1st
alto horn.

Peoria Journal, December 17, 1900

F. R. Brooks ("Easy Ace")-Comedian/W. L. Jackson ("The
Colored Ole Bull")-Violinist/P. G. Lowery-Cornet Soloist/
Pearl Millender-Singer, Dancer/Helen Ogden-Prima Donna,
Soprano/A. L. Prince-Slack-wire artist/The Sherrar Quartet-
Male singing group/W. H. Spencer-Chorus director.

Indianapolis Freeman, June 8, 1901

Lowery Concert Band

Jim Brown-2nd alto horn/Sam Elliott-Traps and snare drum/J.
B. Hall-Baritone euphonium/George Hambright-Clarionet/
Calvin Jackson-1st alto horn/P. G. Lowery-Manager, Band
director, Cornet, Director of vaudeville/Billy May-Tuba/Sam
May-Solo cornet/James Morton-1st trombone/Henry Rawles-Bass
drum/C. Taylor-1st cornet/J. J. Smith-Assistant director,
solo cornet/W. S. Ball-3rd trombone/A. L. Prince-2nd trombone.

Indianapolis Freeman, June 8, 1901

Calvin Jackson-Leader/Tom (?) May-2nd violin/J. J. Smith-
Cornet/G. P. Hambright-Clarionet/James Morton-Trombone/J.
B. Hall-Viola/William May-Bass.

Indianapolis Freeman, June 8, 1901

W. S. Ball, Baritone and Charles B. Foster, Basso-Two

members of the New York quartette/Female quartette members: Mrs. Beadley, Miss Ida Larkins, Miss Cara Scott, Miss Josie Sutton/Billy Bradley-Stage manager.

Indianapolis Freeman, November 2 and 9, 1901

Additions After the Summer Tour

Miss Emma Thompson/Bert and Rosa Rogers/Printus Oliver-Singer, Comedian.

Indianapolis Freeman, November 30, 1901

Vaudeville Troupe

Gordon Collins/Charles Foster/A. L. Prince/Bert and Rosa Rogers/Dan Washington/Miss Weatherby/Miss L. C. Haynes-Prima donna.

Instrumentalists

Sam Elliott-Percussions/James Hall-Euphonium and viola/ George Hambright-Clarinet/C. D. Jackson-Alto horn, Orchestra leader/P. G. Lowery-Cornet, Assistant manager, Band leader/William May-Tuba, Bass/James Marton-Trombone/Henry Rawles-Percussions/J. J. Smith-Cornet.

Indianapolis Freeman, April 11, 1902

Musicians

J. J. Smith/Thomas May/Wilfred Day/George Hambright/Mr. Sweetnam/Henry Eawles/John P. Jones/James B. Hall/James Morton/Fred W. Simpson/William May/Samuel Elliott/Charles Foster.

Indianapolis Freeman, April 21, 1902

Band

Sam Elliott/Charles Foster/James Hall/George Hambright/J. L. Jones/P. G. Lowery/W. C. Sweatman/James Morton/Thomas May/William May/A. L. Prince/Henry Rawles/J. J. Smith.

Vaudeville Company

Four-In-Hand Quartette: Ambrose Davis, Director/William Johnson/Arthur Wilmore/Jack Watkins/Miss Sallie Lee/Miss Essie Williams/Miss Grace Hoyt.

Business Staff

Lowery-Manager, Director of band/J. J. Smith-Assistant band master/W. C. Sweatman-Leader of orchestra/Ambrose Davis-

Stage manager/James Martin-Librarian/Sallie Lee-Agent for the *Freeman*.

Indianapolis Freeman, June 7, 1902

Summer Season Additions

Prentis Oliver-Comedian/Ernest Baker/William Baker-Singer/ George Hambright-Clarionettist/Ambrose Davis (Left show due to illness)/A. L. Prince-Became stage manager/William H. Johnson-Business manager/Prentis Oliver-Sang with quartet.

Indianapolis Freeman, April 18, 1903

Lowery's Enterprise Show No. 2

John Adams-Alto horn/Steve Adams-Baritone (euphonium)/H. Qualli Clark-Director, Cornet, Singer/Albert Hutt-Snare drum/William Johnson-Bass drum, Singer, Stage manager, General manager/Frank Morton-Alto horn/Ted (Fred) Morton-Bass/Harry Morton-Trombone/George Williams-Cornet.

Supporting Singers and Performers

Misses Daisy and Sallie Lee/M. Lea(h) Saunderson/Essie Williams.

Indianapolis Freeman, May 9, 1903

Band

P. G. Lowery-Director, Cornet/George McDade-Cornet, Violin/ Tom May-Cornet/John R. Campbell-Cornet/Carlos Terry-Alto horn/John L. Jones-Alto horn/James Morton-Trombone/Pearl Moppins-Trombone/James Hall-Baritone (euphonium)/Fred Richardson-Clarinet/Sam Elliott-Percussions/Johnny Carson-Percussions.

Vaudeville Company

Mrs. Oma Crosby/Carrie Wood-Soubrette/Miss Maggie Crosby-Soubrette/Harry Garrett-Comedian/George Green-Comedian/ Harry E. Crosby-Stage manager/John McDade.

Indianapolis Freeman, July 4, 1903

Side-show Roster

Vic Hugo-Manager/King Cole-Ventriloquist, Magician/Bessie Devalo-Loop the loop/Del Fuego-Tattooed lady/Mrs. Vic Hugo-Mind-reader, Clairvoyant/Bertha Tipton-Snake enchantress/ Miss Belle Carter-Lady with horse's mane/Maude Alberti-Lady athlete.

Indianapolis Freeman, January 30, 1904

Personnel for 1903-1904 Season

Sam Lucas-Stage manager/Harry Crosby-Assistant stage manager, Stage director, Writer, Principle comedian/Oliver Payne-Programmer/Sam Elliott-Chorus director, Percussionist/George McDade-Orchestra director, Cornetist, Violinist/P. G. Lowery-General superintendent, Owner, Band director, Solo cornetist/Joe Becker and Harvey Lipp-Advance representatives/Carl Hathaway and Al S. Baker-Business Managers/Pearl Crawford-Prima Donna/Oma Crawford-Soubrette/ Sallie Lee-Soubrette/Essie Williams-Soubrette/Jessie Thomas-Soubrette/Ike McBeard-Singer/Gambetter Garrett-Singer.

Band, Orchestra

William May/James Hall/Lowery/Sam Elliott/Pearl Moppin/John Jones/Tom May/S. B. Foster/George McDade/Johnny Carson.

NOTES

1. "The Stage," *Indianapolis Freeman*, December 18, 1897, 5.
2. Ibid.
3. W. C. Handy, *Father of the Blues*, edited by Arna Bontemps, with a foreword by Abble Niles. 1941. Reprint. (London: Sedgwick & Jackson, 1957), 65.
4. Handy, 66.
5. Giles Oakley, *The Devil's Music, a History of the Blues* (New York: Taplinger, 1977), 28.
6. Imamu Amiri Baraka (LeRoi Jones), *Blues People* (New York: William Morrow, 1967), 82.
7. Eileen Southern, *Biographical Dictionary of Afro-American and African Musicians* (Westport, Conn.: Greenwood Press, 1982), s. v. "Lowery, P[erry]. G."
8. *Indianapolis Freeman*, January 16, 1897; January 23, 1897.
9. *Indianapolis Freeman*, January 8, 1898; January 22, 1898; January 15, 1898.
10. *Indianapolis Freeman*, April 2, 1898.
11. *Indianapolis Freeman*, September 24, 1898.
12. *Indianapolis Freeman*, November 5, 1898.
13. *Indianapolis Freeman*, November 12, 1898.
14. *Indianapolis Freeman*, December 3, 1898.
15. *Indianapolis Freeman*, January 7, 1899.
16. *Indianapolis Freeman*, January 28, 1899.
17. For further clarification and explanation of these encoded messages, see Charles P. Fox and Tom Parkinson, *The Circus in America* (Waukesha, Wis.: Flick-Reedy Enterprises, 1969), 24.
18. "The Stage," *Indianapolis Freeman*, March 25, 1899.
19. *Indianapolis Freeman*, April 29, 1899.
20. See P. G. Lowery, "The Cornet and Cornetist of

Today," *Indianapolis Freeman*, January 13, 1900.
    21. "The Stage," *Indianapolis Freeman*, December 30, 1899.
    22. Ibid.
    23. *Indianapolis Freeman*, May 5, 1900.
    24. *Indianapolis Freeman*, November 10, 1900.
    25. *Indianapolis Freeman*, December 29, 1900.
    26. *Peoria Journal*, Peoria, Illinois, December 17, 1900, quoted in the *Indianapolis Freeman*, January 5, 1901.
    27. "The Stage," *Indianapolis Freeman*, February 16, 1901.
    28. *Indianapolis Freeman*, April 27, 1901.
    29. *Indianapolis Freeman*, May 25, 1901.
    30. Eileen Southern, *The Music of Black Americans, A History* (New York: W. W. Norton, 1971), 262-63.
    31. "The Stage," *Indianapolis Freeman*, June 8, 1901.
    32. Ibid.
    33. *Indianapolis Freeman*, June 29, 1901.
    34. Ibid.
    35. *Indianapolis Freeman*, August 24, 1901.
    36. *Indianapolis Freeman*. Excerpts taken from various Lowery notices and ads.
    37. *Indianapolis Freeman*, November 2 and 9, 1901.
    38. *Indianapolis Freeman*, November 16, 1901.
    39. *Indianapolis Freeman*, December 21, 1901.
    40. *Indianapolis Freeman*, July 30, 1898.
    41. *Indianapolis Freeman*, November 30, 1901.
    42. *Indianapolis Freeman*, April 26, 1902.
    43. Oakley, 31.
    44. Tom Fletcher, *100 Years of the Negro in Show Business* (New York: Burdge & Co., 1954), 149.
    45. Ibid.
    46. Fletcher, 152.
    47. "The Stage," *Indianapolis Freeman*, May 10, 1902.
    48. *Indianapolis Freeman*, July 19, 1902.
    49. *Indianapolis Freeman*, October 5, 1901.
    50. Southern, *The Music of Black Americans*, 261-62.
    51. *Indianapolis Freeman*, July 19, 1902.
    52. *Indianapolis Freeman*, August 23, 1902.
    53. *Indianapolis Freeman*, September 6, 1902.
    54. *Indianapolis Freeman*, November 15, 1902.
    55. Ibid.
    56. Ibid.
    57. John and Alice Durant, *Pictorial History of the American Circus* (New York: Barnes, 1957), 132.
    58. Ibid.
    59. Durant, 85.
    60. Oakley, 31.
    61. George McDade was first introduced erroneously as being ten years of age. See "The Stage," *Indianapolis Freeman*, May 16, 1903.
    62. *Indianapolis Freeman*, October 10, 1903.
    63. *Indianapolis Freeman*, July 18, 1903.
    64. *Indianapolis Freeman*, August 8, 1903.
    65. Gene Plowden, *Those Amazing Ringlings and Their Circus* (Caldwell, Idaho: Coston, 1967), 83-84.
    66. "The Stage," *Indianapolis Freeman*, September 5, 1903.

67. *Indianapolis Freeman*, October 17, 1903.
68. *Indianapolis Freeman*, December 19, 1903.
69. Based on information provided by J. B. Wheeler of Knoxville, Tennessee, a close friend of McDade's and the attending mortician at McDade's death. Stated on July 25, 1982.
70. "The Stage," *Indianapolis Freeman*, January 30, 1904.
71. Pearl M. Crawford, "Honor Shown to Pride of Kansas," *Indianapolis Freeman*, February 27, 1904.

REFERENCES

Baraka, Imamu Amiri (LeRoi Jones). *Blues People*. New York: William Morrow, 1967.
Durant, John and Alice. *Pictorial History of the American Circus*. New York: Barnes, 1957.
Fletcher, Tom. *100 Years of the Negro in Show Business*. New York: Burdge, 1954.
Fox, Charles P., and Tom Parkinson. *The Circus in America*. Waukesha, Wisconsin: Flick-Reedy Enterprises, 1969.
Handy, W. C. *Father of the Blues*, edited by Arna Bontemps with a foreword by Abble Niles. 1941. Reprint. London: Sedgwick & Jackson, 1957.
Oakley, Giles. *The Devil's Music: A History of the Blues*. New York: Taplinger, 1977.
Plowden, Gene. *Those Amazing Ringlings and Their Circus*. Caldwell, Idaho: Coston, 1967.
Southern, Eileen. *Biographical Dictionary of Afro-American and African Musicians*. Westport, Conn.: Greenwood Press, 1982.

Newspapers

Indianapolis Freeman
Peoria Journal

Sam Lucas: Comedian and actor with Sprague's Georgia Minstrels (Photo courtesy of the Schomburg Center for Research in Black Culture; The New York Public Library; Astor, Lenox, and Tilden Foundations)

Sam Lucas, 1840-1916: A Bibliographic Study

ELLISTINE PERKINS HOLLY

Samuel Milady, more popularly known as Sam Lucas, was one of the important "pace-setting stars" in breaking new ground for black entertainers.(1) His career as a minstrel star, song writer, and actor on the American stage spanned nearly half a century, and his performing activities included the major forms of nineteenth- and early twentieth-century popular theater.

For many talented black musicians after the Civil War, the minstrel show generally offered the most lucrative form of stage employment; thus, Sam Lucas' name was not unknown to audiences of the 1870s. His versatility as a performer and his ability to capture an audience was recognized by the press and contributed to his early success on the minstrel stage. James Weldon Johnson commented in *Black Manhattan*: "He was a versatile performer and was active on the stage from those early days of minstrelsy down to modern Negro musical comedy."(2) Referring to Lucas as a lifetime showman, Eileen Southern noted that he "always looked the part of the star, whether on or off the stage."(3)

After teaching himself to play the guitar and performing in local minstrel groups and bands, Lucas performed in his first professional minstrel troupe when he was approximately thirty years of age. In the next two decades, Lucas performed with the Lew Johnson Plantation Minstrels, Callender's Original Georgia Minstrels, Sprague's Georgia Minstrels, and Haverly's Minstrels.

Lucas' song writing is documented in *Folio*, the nineteenth-century Boston music journal;(4) however, a complete listing and analysis of his music is presently impossible because of the unavailability of music scores, although I have studied over one hundred songs by Lucas found in the collections of the Library of Congress and Newberry Library, Chicago.

Throughout his years in minstrelsy, Lucas sought other stage opportunities. The play, *Uncle Tom's Cabin*, based on the novel by Harriet Beecher Stowe, showcased his acting talents. The "Tom Show" was a phenomenon of the late nineteenth century and provided theatrical and musical employment for hundreds. Lucas was a member of at least three companies; however, only two apparently were successful. Though documentation for these career ventures is presently limited, he evidently organized the Jubilee Songsters, the Hub Concert Company, and was a member of the Boston Stock Company and the Ideal Combination Company.

Lucas was engaged by the Hyers Troupe about 1875 as a singer and actor in productions of their historical musical dramas. In 1877 a reviewer from Quincy, Illinois, wrote:

> Sam Lucas, in character business, took the audience by storm. In his specialities he has no rival. His business takes better than Kersands or any of the colored minstrels. The *Good-bye to the Old Cabin Home* by him and Emma Hyers was a gem.(5)

Lucas played in vaudeville for about twenty years. A playbill of August 31, 1885, announced Lucas at Austin and Stone's Museum in Boston: "SAM LUCAS, Everybody's favorite character, motto and topical vocalist."(6) Commenting on his career in 1909, Lucas himself wrote: "I joined the ranks of the variety artists, and [have] the distinction of being the first colored man to appear in what is now known as vaudeville. My work consisted of comic and motto songs, monologue and dancing."(7)

During his years in vaudeville, Lucas played many of the large theaters throughout the country: the Bijou Theatre in Boston, Nieblo's Garden in New York, Wonderland in Detroit, and the Olympic Theater in Denver, Colorado. He also played the large and small vaudeville circuits: the Loew Circuit, Kohl, Middleton and Company; Mead's Imperial Vaudeville Company; and Jones and Sutton. Following his marraige to his second wife, the former Carrie Melvin, a talented instrumentalist and vocalist, Lucas traveled with her in an act, "Mr. and Mrs. Sam Lucas." From 1886 to 1900 the duo appeared in variety shows throughout the country. Their act eventually headed one of the Sam T. Jack's Creole Burlesque Companies. Sam and Carrie Lucas remained with the company until 1893, after which the company went abroad for approximately four years.

Tom Riis, in his study of black musical shows, views the years from 1890 to 1915 as a colorful and important era in the history of black musical theater.(8) Lucas apparently moved easily into the musical scene of this period. The young black performers and producers, among whom were Ernest Hogan, Billy Johnson, Bob Cole, J. Rosamond Johnson, and his brother, J. Weldon Johnson, recognized Lucas' talent and his years of stage experience. His role as "Silas Green" in Cole and Billy Johnson's *A Trip to Coontown* received the following review: "Sam Lucas was smooth, and so dry he crackled . . . and sang the most catchy number of the evening with the assistance of a delicious mixed chorus of lads and lassies."(9)

In August 1905, Lucas opened in Ernest Hogan's *Funny Folk* and *Rufus Rastus*. His duo singing role in Bob Cole and the Johnson Brothers' *The Shoo-Fly Regiment* followed a year later: "Sam Lucas and Wesley Jenkins are bringing the house down with their singing and dancing in their number, the 'bode of Edjicashun.'"(10)

Cole and Johnson's *The Red Moon* opened in early 1909. In this show, Lucas performed as part of a quartet with Wesley Jenkins, Henry Gant, and Benny Jones. The show closed in 1910 and was perhaps Lucas' last professional stage appearance. His formal retirement from the stage in 1912 in New York was followed by his active involvement in organizational activities in the theatrical community. In 1914 World Films produced *Uncle Tom's Cabin* with Sam Lucas in the title role and a cast of black players.

Sam Lucas' death in New York on January 9, 1916, brought to an end the career of one of the best known and most popular colored performers in America, called by many the "Dean of the Colored Theatrical Profession."(11)

CHRONOLOGICAL OUTLINE OF THE LIFE AND CAREER OF SAM LUCAS

DATE	ACTIVITY/EVENT/PLACE	SOURCE
1840 Aug. 7	Lucas is born in Washington, Ohio, Fayette County(12)	SKETCH,(13) SONG,BDAM*
	Farm hand until nineteen	
	Barber trade	
	Guitarist and caller with Hamilton's Celebrated Colored Quadrille Band in Cincinnati(14)	SLACK'S, BDAM
1861- 1865	Serves in Union army	
1869	Student at Wilberforce University	SKETCH, BDAM
	Teacher in New Orleans	
	Middleman and caller with Lew Johnson's Plantation Minstrels in St. Louis(15)	
	General performer with Jake Hamilton's Minstrel Company in New Orleans (16)	
1871	Member of Lew Johnson's Group in St. Louis	SLACK'S, SONG
1872	Barber trade in Cincinnati	
1873 July 4	Ballad singer and performer with Callender's Original Georgia Minstrels in Leavenworth, Kansas (17)	CLIP, BLU,SONG
	**First European tour of Fisk Jubilee Singers(18)	

---

*See References for abbreviations.
**An event not directly associated with Lucas.

DATE	ACTIVITY/EVENT/PLACE	SOURCE
1873 Oct.	Performance with Callender's Original Georgia Minstrels at Pike's Opera House, Cincinnati	CLIP, BLU
Nov.	Performances with Callender's Original Georgia Minstrels in cities in Ill., Kan., Ind., Mo.	CLIP, BLU
1874-1875	Performances with Callender's Original Georgia Minstrels	CLIP, BDAM
1876	May Hyers and Sam Lucas in *Out of the Wilderness*, play by Joseph Bradford, in Lynn, Mass.	CLIP
1877	Redpath Lyceum Bureau sponsors Hyers Sisters Dramatic Co. in *Out of Bondage*, a historical musical drama, in Boston; Sam Lucas in role of "Mischievous Henry"(19)	FO, BDAM
1878	Lucas signs with Sprague's Georgia Minstrels. Stars: Kersands, Lucas, Bland	FO, BDAM, BIKU
	Frohman, Stoddart, and Dillon Co. production of *Uncle Tom's Cabin*; Lucas first black in role of Uncle Tom(20)	UTC, BLM
1879	Hyers Sisters and Lucas in *The Underground Railroad*, a historical musical drama, in Boston	FO, HIST
Aug.	Haverly's United Genuine Colored Minstrels, "40 Artists headed by Sam Lucas," at Boston Theater, Boston	BU
1880-1885	Lucas established in Boston(21)	BD
1880 March	Hyers Sisters' Ideal Uncle Tom's Cabin Co. in Boston; Lucas as Uncle Tom(22)	UTC
Sept.	Boston Stock Co.; Lucas attempts to start legitimate theater groups(23)	FO, SKETCH

DATE	ACTIVITY/EVENT/PLACE	SOURCE
1880	"Dude Combination;" Lucas and wife in traveling performing company	SLACK'S
1881	C. H. Smith's Double Mammoth Uncle Tom's Cabin Co.; Lucas as Uncle Tom, Alice Lucas as Emeline(24)	UTC, FO
1882 April	C. H. Smith's Co., *Uncle Tom's Cabin*, Nieblo's Garden Theater, New York City	ANN
May-July	C. H. Smith's Co., *Uncle Tom's Cabin*, Boston Theater	ANN
Aug. 28 opening	Consolidation of Haverly's and Callender's Minstrels-Frohman Bros., Proprietors; performances at Grand Opera House, Chicago	SLACK'S, BDAM
Sept.	"The Sam Lucas Jubilee Songsters," Sunday evening concerts at Indian Village Pavilion, Boston(25)	BDAM, FO
1882-1885	Lucas Hub Concert Company, Boston(26)	BDAM, FO
1882-1883 Sept.	M. G. Slayton Lyceum Bureau; Lucas as principal in Jubilee Organization. Complimentary benefit given Lucas at Paine Hall, Boston	FO
1883	Callender's Colossal Colored Minstrel Festival in Oakland Garden, Boston; Sam Lucas, "New Motto Songs," with Kersands, King, the Hyers Sisters(27)	ANN, HTC
Oct.	"Lucas in a New Budget of Local and Catchy Songs"	HTC,SKETCH
1885 Aug.	Variety Show at Austin and Stone's Museum, Boston; Lucas is character, motto, and topical vocalist(28)	HTC,SKETCH

DATE	ACTIVITY/EVENT/PLACE	SOURCE
1885	The Bergen Star Concert Company at Music Hall, Providence, R.I. featuring Lucas and others; Sam doing impersonations, songs(29)	NYF
1886	The Bergen Star Concert Company at Steinway Hall, New York; "Coloured Talent"	ANN
July	Nattie Lucas and Sam Lucas in Boston; "Grand Entertainment"(30)	ADVO
1886 Aug.	Announcement of marriage of Carrie Melvin and Sam Lucas, Providence, R.I.(31)	FREE, SKETCH
1888 July	Vaudeville, London Theater, New York; "Mr. and Mrs. Sam Lucas"(32)	ANN, SLACK'S
Sept.	Vaudeville, Pacific Coast; "Sam is doing the Pacific Coast"	FREE, SKETCH
1889	Vaudeville, Olympic Theater, Denver; "Mr. and Mrs. Sam Lucas"	FREE, SKETCH
Oct.	Boston Pavilion Uncle Tom's Cabin Co. in Denver; Sam, wife, and child sign with U.T.C. Co.	FREE
Nov.-Dec.	Kohl, Middleton & Co. Circuit in Minnesota; Sam and wife in vaudeville	FREE
1890 Jan.	Kohl, Middleton & Co. Circuit in Chicago, Boston, Philadelphia, New York, Providence, R.I.; Sam and wife in vaudeville	FREE
Feb.-March	Kohl, Middleton & Co. Circuit in Buffalo, Denver, Detroit's Wonderland Theater and Museum, Grand Rapids, Michigan	FREE
Apr. 7-12	Vaudeville, "House Co." Miners Eighth Ave. Theater, New York; "Mr. and Mrs. Sam Lucas"	ANN
Aug.	Mr. & Mrs. Sam Lucas & Co. at London Theater, New York	ANN

DATE	ACTIVITY/EVENT/PLACE	SOURCE
1890–1892	Vaudeville, Sam T. Jack's Creole Burlesque Co. at Procter's Novelty Theater, New York	ANN,SKETCH
1893–1897	Vaudeville, Sam T. Jack's Creole Co. on European Tour; Mr. and Mrs. Sam Lucas, headliners(33)	SKETCH
1897	Bob Cole and Billy Johnson's production of *A Trip to Coontown*; Lucas has role of Silas Green(34)	HTC,BMT
July	Lucas spends summer in Boston	
	Sam and Carrie Lucas in Vogel's *Darkest America*(35)	FREE, SKETCH
1898 Feb.	Vaudeville, "Mr. & Mrs. Sam Lucas" at Olympic, Haymarket Chicago theaters; Alhambra Theater in Milwaukee	FREE
July	Sam Lucas performs with Mead's Imperial Vaudeville Co.	FREE, SKETCH
	Vaudeville, Jones and Sutton; performances in Philadelphia	FREE, SKETCH
Sept.	Vaudeville, Jones and Sutton; performances at Lincoln Park Theater, Mass.	FREE, SKETCH
Oct.	Carrie Lucas in minstrel company production of Isham's *Darktown Aristocracy*	FREE, NYA
1899 Feb.–Dec.	Lucas takes role formerly played by Jessie Shipp in *A Trip to Coontown*; performances in Cleveland, Cincinnati, New York, other cities	FREE, NYA
1900	Lucas plays part of Silas Green in *A Trip to Coontown* at Grand Opera House, Boston	HTC, BMT
1902 Mar. 24	Testimonial benefit given for Lucas at Murray Hill Lyceum, N.Y.(36)	HYA

DATE	ACTIVITY/EVENT/PLACE	SOURCE
1903– 1904	P. G. Lowery's Concert Band & Nashville Students Minstrel Co. in Kan., Mo., Ark., other cities; Lucas is stage manager, performer	FREE
1904	Vaudeville, Moonshiner's Daughter Co., No. 2 in Chicago, other cities in Ill. and Kan.; Lucas has top billing	NYA,FREE, SKETCH
1905 June– July	Lucas sings *Under the Banana Tree* and *Won't You Tickle Me*, Joe Jordan, director, at Pekin Theater, Chicago	FREE,NYA
Aug.	Lucas in Ernest Hogan's *Funny Folk* and *Rufus Rastus*	FREE
Dec.	Lucas in "Grand Star Concert" at Bethel A.M.E. Church, N.Y.	FREE
1906 Aug. 26	Lucas plays "Brother Doolittle" in Cole and Johnson's *Shoo-Fly* *Regiment*; musical opens in Maryland(37)	BDAM,HTC
1907– 1908	Lucas plays "Brother Doolittle" in Cole and Johnson's *Shoo-Fly* *Regiment*	BDAM,HTC
1908– 1910	Lucas and daughter, Marie, in Cole and Johnson's *The Red Moon*(38)	FREE
1909 Jan.	Death of Carrie Melvin Lucas in Boston(39)	FREE
Aug.	Lucas performs at Colored Vaudeville Benevolent Association Benefit	NYA
Sept.	Lucas becomes a member of "Frogs," an exclusive social organization in New York	NYA
1912	Lucas retires from stage; remains in New York	BDAM
1913 Feb.	Lucas performs at New York Frogs Ball singing *I Was All Right in My* *Younger Day*	NYA

DATE	ACTIVITY/EVENT/PLACE	SOURCE
1913 June	Spends summer at New York Sheepshead Bay, guest of Wesley Jenkins	NYA
July	Lucas referred to in New York as "Dean of Colored Theatrical Profession"(40)	NYA
1914	Movie version of *Uncle Tom's Cabin*, World Films. William R. Daly, director; Sam Lucas, Uncle Tom; Irving Cummings; Marie Eline and and a cast of black players(41)	NA,BDAM,BLM
	Lucas speaking, singing in and around New York	NYA
1915	Benefit for Sam Lucas at Lafayette Theater, New York; Marie Lucas, director. "Female Orchestra makes hit at Lafayette Theater"	NYA
1916	Death of Sam Lucas, New York(42)	NYA

APPENDIX A

Troupe Rosters

1. Callender's Original Georgia Minstrels (1872)
Charles Hicks, Business Manager

Anderson, Charley
Benson, Al
Cox, Abe
Devonear, Pete
Easton, Hosey

Grease, Jim
Hicks, Barney
Hieght, Bob
Johnson, Henry
Jones, Sam

Kersands, Billy
Little, Dick
Moore, Hamilton
Pleasants, Billy
Skillings, Prof. George,
   Orchestra Dir.
Smith, Al
Wilson, Billy
Ziebrisky, Jake
Weston, Horace (Banjo)

2. Callender's Original Georgia Minstrels (1873)

Bohee Bros.
Crawford, Bob
Delaney, Charley
Frazer and Allen
Gaine and Thompson
Hunn and Foster
Jackson, Billy
Johnson, Jimmy

Lucas, Sam
Lyle, Billy
McIntosh, Tom
Moore, Neal
Norton, Bob
Ousley, Charley
Stansbury, C. F.
Woodson and Sykes

3. Sprague's Georgia Minstrels (1878)

Bland, James

Kersands, Billy
Lucas, Sam*
Buck and Delaney
Caps, Charley
Watson, Bob
Smith, Lige
Brown and Mills
Taylor, John
Dupre, Charley
Lewis, Charley

Luca, Alex, Voice teacher for
   group
Singer, Charley
Grimes, Frank
Washington, Taylor
Leighton and Warwick
Short, Bob
Stansbury, C. F.
Wright, C.
Haires and John Woods
Moore, Neal

*Date when Lucas joined troupe uncertain

APPENDIX B

EXCERPTS FROM MINSTREL PROGRAMS
HARVARD THEATRE COLLECTION

1. FIRST WEEK OF THE GREAT GEORGIA SLAVE TROUPE
Monday, March 29, 1874
Callender's Original Georgia Minstrels

PART FIRST

TAMBO - KERSANDS/ DEVONEAR/ BONES - LUCAS AND GRACE
OVERTURE - CALLENDER'S GEORGIA MINSTRELS

On My Journey Home..........................Jas Grace
Robin, Tell Kitty I'm Coming...............E. P. Smith
Dar's a Meeting Here To-Night..............P. Devonear
Out of Work.................................A. A. Luca
Daffney, Do You Love Me....................Sam Lucas
Old Aunt Jemima............................Billy Kersands
Sadie Ray..................................Dick Ray

To conclude with the Roaring Sketch & Walk-Around entitled:
Brudder Bones' Baby!

Uncle Ben..................................P. Devonear
Hannah.....................................Jas Grace
Cuff.......................................Al Smith
Slim Jim...................................Sam Lucas
Laura......................................Willie Lyle
The Baby...................................Billy Kersands
                And the members of the Company

PART SECOND

Dick Little and his Banjo - Solo and Song
The Canebreak Spectres
Quartette songs and dances - Devonear, Lucas
Kersands, Al Smith
Christine Nilsson Eclipsed
Willie Lyle the Gay Prima Donna in his Burlesque
A Characteristic and Laughable Plantation Sketch
entitled:
OLD UNCLE JEEMS!

Uncle Jeems	Dick Little
His Boy	Al Smith
Mr. William	P. Devonear

THE NEW ORLEANS DANDY, BILLY KERSANDS AS THE SWELL
of the Levee

George Washington Augustus Smith............S. Lucas
Ben Johnson..................................P. Devonear
Old Jeff.....................................Dick Little
Pete...Al Smith
Cicerto......................................Billy Kersands
Hannah.......................................James Grace
Susannah.....................................Willie Lyle

The Audience is politely requested to remain until the
close of this interesting tableau.
The Whole to Conclude with the Laughable Sketch, written
expressly for this company by D. Marble,
--LIFE AND LOVE IN GEORGIA--

2.   Hooley's Opera House
Brooklyn, New York
January 11, ca1877
C. Callender--Proprietor
Charles & Daniel Frohman--Business Agents

CALLENDER'S FAMOUS GEORGIA MINSTRELS

End Men: Grace, Wilson, Lucas, Devonear

Alex A. Luca--Tenor   E. P. Smith-------Balladist
Alf Smith---- Jig Dancer   Hamilton A. Moore-Orator
             & Comedian   Hosey Easton------Comedian
Willie Lyle--- Prima Donna   Sam L. Lucas------The Great
Dick Little--- Banjo King &   Character
              Basso   Artist

3.   AUSTIN AND STONE'S MUSEUM
August 31, 1885

Programme

Miss Pearl Duncan----Vocalist and Recitationist
Arthur O'Brien and Morris Katie----Irish Sketch Artists
Song, Dances, Wit
Fulmer and Hart----Sketch Artists

Everybody's favorite Character, Motto and Topical Vocalist

SAM LUCAS

The most popular Colored Comedian in the profession, His
name is a household word throughout the nation.

4. Haverly's Nieblo's Garden

J. H. Haverly--Proprietor and Manager
E. G. Gilmore--Assistant Manager

C. H. Smith's Double Mammoth
UNCLE TOM'S CABIN
May 23, 1882

With the largest and Best Company in the World, introducing
Mr. C. H. Smith's original Innovation of Two Topsys, Two
Marks (the Lawyer), Three Donkeys, Ten Siberian Blood
Hounds, One hundred Jubilee Singers, and the

Following Cast of Characters

Uncle Tom............................Mr. Sam Lucas
Simon Legree.........................Mr. Frank A. Tannehill
Phineas Fletcher
Topsy No. 1 with songs and dances....Miss Daisy Markie
Topsy No. 2..........................Miss Lillie Hamilton
Eva..................................Miss Alice Hamilton
Eliza................................Miss Lou Leighton

Other members of the cast: Miss Annie Hay, Mrs. Sanford,
Mrs. Alice Lucas, Miss Nellie Scott, Mr. Cyrus Stuart, Mr.
John L. Hay, Mr. T. E. English, Mr. J. H. Connor, and
others.

During the evening the Orchestra, under the direction of
Mr. Charles Puerner, will render the following selections:

Overture "Bandit's Frolics"..............Suppe
Waltz "Boccacio".........................Strauss
Medley "The Mocking Bird"................Cox
Selection "The Mascotte".................Audran
Song, "Old Folks at Home"................Foster

5. CALLENDER'S COLOSSAL COLORED
MINSTREL FESTIVAL
SEASON OF 1883

Oakland Garden, Boston

Gustav and Charles Frohman----Proprietors

Ed Bowen   Wallace King

Taylor & Reynolds   Billy Green

Dick Little   Lewis Brown

Billy Kersands   Taylor Green

MR. SAM LUCAS - "New Motto Song"

Frazier, Woodson, Young, Hawkins, Cooper, W. Green, Guard,

Evans, Robinson, Reed, Reynolds,

The Famous Hyers Sisters and Wallace King and Lewis Brown

in Vocal Selections, including the quartette

"Greeting to Spring."

NOTES

Factual information about the life and career of Sam
Lucas was found in primary sources in libraries and special
collections at Harvard University and the Boston Public
Library. Newspapers, playbills, programs, individual
histories and autobiographies, clippings, and black
minstrel songbooks were major sources. Additional data
were obtained from secondary sources; however, some dates,
time periods, and events in Lucas' life and career still
remain unaccountable.

1. Ike Simond, *Old Slack's Reminiscences and Pocket
History of the Colored Profession from 1865 to 1891*, with
an introduction by Robert Toll (Chicago: [1892]. Reprint.
Bowling Green State University: Ray B. Browne, 1974), xx.
2. James Weldon Johnson, *Black Manhattan* (New York:
Alfred A. Knopf, 1940. Reprint. New York: Arno Press
and the *New York Times*, 1968), 90.
3. Eileen Southern, *The Music of Black Americans: A
History* (New York: W. W. Norton, 1971), 269.

4. Two songsters are available that provide lyrics to Lucas' songs: *Sam Lucas' Careful Man Songsters* (Chicago: [1881]) and *Sam Lucas' Plantation Songster* (Boston: [1875].

5. *Folio* 22 (May 1877), 211.

6. Playbill, located in Austin's and Stone's Box, Harvard Theatre Collection, Harvard University Library.

7. "Sam Lucas' Theatrical Career Written By Himself in 1909," *New York Age*, January 13, 1916, 6.

8. Thomas Lawrence Riis, *Black Musical Theatre in New York, 1890-1915* (Ph.D. dissertation, University of Michigan, 1981).

9. Unidentified newspaper clipping, February 6, 1900, J. Rosamond Johnson folder, Harvard Theatre Collection, Harvard University Library.

10. *New York Age*, October 31, 1907, 2.

11. *New York Age*, January 13, 1916, 1.

12. Conflicting birthdates and ages appear in references about Sam Lucas.

13. There is little biographical data on Lucas' early years. In 1909 he wrote a sketch of his life for the *New York Age* published on January 13, 1916. Lucas gave few dates in the sketch, some of which are questionable; other information consists of performance activities and locations.

14. Lucas was almost thirty when he began performing professionally. Early experiences are given in Tom Fletcher, *100 Years of the Negro in Show Business* (New York, 1954), 69: "I was with a lot of them. I also used to play and sing on the boats that ran up and down the Ohio River, the packet boats that carried both freight and passengers . . . after dinner, when the passengers were sitting around, I would sing and play. . . . What I picked up doing that kept me going until I could join another show of some kind."

15. Lew Johnson was one of the post-Civil War black minstrel owners whose troupes continued up to the late 1890s. Bert Williams got his start with one of Johnson's companies.

16. The Hamilton Brothers, Dave and Jake, had a famous concert party according to Ike Simond, *Old Slack's Reminiscences and Pocket History of the Colored Profession from 1865 to 1891* (Chicago: n.d.), 3.

17. See Appendix B, sec. 2.

18. The success of the Fisk Jubilee Singers in 1873 had an immediate influence on the minstrel show. Religious songs became a part of the total show; the Olio included jubilee songs and religious singing groups in the form of quartets (see Appendix B, sec. 1).

19. Lucas' association with the Hyers Sisters, Anna and Emma, began formally in 1877 with the production of *Out of Bondage*. Lucas and the Hyers had probably met earlier in Boston. The Hyers' company had several names over the years of its existence: Hyers Sisters' Combination, Hyers Sisters' Opera Co., Ideal Combination Co. Lucas took part in their musical drama, *The Underground Railroad*. Others in the group were Maggie Porter of the Fisk Jubilee

Singers, Mr. and Mrs. John Luca, Wallace King, Billy Kersands.

20. This production of U.T.C. must have been the Stoddart Comedy Company formed by Gus Frohman, George Stoddart, and John Dillon about 1877-1878. The show was short lived. Harry Birdoff, *The World's Greatest Hit: Uncle Tom's Cabin* (New York, 1947), 224-311.

21. A listing in the *Detroit Directory* (Boston, 1880-1884) suggests that Lucas had established residency at 82 Village in Boston, Massachusetts; his occupation is listed as "comedian."

22. "The most unusual of the 'Ideal' companies was formed in Boston, in 1880, the Hyers Sisters' Ideal Uncle Tom's Cabin Co., featuring the colored parts by colored people, the others by whites. When their play opened at the Howard Theatre on March 8, 1880, Sam Lucas, who portrayed Tom, read a new prologue by Mrs. Stowe." Birdoff, 224-311.

23. *Folio* 19 (1880), 372, reported Lucas' efforts to start a serious theater group. Several prominent writers of the time, both black and white, seemed to have been involved in writing plays for him: George Russell Jackson, lyricist; John P. Addams; Joseph Bradford; and Pauline Hopkins, a black author and journalist in Boston.

24. Garff Wilson refers to the Tom Show as a phenomenon of the nineteenth century. This name was given to a traveling circus-like production of *Uncle Tom's Cabin*. Garff B. Wilson, *Three Hundred Years of American Drama and Theatre* (Englewood Cliffs, N.J.: Prentice Hall, 1973), 181-200. The double *Uncle Tom* show was created by C. G. Smith, publisher, composer, and entrepreneur of Boston. The production had two Topsies, two Marks, three donkeys, 10 Siberian hounds, and a large chorus of singers. Birdoff, 224-311.

25. *Folio* 22 (1882), 322, reported the "Jubilee Songsters" concerts were a success, artistically and financially. Selections included many of the new camp-meeting songs, jubilee hymns, and popular melodies.

26. Evidence indicates that Alice Lucas may have been Lucas' first wife; Nattie Lucas was their daughter. The Hub Concert Company members were his wife and daughter, the Walker Male Quintet, Lena Hopkins, and occasionally, the DeWolf Sisters.

27. See Appendix B, sec. 5.

28. Lucas began to perform more in variety shows, dime museum shows, and vaudeville theaters. The dime museums were part of huge vaudeville circuits. A patron could pay a dime and watch a continuous vaudeville show from ten in the morning until eleven o'clock at night. Wilson, 181-200.

29. The Bergen Star Concert Co. was owned and managed by James Bergen, husband of Flora Batson Bergen. Appearing with Miss Batson were other performers, including Lucas, Adelaide G. Smith, the Walker Quintet, and Carrie M. Melvin, contralto and instrumentalist. *New York Freeman*, October 24, 1885.

30. *Boston Advocate*, July 17, 1886: "A grand entertainment will be given in Patriarchate Hall, 465 Washington, on Friday evening, July 30. Miss Nattie Lucas,

daughter of Sam Lucas, will be present and render several selections. Sam Lucas will also favor the audience with his humorous songs and witty sayings."

31. Carrie Melvin Lucas was the younger of two talented daughters of the prominent Melvin family of Newport, Rhode Island. Before her marriage, her early concerts were with Madame Selika. She played the violin, cornet, banjo, guitar, and mandolin. *Indianapolis Freeman*, January 9, 1909.

32. Mr. and Mrs. Sam Lucas were a vaudeville and variety show act from 1888 to 1890. *New York Age*, January 13, 1916.

33. Sam T. Jack was a theater owner and manager of several performing groups in New York and Chicago. Lucas said he met Jack in Denver and suggested the idea of a colored show. *The Creole Show* opened with Sam Lucas, Fred Piper, and others in 1890. For the first time, this show featured a female interlocutor and beautiful black girls in the traditional semi-circle. James Weldon Johnson, *Black Manhattan*, 1968. The Lucases remained with the show three years and then went abroad. Documentation as to the length of time the Lucases spent abroad is not presently available.

34. *A Trip to Coontown* broke the minstrel tradition by having the cast of characters extemporize the plot. The show was organized, produced, and managed by blacks. The cast included Bob Cole, Billy Johnson, Sam Cousins, the Freeman Sisters, Alice MacKay, Sam King, Tom Craig, and others. Unidentified newspaper clipping: February 6, 1900. Harvard Theatre Collection, n.d., n.p.

35. In SKETCH, Lucas notes that he and his wife did not remain with the "Darkest America" Company.

36. The *Indianapolis Freeman*, April 5, 1902, reported that the testimonial benefit given on March 24, 1902, for Lucas netted over two hundred dollars. Performers included Abby Mitchell, Simpson and Pittman, Smart and Williams, Billy Johnson, Paul L. Dunbar, and Aida O. Walker. A press dispatch stated that Lucas was dying of consumption.

37. Bob Cole joined J. Rosamond Johnson to write and produce the musical comedy, *The Shoo-Fly Regiment*. Opening in July 1906, the cast included Tom Brown, Bob Kelley, Theo. Panky, Inez Clough, Anna Cook, Sam Lucas, and others. He and Wesley Jenkins performed "Bode of Edjicashun." Marie Lucas, daughter of Sam, was also in the show.

38. Bob Cole and J. Rosamond Johnson collaborated on another hit musical, *The Red Moon*. Lucas, Wesley Jenkins, Henry Gant, and Benny Jones performed in a comical quartet. The *New York Age*, October 1, 1908, reported that "the Grand Old Man, Sam Lucas, is still as spry and funny as ever. All he talks of is that diamond ring George Walker gave him recently."

39. The *Indianapolis Freeman*, January 1909, reported that Carrie Lucas was shot. The Lucases were separated at the time of her death.

40. Lucas was a respected member of the theater profession. Many called him "Dad." Toll remarked that "Sam Lucas had the most varied and distinguished career of any black minstrel who began his career before 1890." Simond, 36.

41. "The featuring of a Negro actor, Sam Lucas, rather than a white actor in blackface, created a precedent." Harry Ploski and Warren Marr, II, *The Negro Almanac: A Reference Work on the Afro-American* (New York: Bellwether Publishing Co., 1976), 788.

42. Sam Lucas' death was reported in major newspapers across the country. The *Indianapolis Freeman* (January 17, 1916, 1) noted the tribute to Lucas given by Gustav Frohman, an early minstrel proprietor and theatrical entrepreneur: "I met Lucas in 1873 in St. Louis and gave him his first rehearsal . . . it was in 1875 in Beethoven Hall in Boston when Lucas first attracted the attention of the public as an actor." The *New York Age* (January 13, 1916, 1) stated that "Sam Lucas enjoyed the unique record of having been a member of the theatrical profession for nearly half a century."

REFERENCES

The titles in the following list represent the research materials most relevant to this study. Abbreviations for sources are included.

Birdoff, Harry. *The World's Greatest Hit: Uncle Tom's Cabin*. New York: S. F. Varni, 1947. (UTC)
Bordman, Gerald. *American Musical Theatre: A Chronicle*. New York: Oxford University Press, 1978. (BORD)
Boston Directory. Boston: Sampson, Davenport and Co., 1880-1886. (BD)
Clark, Peter H. *The Black Brigade of Cincinnati: Being a Report of Its Labords and a Muster-Roll of Its Members; Together with Various Orders, Speeches, Etc. Relating to It*. Cincinnati: printed by Joseph B. Boyd, 25 West Fourth Street, 1864. (CLARK)
Cuney-Hare, Maud. *Negro Musicians and Their Music*. Washington, D.C.: Associated Publishers, 1936.
Fletcher, Tom. *100 Years of the Negro in Show Business*. New York: Burdge and Co., 1954. (100 yrs.)
Hamm, Charles. *Yesterdays: Popular Song in America*. New York: W. W. Norton, 1979. (YES)
Handy, W. C. *Father of the Blues: An Autobiography*, edited by Arna Bontemps, with a foreword by Abble Niles, 1941. London: Sedgwick & Jackson, 1957. (FAB)
Johnson, James Weldon. *Black Manhattan*. New York: Alfred A. Knopf, 1940. Reprint. New York: Arno Press and the *New York Times*, 1968. (BLM)
Lucas, Sam. *Sam Lucas' Plantation Songster*. Boston, 1875. (SONG)
Lucas, Sam. "Sam Lucas Theatrical Career Written by Himself in 1909." *New York Age,* January 13, 1916. (SKETCH)
Odell, George. *Annals of the New York Stage*. 15 vols. New York: Columbia University Press, 1927-49. (ANN)
Patterson, Lindsay. *Anthology of the American Negro in the Theatre*. New York: Publisher's Co., 1967. (PAT)

Ploski, Harry, and Warren Marr, II, ed. and comp. *The Negro Almanac: A Reference Work on the Afro-American.* New York: Bellwether Publishing Co., 1976. (NA)

Riis, Thomas Lawrence. *Black Musical Theatre in New York, 1890-1915.* Ph.D. dissertation, University of Michigan, 1981. (BMT)

Simond, Ike. *Old Slack's Reminiscence and Pocket History of the Colored Profession from 1865-1891.* Chicago, n.d. Reprint. Bowling Green, Oh.: Bowling Green University, 1974. (SLACK)

Southern, Eileen. *Biographical Dictionary of Afro-American and African Musicians.* Westport, Conn.: Greenwood Press, 1982. (BDAM)

_____. *The Music of Black Americans: A History.* New York: W. W. Norton, 1971. (HIST)

Newspapers and Journals

Black Perspective in Music 2 (Fall, 1974). (BPIM)
Boston Advocate, 1885-1886. (BA)
Denver Star, 1916. (DS)
Douglass' Monthly 1-5 (1861-1863). Reprint. *Negro Periodicals in the United States, 1840-1960.* New York: Negro Universities Press, 1969. (DM)
Folio, 1870-1888. (FOI)
Indianapolis Freeman, 1886-1916. (IF)
New York Age, 1886-1920. (NYA)
New York *Clipper,* 1872-1878. (NYC)
New York Freeman, 1881-1885. (NYF)

Special Collections: Programs, Clippings, Scrapbooks

Allen A. Brown Collection, Boston Public Library (ABC)
The Edna Kuhn Loeb Music Library, Harvard University (EKL)
Boston Public Library (BPL)
Harvard Theatre Collection, Harvard University Library (HTC)
Houghton and Widener Libraries, Harvard University

The Singing Tours of the
Fisk Jubilee Singers:
1871-1874

Louis D. Silveri

The year 1871 was an auspicious one for American music.
From out of the war-torn South came a small troupe of ex-
slaves who introduced a new era in American musical
culture. It was already six years after Appomattox, and
the nation was still far from adjusting to the new
realities. The massive task of reconstruction included the
need to educate millions of former slaves who lived in
social, economic, and political limbo. Fortunately, public
and private efforts had been undertaken to aid them in the
transition from slavery to freedom.

The federal government established the Freedmen's
Bureau in 1865 to care for immediate needs of food,
shelter, and clothing for the ex-slaves. In time the
Bureau also found employment for them, provided legal
assistance, and established schools for both children and
adults. Assisting the Bureau were private secular and
religious organizations, especially in the field of education, such as the American Missionary Association.

The AMA was founded in Albany, New York, in 1846. It
devoted much time, effort, and resources to the slave
question and to the uplifting of freedmen after 1862. By
1871 it had under its care in the South 23 churches, 147
common schools, 16 graded schools, and 7 "institutions of
learning."(1) Of the four million freedmen, only one in
forty thousand was in college. Of these, eighty percent
were in institutions founded for black people by Northern
individuals and institutions with assistance from the
Freedmen's Bureau. Among these was Fisk University in
Nashville, Tennessee.(2)

Fisk University opened in 1866 and was named for
General Clinton B. Fisk, former head of the Freedmen's
Bureau in Nashville. It was chartered in 1867, and its
enrollment, but not its resources, grew every year. By
1871 the school officials were desperate; the students did
not have the resources to pay for their education, and the
facilities were outmoded and crowded.

It is fortunate for posterity that religious educators
believed it important to include musical expression in the
curriculum, or at least to encourage extra-curricular

musical endeavors.   Serving as treasurer and musical director of Fisk was George White, a young war veteran from upstate New York.   He had conducted choirs and given music lessons for many years in both the North and South.   During the years following the war he had assembled and trained a student choir whose performances were well received by local audiences.   White suggested that the trustees authorize a singing tour of the North to raise money for the school.   At first the trustees saw no hope in the plan; there was no money for expenses, and who would pay to listen to a group of colored singers from the South? George White persisted.   He was sure he could find sympathetic audiences among church groups and that people would pay to hear the beautiful voices he had trained.   The trustees finally agreed to give the tour their official blessing--but little else.   They gave the few dollars the school could spare, and White contributed some of his own funds to begin the tour.(3)

Twelve people embarked on the tour: White, the musical director; a chaperone named Miss Wells; her eight-year-old ward Georgie Wells; and nine singers. Seven of the student singers were ex-slaves, ranging in age from 14 to 23. Five were female and four were male.   They called themselves "The Colored Christian Singers."(4)

Even after four years of war and six years of peace and reconstruction, many in the North knew little about the ex-slaves and continued to cling to their prejudices and stereotypes about Afro-Americans.   The Fisk Singers were buffeted by a confusion of acceptance and rejection in transportation, accommodations, churches, restaurants, and concert halls.   Despite these problems, the troupe courageously continued the tour until they achieved recognition.

The Singers left Nashville on October 6, 1871.   In an informal presentation at the Cincinnati Exposition, they sang *The Star-Spangled Banner; Red, White and Blue; Away to the Meadows;* and other favorites of the day.(5) They drew a large crowd which was probably more curious about this odd-looking group than appreciative of their music.

They next appeared by invitation in a local church.   A city newspaper reported an overflow crowd and listed the six songs performed. Three were traditional hymns: *Broken Hearted Weep No More; Singing for Jesus;* and *My Lord Says There's Room Enough.* Three were slave songs or spirituals: *Children, You'll Be Called Upon to March in the Field of Battle; O Redeemed, Redeemed, I'm Washed in the Blood of the Lamb;* and *Go Down Moses.* Reviews of the concert appeared the following day in three newspapers.   They ranged from a brief account identifying the group as "a band of negro minstrels . . . genuine negroes," to another with the heading, "NEGRO MINSTRELSY IN CHURCH--NOVEL RELIGIOUS EXERCISE." A friend of one reviewer supposedly left in disgust, muttering "no bones, no end man, no middle man." The reviewer stated that his friend should have stayed. He could have heard "some very fine music, at times funny, but deep and rich."   The third review was perceptive and prophetic.   The reviewer called *Go Down Moses* the masterpiece of the evening:

rough in language, it was richly melodious and
showed that analogy between the feeling of the slaves
of the South and that of the captive Israelites. The
unaffected simple fervor breathing forth the soul were
remarkable and touching qualities of the performance.
What might be done with such voices, subjected to
early, thorough, and skillful culture, the singing of
last night afforded a faint intimation.(6)

This reviewer recognized that he had not attended a
minstrel show, that he had heard and seen something
special. The spirituals and the mode in which they were
sung were unique and captivating, but he did suggest that
this raw material be refined through an acculturation
process, making it more acceptable to the concert stage of
the day. Singing spirituals in the field was one thing--
singing them to sophisticated audiences was something else.
George White would have to confront this issue again and
again.
On October 17 the first concert with an admission fee
was held in Mozart Hall. The *Cincinnati Gazette* reported
that the audience contained many leading white citizens and
a large number of colored people. The repertory continued
to be a mixture of sacred anthems, Irish ballads, sentimen-
tal and patriotic songs, and a few spirituals. The
reviewer made no comment about the spirituals that were
sung, writing only that "many were pleased with the sweetness of the voices, accuracy of the execution, distinctive-
ness of enunciation, and precision of time." The fact that
the reviewer was reminded of the Hutchinson and Gibson
Singers as he listened to the Fisk Singers, and that the
attending audience was small, necessitated a rethinking of
the group's image. Proceeds from this concert barely paid
expenses. Even though they were heavily in debt and badly
clothed, the remaining forty dollars of proceeds was
donated to the victims of the devastating fire that had
recently swept Chicago.(7)
Fortunes had not improved two days later when less than
twenty people showed up for a concert at Black's Opera
House in Springfield, Ohio. However, Mr. White made a
visit to the Synod of the Presbyterian Church then in
session in the city and requested that they hear his group
sing. The half hour granted extended to an hour. At least
seven songs were sung, four of which were spirituals. The
audience was especially pleased with *Go Down Moses* and
Turn Back Pharoah's Army. The Singers came away with a
donation of $105 and a resolution

that the singing of the songs of Zion by the students
of Fisk University has profoundly stirred our hearts,
and awakened anew our sympathy for the freed people of
the South. We heartily commend Professor George L.
White and his company to the favor of the Christian
community, and feel assured that their appearance before the public will tend greatly to increase the
interest that is felt in the religious education of the
millions of our fellow countrymen who, by the wondrous

providence of God have so recently been released from
the fetters of bondage.(8)

The reception by the Synod gave the Singers encouragement as they headed for Wilberforce University in Xenia,
Ohio.   When two concerts netted only $84, the next two
weeks tested the resolve of Mr. White and his ragged group.
Little money was coming in and debts continued to mount.
George White was not only musical director but also advance
agent, advertising agent, ticket seller, and porter.   He
was feeling the strain of these jobs and the embarrassment
of answering the entreaties from university officials with
empty palms, but he remained convinced that success would
result from the right kind of exposure.
Mr. White met with that kind of exposure when the
Council of the Congregational Church, meeting in Oberlin,
invited them to give a performance.   The Council was
impressed with the singing and the mission of the Singers.
G. Stanley Pope, secretary of the American Missionary
Association and a member of the Oberlin Theological
Seminary, agreed to serve as advance agent for the next few
months.   The Council urged George White to work his way to
New York.(9)
Although the Oberlin meeting provided some hope, the
situation did not improve during the next two weeks of
performances in Ohio.   While in Columbus, George White,
during "an anxious and almost sleepless night," decided to
rename his group the Jubilee Singers in hopes of adding a
new dimension to their appeal.   There was still no indication that White thought of concentrating on the spirituals
that were so appealing to almost every audience.(10)
In early December the Jubilee Singers were in Elmira,
New York, where they met and sang for the Reverend T. K.
Beecher.   Reverend Beecher sent a letter of commendation to
his famous brother, Reverend Henry Ward Beecher, pastor of
Plymouth Church in Brooklyn, New York.   By mid-December the
Singers were in New York City where they were welcomed by
the   officials of the American Missionary Association
(AMA).(11)
The first performance in the metropolitan area occurred
at an evening prayer service in Beecher's church.   In the
audience was Mr. Gustavus D. Pike, an AMA official who
replaced Mr. Pope as the group's agent and had an important
role in recording the history of the tour.   He later wrote:

A motley group!   The girls dressed in waterproofs and
clothed about the neck in long woolen comforters to
protect their throats, stood in a row in the front.
The young men occupied positions closely in the rear,
the class standing solid . . . in order to secure the
most perfect harmony.   The first hymn was *O How I Love
Jesus*, and I shall never forget the rich tones of the
young men as they mingled their voices in a melody so
beautiful and touching I scarcely knew whether I was
"in the body or out of the body."   Slave songs followed, occupying about twenty minutes.(12)

Pike's failure to comment on the slave songs was in sharp

contrast to the comments of those who heard them in the next few weeks.

Reverend Beecher held a benefit concert for the Jubilee Singers in his church on December 18, making sure that a large audience would be in attendance. The concert was reviewed in the New York press with little understanding. The *New York Herald*'s lead was "BEECHER'S NEGRO MINSTRELS . . . THE GREAT PLYMOUTH PREACHER AS AN END MAN . . . A FULL TROUPE OF REAL LIVE DARKIES IN THE TABERNACLE OF THE LORD . . . ROLLICKING CHORUSES BUT NO SAND SHAKING OR JOY DANCING." The reviewer derided the audience as "people of a superior race, or fancy they belong to a superior race, who like to patronize those whom they fancy to be of an inferior or docile race." He did believe, however, that Maggie Porter had "an exquisite voice." The *New York World* complained that "only 4 of 19 songs were camp meeting songs and poor work was made of others. This amateur group of Negro Minstrels should sing camp meeting and nigger melodies rather than opera." The *Clipper* announced "their attractive and original concerts. A feature . . . is their sacred chants and plantation hymns."(13)

The Jubilee Singers sang at prayer meetings and in concerts until the end of January. The Reverend Theodore L. Cuyler of the Brooklyn Lafayette Avenue Church wrote a perceptive letter to the New York *Tribune* about the group. Cuyler related that he had never seen a cultivated Brooklyn audience so moved: "The wild melodies of these emancipated slaves touched the font of tears, and gray-haired men wept like little children." The Jubilee Singers had

> a fresh collection of the most weird and plaintive hymns sung in the plantation cabins in the dark days of bondage . . . the very embodiment of African heart music. . . . The harmony of these children of nature and their musical execution were beyond the reach of art.

Cuyler requested a universal welcome in the North for "these living representatives of the only true, native school of American music." In addition, he related that a friend of his, a Scottish minister recently visiting in America, told his fellow Scots on his return that he had found the ideal church in America. It was made up of Methodist praying, Presbyterian preaching, and Southern negro singing.(14)

The five weeks spent in New York City represented a turning point for the Jubilee Singers, their music, and Fisk University. They became better acquainted with officials of the American Missionary Association who took care of their needs while in the city, found endorsements, and helped to plan and manage their future performances. Henry Ward Beecher became an important patron who encouraged people to give financial support to the Singers' cause. Word-of-mouth advertising brought good attendance from within the church community, and newspaper reviews, while often devoid of any understanding of this musical phenomenon, excited the curiosity of readers. George White concluded that there were two reasons for their growing

popularity: people came to their performances to hear the
beautiful voices of the students and to hear the songs they
brought with them out of slavery. The spirituals became
the feature presentations of their performances, and White
began to think about preserving them in written form.

The Jubilee Singers began a New England tour in late
January with Mr. Pike as agent. Since they were nearly
free of debt and had many endorsements, Pike believed they
could expect $500 above expenses every week.(15)

On February 15 they sang a concert in the New Haven
Music Hall, where one of the largest audiences ever
assembled in that city gave, through admission fees and
donations, about two thousand dollars--by far the largest
income from a performance to date. Unfortunately, the
editor of the *Loomis Musical Journal* had harsh words for
the Singers:

> their performance is a burlesque on music, and almost
> on religion. We do not consider it consistent with
> actual piety to sit and be amused at an imitation of
> the religious worship formerly engaged in by ignorant
> but Christian people; and as for calling their effort a
> concert, it is ridiculously absurd.(16)

Such criticism did not daunt the Singers, because they
drew large and enthusiastic audiences through most of the
remainder of the tour. Moreover, George White commissioned
Theodore F. Seward, editor of the New York *Musical Gazette*,
to notate the spirituals for publication. His work, *The
Jubilee Songs*, appeared in March as a twenty-eight-page
booklet containing sixty-one songs. Seward wrote an introduction that constituted the first explanation of the goals
of the Jubilee Singers and the first analysis of the songs
they sang.

Seward noted that the songs "touch a chord which the
most consummate art fails to reach." He attributed some of
this to the skill of the singers as well as the condition
of slavery from which they came; but he believed the power
was mainly in the songs themselves, whose origins were
unique. They were not "composed" like ordinary music, but
sprang to life "as a gift from God to keep them from the
state of hopeless apathy." He remarked that the compli-
cated and at times strikingly original rhythm was
emphasized during performance by foot stamping and body
swaying in even measure and in perfect time. He found the
variety of forms presented in the songs to be "truly
surprising."

Seward assured the public that the music was taken down
during repeated interviews with the singers:

> Some of the phrases and turns in the melodies are so
> peculiar that the listener might not unreasonably
> suppose them to be incapable of exact representation by
> ordinary musical characters. It is found, however, that
> they all submit to the laws of musical language, and if
> they are sung or played exactly as written, all the
> characteristic effects will be produced.(17)

The Jubilee Songs was not the first publication of slave songs. In 1867 William Francis Allen, Lucy McKim Garrison, and Charles Pickard Ware published Slave Songs of the United States, a compendium of 137 songs with extensive descriptions of the music and how it was performed. The Allen collection was gathered during and after the war. In the same year Thomas Wentworth Higginson's article, "Negro Spirituals," was published in the Atlantic Monthly. This article contained thirty-six of the many songs he collected while commanding a black regiment during the Civil War. There was little duplication in these three publications, suggesting the existence of a vast treasure trove of slave songs.(18)

The Jubilee Singers toured New England during the spring of 1872, spending much of this time in Boston. Their first performances in that city were not successful. The New York Clipper reported that they had appeared in five concerts at Tremont Temple

> but no marked impression on the community was made. They are chiefly of interest because they are genuine negros and give genuine negro songs, but their voices are certainly nothing very remarkable.

Mr. Pike saw the problem as nothing more than proper timing:

> By giving 5 concerts in one week in a place where the company has its reputation to make, a supply is brought in advance of the demand, and hence success is quite uncertain. Toward the close of the week people began to flock in, and it was apparent the tide was turning in our favor and two more concerts were arranged.(19)

The troupe made a quick trip to the nation's capital to help influence a bill pending in Congress to transfer some federal land in Nashville to Fisk University. Pike wrote that he was met

> almost everywhere with the assurance, given not in words, but in looks and acts, that Washington people could not be told anything about the singing of the negro. They had lived with colored people and it was difficult to find credit for my commendations. But never did I see people so taken by surprise.

Many government officials attended their concerts, and they were summoned to the White House by President Grant who heard their renditions with great interest.(20)

The Jubilee Singers finished their first tour on May 2, when they left New York City for Nashville. The seven-month tour had raised an astounding twenty thousand dollars for the university, a success by any standard, but raising money was not the only accomplishment of the Singers. Perhaps more importantly was the introduction to the world of a unique music. According to the Illustrated Christian Weekly, they were

likely to sing themselves into history . . . with
native simplicity they sang the quaint, grotesque,
yearning, melodies of old slave life and carried them
home to the hearts of people.(21)

The success of the Jubilee Singers had induced Patrick
Gilmore to invite them to his World Peace Jubilee
extravaganza, held in Boston in July 1872. Gilmore had
amassed a twenty-thousand-voice choir, two thousand
instruments, one hundred anvils, unnumbered bells, and
field artillery. National and international attention
focused on this unusual event, and the audience was often
as large as forty thousand. The Jubilee Singers appeared
first with another group of blacks from Boston, singing *The
Battle Hymn of the Republic*. The result was described by
an enthusiastic observer:

> The first verses were taken by the Boston singers. But
> for some unexplained reason the key was given to the
> orchestra in E-flat, cruelly high under such circum-
> stances, and the first verses were a painful failure.
> The Jubilee Singers came in with the verse beginning
> "He hath sounded forth the trumpet that shall never
> call retreat." Every word of that first line rang
> through the great Coliseum as if sounded out of a
> trumpet. The great audience was carried away on a
> whirlwind of delight. . . . When the grand old chorus
> "Glory, Glory, Hallelujah" followed, with a swelling
> volume of music from the great orchestra, the thunder
> of the bands, and the roar of the artillery, the scene
> was indescribable. . . . The coliseum rang with the
> cheers and shouts of "The Jubilees, The Jubilees
> forever!" Mr. Gilmore brought the Singers from their
> place below, and massed them upon his own platform,
> where they sang the remaining verses.(22)

The Jubilee Singers were called upon several more times
during the seventeen-day affair, receiving great acclaim
for their rendition of spirituals. These Peace Jubilee
performances enhanced the reputation of the Jubilee Singers
and brought them to the attention of a wider audience.
The success of the tour convinced Fisk University
officials to approve a second one. The university had
purchased twenty-five acres of land in Nashville and
planned to erect Jubilee Hall on the new campus. The
popularity of the Singers would almost guarantee another
financially and artistically successful tour.
The second tour began in June 1873 and continued into
the spring of 1874; indeed, it was successful, raising
another twenty thousand dollars. Moreover, while on this
tour, word came to the group from England of the growing
interest of the British in this musical phenomenon. It was
decided that the Jubilee Singers would go abroad as soon as
their commitments were fulfilled in America.(23)
The New York *Musical Gazette* perceptively reported the
sociological advantages of the Fisk Singers coming North
again: "for the manners and customs of slave life will
soon be forgotten. . . . The songs they sing are veritable

mementoes of a day that is past." The same periodical
published another analysis of the Jubilee Songs while the
singers were on their second tour. Mr. W. Matthews, who
had attended performances, was more than a little
perplexed, stating that the collection as a whole was
"altogether peculiar. The entire book does not afford a
single instance of a consistent, well sustained melody."
He noted "the entire absence of connected thought" in the
songs where there are "never 3 stanzas in succession that
necessarily depend on each other. The music is every bit
as illogical as the words." With all this, he pointed out,
"somehow or other these songs afford a rare musical
delight. . . . each one is a rapture, a revery."(24)

The *Folio* commented on their last performance in
Boston, reporting that they could not be judged by any of
the ordinary rules of criticism, thus making it difficult
to describe the secret of their power:

> Their taste runs to minors to a degree not common,
> except among singers of considerable culture, and the
> compositions exhibit peculiarities of accent found no
> where else. Many of their old plantation, or camp
> meeting hymns, read like the veriest nonsense yet are
> rendered in a style which excites a perfect storm . . .
> of genuine, sympathetic admiration.(25)

The *Independent* gave the Jubilee Singers a send-off to
England with this observation:

> Our English cousins sometimes ask for purely American
> art. No product more perfectly indigenous has ever
> been carried across the ocean. We shall be greatly
> disappointed if these weird, grotesque, but marvelously
> pathetic songs--which reveal more perfectly than any
> history or picture could do the soul of slavery--do not
> touch the British in a very soft spot.(26)

The Jubilee Singers visited and sang for many of the
British nobility, including Queen Victoria, as well as
Prime Minister Gladstone. They sang in Scotland, Wales,
Ireland, and England, in churches and concert halls. Their
performances elicited much comment from the British press
throughout their year-long stay, and prompted the publication in London of another volume of songs in 1874. Entitled *Slave Songs of the Fisk Jubilee Singers*, the work
contained sixty-six songs, only seven of which had not
previously been published.

British reaction to the Jubilee Singers was summarized
in the comments of Professor Colin Brown, who wrote the
preface to the British collection. Like most serious
critics he was deeply moved by their performances and a bit
overwhelmed: "Why should such simple music, modest and
unassuming singing, and unpretentious performances produce
so great an effect on the audience?" One reason was the
character of the songs, which he found to be "purely natural. . . . They are the spontaneous growth of genius, and
are sung with intense earnestness. Every line tells something of their people's history." Brown believed the

critics did not usually appreciate "the deep religious
feeling underlying most of their songs, which is often the
true secret of their power." As to the manner of their
singing, "It must be heard before it can be realized. The
richness and purity of tone, both in melody and harmony,
the contrast of light and shade, the varieties of gen-
tleness and grandeur in expression . . . fill us with
delight." The irony of these plain singers taking Britain
by storm was not lost on Dr. Brown: "How strange it is
that these unpretending singers should come over here to
teach us what is the true refinement of music, and make us
feel its moral and religious power."(27)

The British tour was a resounding artistic and
financial success. A sum of fifty-thousand dollars was
raised for the university. When the Singers arrived home
in May 1874, they learned that thirty thousand copies of
*The Jubilee Singers and Their Campaign For Twenty Thousand
Dollars*, the story of their first tour written by Gustavus
Pike, had been sold.(28)

Other institutions were quick to imitate the Fisk
University Singers. Hampton Institute had a touring group
of singers as early as 1873 and for several years there-
after, but it was George White's vision, plus the talent
and determination of his original group of singers, that
opened the door to an enduring musical legacy. The music
transcended language barriers and national boundaries.
When the noted English composer Frederick Delius, as a
young man, took possession of an orange grove his father
bought him in Florida's interior in 1884, he became en-
thralled with the folk songs and spirituals sung by his
black neighbors. His biographer points out that although
his work "was grounded in European musical art forms they
are saturated with a quality of sound not heard before in
the orchestra. . . . A quality derived from and redolent of
negro hymnology and folk song."(29)

Sometimes Americans had to be reminded of this
legacy, as the Czech composer Anton Dvořák did in 1893 when
he said:

In the negro melodies in America I discover all that is
needed for a great and noble school of music. . . .
There is nothing in the whole range of composition that
cannot be supplied with themes from this source. This
must be the real foundation of any serious and original
school of composition to be developed in America.(30)

This negro folk music did become part of the repertory
of church choirs, concert artists, and symphony orchestras
in America, and many composers derived inspiration from
this tradition for their own compositions. To echo
Professor Colin Brown, it is ironic that a lowly and
despised class of "unpretending singers," coming out of
slavery, "should teach us what is the true refinement of
music, and make us feel its moral and religious power."

NOTES

1. *American Missionary Association Magazine*, January 1871. Hereafter cited as *AMA Magazine*.

2. Gustavus D. Pike, *The Jubilee Singers and Their Campaign for Twenty Thousand Dollars* (Boston: Lee and Shepard, 1873). This is the best source on the first tour. Contains very good information on the founding and early years of the school. Has photographs of George White and the following singers: Greene Evans, Isaac Dickerson, Maggie Porter, Minnie Tate, Jennie Jackson, Benjamin Holmes, Thomas Rutling, Eliza Walker, and Ella Shepard. It contains words and music to sixty-one Jubilee songs with a preface to the music by Theodore F. Seward, the composer, music critic, and one-time editor of the New York *Musical Gazette*. Pike, an American Missionary Association official, accompanied the singers on part of their first tour. He wrote the book from his own observations and from those who participated in the campaign. Eileen Southern, *The Music of Black Americans: A History* (New York: Norton, 1971). This is the best source on the role of the singers in the development of the black tradition.

3. Pike, 12.

4. Pike, 14.

5. Pike, 42.

6. Pike, 75. Pike is the best source for the itinerary. Also useful is the New York *Clipper* and George Odell, *Annals of the New York Stage* (New York: Columbia University Press, 1927-49).

7. *Cincinnati Gazette*, October 18, 1871.

8. Springfield *Daily Republican*, October 21, 1871. *AMA Magazine*, December 1871.

9. Pike, 97.

10. Pike, 99.

11. Pike, 102.

12. Pike, 108-109.

13. New York *World*, January 6, 1872; New York *Herald*, January 6, 1872; New York *Clipper*, January 6, 1872.

14. New York *Tribune*, January 17, 1872.

15. Pike, 119.

16. As reported in the New York *Musical Gazette*, April 1872

17. The booklet was incorporated into Pike's *The Jubilee Singers*.

18. William Francis Allen, et al., *Slave Songs of the United States* (New York: A. Simpson, 1867). Thomas Wentworth Higginson, "Negro Spirituals," *Atlantic Monthly* (June 1867): 685-94.

19. New York *Clipper*, March 23, 1872; Pike, 144.

20. Pike, 124.

21. New York *Clipper*, May 4, 1872.

22. J. B. T. Marsh, *The Story of the Jubilee Singers* (Cleveland: Cleveland Publishing Co., 1892), 40-41. This volume contains abridgements of the two Pike histories and accounts of subsequent tours. It contains 138 songs with the same Seward notes contained in the first Pike volume.

23. Gustavus D. Pike, *The Singing Campaign for Ten Thousand Pounds; The Jubilee Singers in Great Britain*

(American Missionary Association, 1875). Seventy-one songs
are included in this volume with the same Seward notes.
    24. New York *Musical Gazette*, October 1873.
    25. *Folio*, May 1873.
    26. *AMA Magazine*, May 1873.
    27. *Slave Songs of the Fisk Jubilee Singers* (London:
W. H. Guest, 1874).
    28. Pike, *The Singing Campaign for Ten Thousand Pounds*.
By 1893 Pike's books had sold 180,000 copies.
    29. Eric Fenby, *Delius* (New York: Thomas Y. Crowell,
1971).
    30. New York *Herald*, May 21, 1893.

REFERENCES

Johnson, James Weldon, and J. Rosamond Johnson. *American
    Negro Spirituals*. New York: Viking Press, 1953.
Krehbiel, Henry Edward. *Afro-American Folk Songs*. New
    York: Frederick Unger, 1962.
Locke, Alain. *The Negro and His Music*. Port Washington,
    N.Y.: Kennikat Press, 1968.
Lovell, John, Jr. *Black Song: The Forge and the Flame*.
    New York: Macmillan, 1972.
Marsh, J. B. *The Story of the Jubilee Singers*. Cleveland:
    Cleveland Publishing Co., 1892.
Odell, George. *Annals of the New York Stage*. 15 vols.
    New York: Columbia University Press, 1927-1949.
Pike, Gustavus D. *The Jubilee Singers and Their Campaign
    for Twenty-Thousand Dollars*. Boston: Lee and Shepard,
    1873.
___. *The Singing Campaign for Ten Thousand Pounds, or The
    Jubilee Singers in Great Britain*. New York: American
    Missionary Association, 1875.
Slave Songs of the Fisk Jubilee Singers. London: W. H.
    Guest, 1874.
Trotter, James M. *Music and Some Highly Musical People*.
    New York: Lee and Shepard, 1881.
Work, John Wesley. *Folk Songs of the American Negro*.
    Nashville: Fisk University, 1915.

Newspapers and Journals

American Missionary Association Magazine
Cincinnati *Gazette*
Folio
New York *Clipper*
New York *Herald*
New York *Musical Gazette*
New York *Tribune*
New York *World*
Springfield (Ohio) *Daily Republican*

Black Male Concert Singers
of the Nineteenth Century:
A Bibliographic Study

RONALD HENRY HIGH

During the nineteenth century, changes took place in the history of Western singing. Both the virtuosity of early Romantic opera and the intimacy of the solo song demanded voices that could meet the demands of the repertory. Although there were limited opportunities for black singers in opera performances and lieder recitals, some artists were featured in sacred music concerts sponsored by black churches; numerous singers became professional church soloists and choir members. Other professional musicians found employment in minstrel shows, traveling concert troupes, musico-dramatic productions, and eventually Afro-American opera companies.

A nineteenth-century institution that not only trained singers but also provided opportunities for concert singing was the conservatory. Several black artists were admitted to the Boston, Oberlin, and National Conservatories, and other black musicians studied privately with artists/teachers at schools such as the New England Conservatory. When these teachers presented their students in public recitals, they sang repertory similar to that being performed by established artists in the United States and abroad.

Thomas J. Bowers, the first significant black male concert singer, was the most important protégé of Elizabeth Taylor Greenfield (ca1824-1876). Greenfield, the first black concert singer in America, toured extensively in the United States and England before establishing a music studio and opera troupe in Philadelphia.

Bowers, born in Philadelphia about 1823, showed musical ability at an early age.(1) His father, a warden of St. Thomas Episcopal Church of Philadelphia, obtained a piano for his eldest son, John C., so he could instruct Thomas and the other children of the family in the home. Thomas learned to play the piano and organ so well that by the time he was eighteen, he succeeded his brother as organist at St. Thomas Church; his younger sister, Sarah Sedgewick, became a concert soprano.

After refusing an opportunity to join the Frank Johnson Band, Bowers began his professional career at Samson Street

Hall in Philadelphia with Elizabeth Greenfield in 1854.
The concert was so successful that a critic for the
Philadelphia Press not only requested a repeat performance, but also named Bowers "The Colored Mario," comparing
him favorably with the great Italian tenor, Giovanni Mario
(1810-1883).(2) In addition, Colonel J. H. Wood, Greenfield's manager, engaged him for a concert tour of New York
state and Canada. When Wood insisted that he appear under
the title, "Indian Mario," or "African Mario," Bowers
refused, preferring to use the simpler professional cogno-
men of "Mareo [sic]."(3)
     During his long career, Thomas Bowers ultimately sang
in most of the Eastern and Midwestern states to critical
acclaim. On February 2, 1854, the *Daily Pennsylvania*
reported: "He has naturally a superior voice, far better
than many of the principal tenors who have been engaged for
star opera troupes. He has, besides, much musical
taste."(4)
     Described by Trotter as "an ideal tenor, and a real
artist," Bowers apparently possessed a voice of great power
and beauty, with a range of almost two octaves. Some
critics regarded him as being "unequalled by any of the
great operatic performers."(5) Reviewers continued to
herald his accomplishments until late in his career. On
June 2, 1883, he received a glowing review for his performance in a Philadelphia Musicale:

     The solo, "Ah! I have sighed, to rest me," by Mr. T. J.
     Bowers, Philadelphia's finest tenor, was received with
     rapturous applause, and he was compelled to repeat,
     which he did by singing a duett, "Life's Dream Is
     O'er," with Miss Ida E. Gilbert.(6)

     Bowers' repertory consisted of classical songs and
ballads, as well as many of the tenor arias from standard
operas and oratorios, including "Spirto Gentil" from *La
Favorita*, "Ah! I have Sighed" from *Il Trovatore*, and "How
So Fair" from *Martha*.(7)
     Bowers' obituary, which appeared in the *New York
Freeman* following his death on October 3, 1885, summarized
his career:

     Mr. Bowers was the last of the name in the male line
     that has figured so conspicuously in public affairs, in
     business and in the social relations of Philadelphia
     for nearly a century. Mr. Bowers himself was promi-
     nently identified with musicale matters and at one time
     the very best singer among colored people.(8)

In addition to being a successful singer, Bowers was also a
prominent coal merchant. He was worth approximately
$25,000 at the time of his death.
     Another black tenor, Wallace King, had a voice of
operatic magnitude, but he performed primarily in singing
troupes and in minstrelsy. King, born around 1840 in
Newark, New Jersey, was discovered and initially trained by
Professor J. H. O'Fake, a noted voice and piano instructor,
who taught in the homes of some of the wealthiest families

in New Jersey.(9) King served as janitor of the Merchant's
National Bank and of the Central Methodist Church in
Newark. William Tomlins, the church organist, gave King
lessons after he was denied admission to one of the local
conservatories. King later reapplied for entrance to the
conservatory and was again denied.(10)

An important impetus for Wallace King's career was his
affiliation with the famous Hyers Sisters, organizers of a
concert company and later an opera bouffe troupe. The
group was well-known for its performance of the musical
drama, *Out of Bondage*, in which King featured as a singer
and actor. He played the role of Prince, the happy slave,
and received critical acclaim throughout the 1876-77
season. Reviews from various newspapers were reprinted in
the Redpath *Lyceum Magazine*:

> Wallace King, the tenor, and J. W. Luca, the basso,
> displayed voices of unusual excellence. . . . The tenor
> especially being of the finest which it has been our
> pleasure to hear in a long time.(11)

> Mr. King's tenor is the sweetest it has been our
> fortune to listen to.(12)

> Mr. King, as a tenor, probably has no superior in the
> country.(13)

Wallace King had a very active, successful career in
the 1880s in both Europe and the United States. On January
24, 1882, he appeared with Haverly's Minstrels in Glasgow,
Scotland.(14) In 1883 he performed with the Callendar
Spectacular Minstrels and received commendation: "The
singing of Messrs. Wallace King and Lewis Brown were
prominent features, and merited bountiful applause given
them."(15) On May 26, 1883, the *New York Globe* announced
that a "Colored Opera Troupe" would open in the city and
that the Hyers Sisters and Wallace King would be among the
performers.

Wallace King was especially noted for his singing of
When My Rover Comes Again, *A Boy's Best Friend Is His
Mother*, *The Excelsior*, and *Cricket on the Hearth*. In May
1884 King went to London with the Callender Troupe and his
repertoire delighted audiences there:

> Then came the old favorite tenor, Wallace King in *A
> Boy's Best Friend is His Mother*, which so pleased the
> audience that Mr. King was compelled to sing another
> verse after his encore, and it has been the same
> nightly ever since.(16)

On January 15, 1885,King appeared in Providence, Rhode
Island, at the first Grand Concert of the Acme Glee Club.
The audience applauded as he sang *Sweet Dreaming Faces* and
My Sweetheart When a Boy.(17) During the 1885-86 season,
King performed with the Kersands Minstrels at the Miner's
Eighth Avenue Theatre in New York. Other performers
included Billy Speed, Billy Wilson, Charles Johnson, Billy
Kersands, and Frank Mallory.(18)

The *Cleveland Gazette* of May 1, 1886, announced his appearance at D. C. Hart's Academy of Music:

> Mr. Wallace King . . . has appeared before all the crowned heads of Europe, and possibly before more people than any other singer ever visiting this country. . . . The silver-voiced tenor, Mr. Wallace King, appears at every performance, and every one should hear the sweet melody of this world-famed singer's voice.

King also appeared in 1886 in Dayton, Ohio, with the Hyers Sisters' Dramatic Company, and in Sioux City, Iowa, with Donavin's Colored Dramatic Company.

In 1888 King joined the Hicks-Sawyer Minstrels and traveled with them to Australia and the Far East. He died from Bright's Disease on February 20, 1903 in Oakland, California.

Perhaps the most famous black male singer, song writer, and actor of the nineteenth century was Samuel Milady, better known as Sam Lucas (1840-1916).(19) During his illustrious career, he performed with such companies as Hamilton's Celebrated Quadrille Band, Lew Johnson's Plantation Minstrels, Callender's Original Georgia Minstrels, the Hyers Sisters' Comic Opera Company, Sprague's Georgia Minstrels, Haverly's United Genuine Colored Minstrels, and his Hub Concert Company of Boston.

Among Lucas' most notable accomplishments were: in 1878 he became the first black to play the role of Uncle Tom in *Uncle Tom's Cabin*; in 1898-99, he played in the first Negro musical, *A Trip to Coontown*; and he participated in the transition from minstrelsy to Negro musical comedies by starring in Sam T. Jack's *Creole Show* in 1890.(20)

Lucas' career ended in 1912, and he died in 1916. At the time of his death, he was called "Dean of the Colored Theatrical Profession"(21) and the "Grand Old Man of the Negro Stage."(22)

Another area of musical performance during the nineteenth century that helped to establish the careers of black male singers was that of the "singing families." These troupes traveled widely and sang songs that became popular with the American people. The singing families were at the height of their popularity from the early 1840s to the 1860s, offering instrumental and vocal music.(23)

The best known of the early white troupes, the Hutchinson Family, may have provided inspiration for the Luca Family. The Luca Family included Alexander C. Luca, Sr., the father; Lisette, the mother; John W., Simeon, Alexander C., and Cleveland, the sons; and an aunt, Diane.(24)

The *Rochester North Star* called attention to this family in the early days of their career:

> This interesting band of musical children are [sic] entertaining the public with exhibitions of their powers, vocal and instrumental, they were warmly

greeted at several anniversary meetings in New York City.(25)

The Luca Family's performance for the Anti-Slavery Society in New York in May 1850 was well received by an audience of more than five thousand people. During 1852 the Family toured for three months in Connecticut, Massachusetts, New York, and Pennsylvania to critical acclaim; Cleveland, the pianist, garnered much attention for his exceptional virtuosity. Unfortunately, Simeon, a tenor and violinist, died in 1854. Miss Jennie Allen, a contralto from New York, was hired as his replacement.(26)

The Luca Family traveled more extensively in 1857, obtaining more artistic and financial success. Trotter cited a review from the *Niagara Courier*, Lockport, New York, published on September 2, 1857:

> their performance was such as to elicit the enthusiastic approval of all present. . . . The two brothers John and Alexander have superb voices, guided by a correct knowledge of music, and enriched by cultivation. Madame Luca . . . sang well, and gave abundant assurance of superior vocal powers. But the great feature of the entertainment was the performance of C. O. Luca on the piano. . . . Such superior musical powers must win for them a reputation that will bring its recompense.(27)

The Lucas met the Hutchinson Family in Ohio in 1859 and toured with them for more than a month. Different newspapers printed favorable reviews of the troupes:

> The concert given in this place on Saturday night last by the Hutchinsons and Lucas was among the best musical entertainments ever given here. The audience was large, and the artists sang with spirit.

> Where all sang so well, it is difficult to select the best. . . . The Lucas are charming musicians, both in-instrumental and vocal; and, when two such companies unite, there will be superior concerts.(28)

> The performance could not, coming from troupes possessing talent varied and of the higher order, be otherwise than good. These bands, when they united, made a palpable hit. The combined concerts are almost invariably successes.(29)

In 1860 the combined troupes disbanded when President Roberts of Liberia induced Cleveland Luca to go there to teach music.(30) Alexander, tenor and second violinist, continued his career in minstrel troupes and taught voice for Sprague's Georgia Minstrels. He died on September 29, 1883.

John W. Luca, baritone and cellist, continued to have an active performance career. He moved to Washington, D.C., in 1861, where he sang in the Presbyterian church and for numerous events until the war ended. He then went to

Baltimore where he sang in the St. Francis Xavier "Roman"
and Bethel churches before returning to New York in 1870.
There, he performed concerts until he joined the Hyers
Sisters in 1871 as musical director and stage manager. His
1876-77 performances with the Hyers Sisters in the musical
drama, *Out of Bondage*, received favorable mention from the
press:

> "Uncle Eph," Mr. J. W. Luca, was the best "Uncle Tom"
> we ever saw.(31)

> The Uncle Eph of Mr. J. W. Luca is a fine bit of old
> Negro business.(32)

> Mr. Luca has a barytone [sic] voice equalled by few
> barytones in the country.(33)

John remained with the Hyers Sisters until about 1884,
when he moved to St. Paul, Minnesota. He established a
music studio, conducted church choirs, and continued to
sing concerts and produce stage works until his death in
1910.(34)

In contrast to Bowers, King, Lucas, and the Luca
Family, the conservatory-trained Sidney Woodward sang pri-
marily in concerts and on the opera stage. He was born on
October 16, 1860, in Stockbridge, Georgia, and showed
musical talent at an early age. Aided early in his career
by Norris Wright Cuney, Collector of Customs in Galveston,
Texas, and Madame Nellie Brown Mitchell, Woodward went to
Boston in 1890 where he studied voice with Madame Edna Hall
and B. J. Lang, distinguished faculty members of the New
England Conservatory.(35)

In 1891 Woodward sang at the anniversary of the Young
People's Society of Christian Endeavor of the Phillips
Congregational Church, South Boston.(36) In that same
year, Woodward appeared with Flora Batson and other artists
at the A.M.E. Church on North Russell Street in Boston.(37)

Sidney Woodward became tenor soloist and a member of
the quartet at Second Congregational Church, Boston,(38)
before singing his debut recital at Chickering Hall,
Boston, on February 15, 1893. The concert was reviewed by
the noted critic, Philip Hale:

> Mr. Woodward has a tenor voice . . . [that] lends
> itself easily to the demands of expression. . . . He
> sings as a rule with ease; his tones are firm and
> sustained; his attack is decisive, and he does not
> often abuse the portamento; he knows the meaning of the
> word legato; he phrases intelligently; he holds himself
> in control; and his enunciation is admirable. He made
> a favorable impression at the very beginning by the
> modesty and intelligence displayed in his version of
> Beethoven's *Adelaide*, and the impression was strength-
> ened by his pleasing singing of songs by Bradsky,
> Adams, Helmund, Newcomb and De Koven.(39)

On August 25, 1893, Woodward performed at the World's
Fair in Chicago on "Colored American Day." A reporter for

the *Cleveland   Gazette*, October 21, 1893, described
Woodward's performance:

> Sidney Woodward . . . who began his musical career in
> Memphis . . . is to-day the talk of all New England.
> He holds the enviable position of tenor soloist in the
> leading Congregational church in Boston, and weekly
> wins the encomiums of one of the most critical
> audiences in America. . . . Mr. Woodward, in the first
> place is a musician, both in point of judgment and
> power of execution. He possesses one of those rich,
> pure, ringing tenor voices that is susceptible of the
> most delicate shadings. . . . One recalls with pleasure
> the thundering applause that followed his rendering of
> Verdi's recitation and aria, "I Due Foscari." This was
> on August 25, in the world's fair grounds, and the
> people assembled there, in Festival Hall, demanded from
> Mr. Woodward three encores, which he gave with ever
> increasing favor. This wonderful singer must succeed,
> and we are glad to know that . . . he purposes to
> perfect his musical education by study in Italy.

Woodward joined John Isham's new production of *Oriental
America* in 1896. A review from the Washington, D.C.,
Morning Times which appeared in the *Indianapolis Freeman*,
November 7, 1886, described Woodward's performance: "The
famous colored tenor, Sidney Woodward, fully justified all
that has been written about him. He has a good presence
and is in every way in voice and manner an ideal tenor.
His rendition of the aria from *Rigoletto* was enthusias-
tically received."
Woodward continued his study at the Royal Conservatory
in Dresden, Germany, where he was awarded a certificate of
proficiency. Later, he made a continental tour, singing
with great success in the principal cities of Germany,
Russia, Holland, Belgium, and the United Kingdom.(40)
While in England, Woodward sang before Queen Victoria at
Buckingham Palace.
Following Woodward's return to the United States, he
taught at Florida Baptist Academy in Jacksonville, Clark
College in Atlanta, Georgia, Atlanta University, and the
Music Settlement School for Colored in New York (1916-
1921). He died on February 13, 1924, in New York.
Other significant black singers of the nineteenth
century included in the bibliographic study are: William
Edward Lew (1865-1949); George Lewis Ruffin; Henry "Harry"
Williams (cal850-cal940); Sampson Williams; Theodore Drury
(cal860-cal940); and Henry "Harry" Thacker Burleigh (1866-
1949).
In conclusion, nineteenth-century black male concert
singers were involved in minstrelsy, oratorio, opera,
teaching, church work, management, and stage direction.
Many of them studied and performed abroad as well as in the
United States; most possessed solid techniques and great
flexibility. Because of these vocal attributes, some of
the singers were favorably compared to the leading artists
of the day. By the end of the century, black male concert

singers had successfully blazed new pathways in all areas
of musical performance.

APPENDIX A

Annotated Chronology of Newspaper Articles (ACNA)

of Black Male Concert Singers

Thomas J. Bowers

Daily Pennsylvania	Feb. 9, 1854		Review of Samson Hall concert (Trotter)
New York Globe	Jan. 20,1883,	3	Relative's funeral
	Jan. 27,1883,	3	Tribute to J. W. Bowers
	June 9,1883,	4	Philadelphia Musicale
	Nov. 17,1883,	1	Bowers as coal merchant
	Dec. 22,1883,	3	Death of Mrs. E. J. Bowers
	May 17,1884,	4	Attends testimonial to H. Vinton Davis
New York Freeman	Oct. 17,1885,	1	Bowers' obituary
Cleveland Gazette	Oct. 24,1885,	2	Announcement of Bowers' wealth and death

H. T. Burleigh

Burleigh was mentioned in many newspapers. His vocal
repertory is discussed in:

New York Age   Sept. 14,1916, 6 Lucien White

Theodore Drury

New York Age	May 18,1889,	2	Rising young baritone
	June 1,1889,	2	St. Mark's Lyceum performance
	June 27,1889		Favorable comments of Drury Co.
	Oct. 5,1889,	3	Advertisement of Opera Company
	Mar. 8,1890,	3	"Infelice" aria
	Jan. 4,1900,	5	Photo and favorable comments
Indianapolis Freeman	April 14,1900,	5	Accomplished baritone, Opera Company
	May 24,1902,	5	Review of *Faust*, New York

Wallace King

Redpath *Lyceum Magazine*	1877-1878, 71-74	*Out of Bondage*
New York Globe	May 19,1883, 3	Appearance with Callender Minstrels
	May 26,1883, 3	Appearance with Colored Opera Troupe
	June 2,1883, 3	Correction
	June 16,1883, 3	Review of performance with Callender
	Feb. 23,1884, 3	Review of Callender, 14th Street Theatre
	June 28,1884, 1	Report of May 19 London appearance
New York Age	Jan. 10,1885, 1	Performs for Acme Glee Club, Providence, R.I.
	Jan. 24,1885, 4	Review of above appearance
New York Freeman	Apr. 11,1885, 1	Benefit concert, Charles St.Church, April 16
Cleveland Gazette	May 1,1886, 2	Portrait; performance D. C. Hart's Academy
	June 5,1886, 1	Announcement of appearance with Donavin's Co.
	Sept. 4,1886, 3	Appears with Hyers Sisters, Dayton, Ohio
	Nov. 20,1886, 4	Performs with Donavin, Sioux City, Iowa
	Dec. 4,1886, 1	Accident reported enroute to Des Moines, Iowa
Boston Advocate	Jan. 1,1887, 1	Discussion of career with Wisconsin reporter
Cleveland Gazette	Mar. 5,1887, 1	Brief biographical statement
Indianapolis Freeman	Mar. 14,1903, 5	Obituary

The Luca Family

Rochester North Star	June 2,1848, 2	Early appearances in New York
Voice of the Fugitive	Aug. 27,1851, 2	N. Y. Central College, McGrawville Sandwich, Ont. (Abajian)
Rochester Frederick Douglass' Paper	Jan. 27,1854, 2	Family refused accommodations
Niagara Courier	Sept. 2,1857, n.p.	Ringueberg Hall review (Trotter)

Ohio newspapers:
Wooster	Feb. 18,1859	Arcadame Hall Performance (Trotter)
Fremont	Feb. 25,1859	Lucas/Hutchinsons (Trotter)
Cleveland	Feb. 28,1859	Lucas/Hutchinsons (Trotter)
Norwalk	Mar. 1,1859	Review of Lucas/ Hutchinsons (Trotter)
Sandusky	Mar. 1,1859	West Hall Concert with Hutchinsons (Trotter)
New York Globe	Sept. 29,1883, 3	Alexander Luca, Jr.'s death
Cleveland Gazette	Jan. 26,1884, 2	Zainesville, A. Lucas, Sr.'s illness
	Oct. 4,1884, 1	A. Luca's illness; mentions other children
	Mar. 7,1885, 1	Obituary of A. Luca, Sr.
New York Age	Mar. 14,1885, 2	Announcement of A. Luca's death
St. Paul *Western Appeal*	1888	St. Paul musician, local news (Abajian)
	June 8,1889	John W.'s activities
Indianapolis Freeman	Nov. 27,1909, 6	Letter by John W., family history
	Dec. 3,1910, 6	John W. Luca tribute

Sam Lucas

Redpath *Lyceum Magazine*	1877-1878, 71-74	*Out of Bondage*
New York Age	Jan. 30,1916, 1	Obituary

George L. Ruffin

New York Age	Mar. 8,1890, 4	Member, "Society for Collection of Negro Folklore"
Indianapolis Freeman	May 24,1902, 5	Review of role of Valentine (*Faust*)

Harry Williams

Cleveland Gazette	May 29,1886, 4	Testimonial concert

Sampson Williams

New York Freeman	Mar. 3,1883, 3	Abroad with Selika
	Jan. 2,1886, 3	Review of recital with Selika, Dec. 24
	Jan. 23,1886, 1	Hartford debut, repertory mentioned
	Mar. 27,1886, 1	New Bedford concert, March 23, repertory
	Mar. 27,1886, 4	Ad for "Prima Baritone"
	Apr. 3,1886, 4	Boston concert, Parliamentary Fund
	May 1,1886, 1	Easter in Baltimore, repertory
	Sept. 18,1886, 3	Concert with Selika, Steinway Hall, Nov. 4
Cleveland Gazette	Mar. 5,1887, 3	Concert with Selika, Columbus, Ohio; Repertory
	Apr. 28,1888, 1	Recital with Selika, Louisville, KY; Repertory
Indianapolis Freeman	Mar. 2,1889, 5	Selika, Williams, Hallie Q. Brown, Savannah, GA
Cleveland Gazette	July 1,1893, 3	Selika and Williams open voice studio

Sidney Woodward

Indianapolis Freeman	May 24,1890, 6	Rising young Boston tenor
Boston Globe	Feb. 1,1891, 16	Concert, Young People's Society, Boston
	Feb. 15,1891, 10	AME Zion, Concert with F. Batson, Boston
Boston Journal	Feb. 13,1893, 5	Announcement of Chickering Hall Recital, Boston
	Feb. 15,1893, 5	Advertisement of Chickering Hall performance
	Feb. 16,1893	Chickering Hall review by Philip Hale (Scrapbook - BPL)
Indianapolis Freeman	Aug. 19,1893, 1	Mentions performance at Bethel Church, Chicago
Chicago Tribune	Aug. 25,1893, 3	Announcement of World's Fair artists
Cleveland Gazette	Oct. 21,1893, 1	Sings at Chicago World's Fair
Indianapolis Freeman	Aug. 15,1896, 5	Isham's *Oriental America*
	Nov. 7,1896, 6	Performs *Rigoletto* aria

New York Age	Sept. 28,1916, 6	Music Settlement School; Nordica comments; career
	Oct. 5,1916, 6	Faculty of Music School Settlement
	Dec. 3,1921, 5	Festival for thirty-first year as singer
	Dec. 10,1921, 5	Festival for thirty-first year as singer
	Dec. 17,1921, 5	Lucien White mentions Carnegie Hall performance
	Dec. 24,1921, 5	Review of Carnegie Hall performance
	Feb. 23,1924, 7	Obituary

APPENDIX B

Repertory of Black Male Concert Singers

Thomas J. Bowers (tenor)

Classical songs, ballads, operatic and oratorio arias

"Spirto Gentil," *La Favorita*, Donizetti
"Ah! I Have Sighed," *Il Trovatore*, Verdi
"How So Fair," *Martha*, Flotow
"The Light of Other Days," Balfe
"Life's Dream Is O'er" (duet)

Sources: Trotter
              New York Globe, June 9, 1883, 4

H. T. Burleigh (baritone)

"The Palms," Fauré
"The Young Warrior"
"The Soldier"
"The Kashmere Song"
"Worth While"
"Her Eyes Twin Pools"
"The Glory of the Day"
Negro Spirituals

Sources: *New York Age*   September 14,1916, 6
                                            Lucien White
          Music of Black Americans, Southern

Theodore Drury (baritone/tenor)

Arias from *Faust* for Tenor
"Infelice," *Ernani*, Verdi

Sources: *New York Age*   June 1,1889, 2
                                      Mar. 8,1890, 3
                                      Jan. 4,1900, 5
           Indianapolis Freeman   May 24,1902, 5

Wallace King (tenor)

"When My Rover Comes Again"
"A Boy's Best Friend is His Mother"
"My Sweetheart When a Boy"
"Sweet Dreaming Faces"
"Come into the Garden, Maud"
"The Excelsior" (duet)
"Sleep Well"
"Greetings to Spring" (quintet)
"Shadows Deepen on the Castle Wall"
"Cricket on the Hearth"
"Rock Me to Sleep, Mother"
"Some Day"

Sources: Redpath *Lyceum Magazine* 1877-1878
           Old Slack's Reminiscence
           New York Globe   June 16,1883, 3
                                      June 28,1884, 1
           New York Freeman   Jan. 24,1885, 4
           Indianapolis Freeman   Mar. 14,1903, 5

The Luca Family

"Fantasia," *Lucia*, Donizetti   John Luca, baritone
Duet, Millard   with Anna Hyers
"The Excelsior" (duet)
"The Old Toper"

Sources: Trotter
           Redpath *Lyceum Magazine* 1877-1878

Sam Lucas (tenor)

Arias from *Il Trovatore*, Verdi
Arias from *Ernani*, Verdi
Lucas' Plantation Songster
       "Old Uncle Jasper"
       "Emancipation Day"
       "Grandfather's Clock"
       "I'll Love My Love in de Mornin'"
       "Carve dat Possum"

"The Dear Old Home We Love so Well"
"Daffney, Do You Love Me?"
"Shivering and Shaking out in the Cold"
"I'se Gwine Back to Dixie"
"I'se Gwine in de Valley"
"The Old Log Cabin in the Dell"
"The Old Home Ain't What it Used to Be"
"On Board of the Mary Jane"
"Shew Fly"
"The Old Man Ain't What He Used to Be"
"Weeping for Lost Ones"
"Oh, no, I'll Never Marry"
"The Letter in the Candle"
"Little Footsteps"
"Since I Saw de Cotton Grow"
"My Dear Savannah Home"
"Since Terry First Joined the Gang"
"Sadie Ray"
"Dar's a Meetin' Here To-Night"
"My Dear Old Southern Home"
"Old Jemima"
"I Hope I May Jine de Band"
"Oh, Git Away"
"Bring a Char for Uncle Moses"
"Who Struck My Mother's Only Son?"
"Hildebrandt Montrose"
"Sunrise in the Morning"
"Rollicking Dollie Day"
"Homeless To-Night"
"Silver Bells of Memory"
"Hannah, Boil Dat Cabbage Down"
"You Never Miss the Water till the Well Runs Dry"
"Behind the Scenes"
"Maggie, Darling, now Good-Bye"
"Oh, The Peanuts"

Sources: *Lucas' Plantation Songster*
           Old Slack's Reminiscence
           Redpath *Lyceum Magazine*, 1877-1878

George L. Ruffin (baritone)

Arias from oratorios
Arias from *Carmen*, Bizet
"Avant de quitter," *Faust*, Gounod

Source: *Indianapolis Freeman*, May 24, 1902, 5

Harry A. Williams (tenor)

Trio, *Messe Solennelle*, Rossini
"Salve dimora," *Faust*, Gounod
"Romance, I Love," Mattel
Quartet, *Rigoletto*, Verdi

Source: *Cleveland Gazette*   May 29,1886, 4

Sampson Williams (baritone)

"Let Me Love Thee," Arditi
Duet, *Il Trovatore*, Verdi
"Wandering Minstrel," Mazzoni
"Name the Day"
"Lady, thus Hear Me" (duet)
"Jerusalem"
"Only Thee" (duet)
"The Scout," Campani
Romanza, "Non a Ver," Mattel

Sources: *New York Freeman*   Jan. 2,1886, 3
                                        Jan. 23,1886, 1
                                        Mar. 27,1886, 1
                                        May 1,1886, 1
           Cleveland Gazette   Mar. 5,1887, 3
                                        Apr. 28,1888, 1

Sidney Woodward (tenor)

"The Pilgrim," Adams
"Ave Maria," Millard
"Adelaide," Beethoven
"Romanza," *La Favorita*, Donizetti
"I Due Foscari," Verdi
"La donna mobile," Verdi
Songs by Bradsky, Adams, Helmund, Newcomb, DeKoven
Arias from the opera, *Uncle Tom's Cabin*, Will Marion Cook

Sources: *Boston Globe*   Feb. 1,1891, 16
           Boston Journal   Feb. 16,1893 (P. Hale)
           Chicago Tribune   Aug. 25,1893, 3
           Cleveland Gazette   Oct. 21,1893, 1
           Indianapolis Freeman   Nov. 7,1896, 6
           New York Age   Dec. 24,1921, 5

NOTES

    1. Sources cite conflicting dates for the birth of
Bowers. In the biography of Bowers included by James
Monroe Trotter in his work *Music and Some Highly Musical
People* (Boston: Lee and Shepard, 1881), 131, Bowers' date
of birth is given as 1836. Eileen Southern gives ca1826 in
The Music of Black Americans: A History, 2d ed. (New York:
Norton, 1983), 104; and 1823 in *Biographical Dictionary of
Afro-American and African Musicians* (Westport, Conn.:
Greenwood Press, 1982). At this time there is no con-
clusive evidence for the exact date of birth.
    2. Trotter, 133.

3. Trotter, 134.

4. Trotter, 136.

5. Ibid.

6. *New York Globe*, June 2, 1883.

7. Trotter, 135.

8. *New York Freeman*, October 17, 1885, 1.

9. *Indianapolis Freeman*, March 14, 1903, 5.

10. A reprint of an interview with Wallace King in the *Evening Wisconsin* on December 21, 1886, appeared in the *Boston Advocate*, January 1, 1887, 1.

11. The Redpath *Lyceum Magazine* printed a review of King's performance, which appeared in the *Elmira (N.Y.) Gazette*, October 24, 1876.

12. *Collinsville (Pa.) Head-Light*, October 14, 1876. An excerpt from this newspaper describing King's performance appeared in the Redpath *Lyceum Magazine*.

13. *Titusville (Pa.) Courier.* Excerpt appeared in Redpath *Lyceum Magazine*.

14. Eileen Southern, *The Music of Black Americans: A History*, 2d ed. (New York: Norton, 1983), 230.

15. *New York Globe*, May 19, 1883, 3.

16. *New York Globe*, June 28, 1884, 1.

17. *New York Freeman*, January 24. 1885, 4.

18. George Odell, *Annals of the New York Stage*, 15 vols. (New York: Columbia University Press, 1927-49), 8:115.

19. Conflicting dates of birth for Lucas are given in the sources. Southern in *The Music of Black Americans*, 327, gives the date as 1840. According to the Compiled Military Records, (National Archives, Washington, D. C.) Lucas was born August 7, 1842. This record, however, may have been filed when Lucas was an old man, and the date may not be accurate. I am indebted to Sherrill Martin for the information concerning Lucas' military record.

20. Ike Simond, *Old Slack's Reminiscence and Pocket History of the Colored Profession from 1865-1891* (1891. Reprint. Bowling Green, Oh.: Bowling Green University Popular Press, 1974), 20.

21. *New York Age*, January 13, 1916, 1.

22. James Weldon Johnson, *Black Manhattan* (New York: Alfred A. Knopf, 1940), 90.

23. John Tasker Howard, *Our American Music* (New York: Thomas Y. Crowell Co., 1965), 173.

24. *Indianapolis Freeman*, November 27, 1909.

25. *Rochester North Star*, June 2, 1848, 2.

26. Trotter, 91.

27. Trotter, 99-101.

28. Trotter, 103.

29. Ibid.

30. *Indianapolis Freeman*, November 27, 1909, 6. A letter from John W. Luca.

31. *Logansport (Ind.) Daily Journal*, June 6, 1877. Reprinted in the Redpath *Lyceum Magazine*.

32. *Providence (R.I.) Star*, March 7, 1877.

33. *Saco (Me.) Daily Times*, October 18, 1876. Reprinted in the Redpath *Lyceum Magazine*.

34. Eileen Southern, *Biographical Dictionary of Afro-American and African Musicians* (Westport, Conn.:

Greenwood Press, 1982), 251.
    35. *New York Age*, September 28, 1916, 6.
    36. *Boston Globe*, February 1, 1891, 16.
    37. *Boston Globe*, February 15, 1891, 10.
    38. *New York Age*, September 28, 1916, 6.
    39. *Boston Journal*, February 16, 1893.
    40. *New York Age*, December 24, 1921, 5.

REFERENCES

Hare, Maude Cuney. *Negro Musicians and Their Music*.
    Washington, D.C.: Associated Publishers, 1936. Re-
    print. New York: Da Capo Press, 1974.
Howard, John Tasker. *Our American Music*. 4th ed. New
    York: Thomas Y. Crowell, 1965.
Hughes, Langston, and Milton Meltzer. *Black Magic: A
    Pictorial History of the Negro in American Entertain-
    ment*. Englewood Cliffs, N.J.:   Prentice-Hall, 1967.
Johnson, James Weldon. *Black Manhattan*. New York: Alfred
    A. Knopf, 1940. Reprint. New York: Arno Press and the
    New York Times, 1968.
Lucas, Sam. *Sam Lucas Plantation Songster*. Boston:
    White, Smith & Co., n.d.
Madeira, Louis C. *Annals of Music in Philadelphia and
    History of the Musical Fund Society*. Philadelphia: J.
    B. Lippincott Co., 1896.
Odell, George. *Annals of the New York Stage*. 15 vols.
    New York: Columbia University Press, 1927-49.
Simmons, William J. *Men of Mark: Eminent, Progressive and
    Rising*. Cleveland: G. M. Rewell, 1887.
Simond, Ike. *Old Slack's Reminiscence and Pocket History
    of the Colored Profession from 1865-1891*. 1891.
    Reprint, with preface by Francis Lee Utley and intro-
    duction by Robert C. Toll.   Bowling Green, Oh.:
    Bowling Green University Popular Press, 1974.
Southern, Eileen. *Biographical Dictionary of Afro-American
    and African Musicians*. Westport, Conn.:   Greenwood
    Press, 1982.
___. "Musical Practices in Black Churches in Philadelphia
    and New York ca. 1800-1884." *Journal of the American
    Musicological Society* 30 (1977):   68-70.
Trotter, James Monroe. *Music and Some Highly Musical
    People*. Boston: Lee and Shepard, 1881.

Newspapers

Boston Advocate, 1887
Boston Globe, 1891-1893
Boston Herald
Boston Journal, 1892-1893
Chicago Tribune, 1893
Cleveland Gazette, 1883-1900
Freedom's Journal, 1827
Indianapolis Freeman, 1886-1916

New York Age, 1883-1900; 1905-1924
Philadelphia Public Ledger, 1836-1845
Rochester North Star, 1848;
  also *Frederick Douglass' Paper* (Rochester), 1848
St. Paul Appeal, 1889

Newspaper Clippings

Boston Concert Life Programmes, Boston Public Library,
    Music Section
Chickering Hall Concert Files, Harvard Theatre Collection
Lillian Nordica Programme File, Harvard Theatre Collection
Philip Hale Clippings (1/28/1889-12/25/1889), Musical and
    Dramatic Criticism Scrapbook, Boston Public Library,
    Microfilm
Programme Books and Catalogs from the 1880s-1900s, New
    England Conservatory, Boston

Keyboard Music by Nineteenth-Century Afro-American Composers

ANN SEARS

Piano music by nineteenth-century Afro-American composers is rarely heard in concert halls nor is this repertory discussed in the standard histories of American music. Despite its absence from contemporary scholarly works and concert programs, many black composers created works for the piano during the previous century. The piano was an omnipresent instrument in the nineteenth-century parlor, and the majority of composers wrote for it. Keyboard music, therefore, provides an instructive vehicle for examining black music of this period. The goal of this study is the rediscovery of these keyboard works.

With the exception of those complete pieces reproduced in Eileen Southern's landmark history, *Music of Black Americans: A History*, and the journal, the *Black Perspective in Music*, few nineteenth-century keyboard pieces by black Americans are readily available. The appended catalogue which includes locations of scores will help make this music accessible.

Antebellum composers such as Frank Johnson (1792-1844), James Hemmenway (1800-1864), Edward de Roland (1803-1894), Isaac Hazzard (1804-1864), William Brady (d. 1854), Henry Williams (1813-1903), and A. J. R. Connor (d. 1850) flourished in the cultural centers of Boston, New York, and Philadelphia.(1) Examples of their works clearly indicate that they were much more than journeymen musicians. Like the compositions of their white contemporaries, the piano music of these early composers consisted largely of keyboard arrangements of ceremonial music and functional dance music.

The compositions utilize the symmetrical forms of dance music--cotillion, quadrille, waltz, polka, quick step, gallop, schottische, and march. Instructions for the dance steps are frequently printed in the piano score. Since much of this music was intended for use by America's growing number of amateur musicians, its musical and technical demands are slight. The textures are usually thin, particularly the left-hand accompaniment figures. When dynamic markings are present, they modify large sections of music. Indications of crescendo or descrescendo are

infrequent, and pedal markings do not appear. This music
could be played on any keyboard instrument, for it utilizes
hardly any of the unique sound capabilities of the piano.

Frank Johnson was one of the most prolific antebellum
composers of keyboard music. A typical set of keyboard
pieces is *Quadrille, de contredanses suivi d'une valse pour
le piano forte composé & arrangé sur des motifs de l'opéra
de Bellini La Sonnambula.* Considering Johnson's awareness
of current musical fashions, it is not surprising that he
took advantage of the attractive melodic material provided
by this still-new opera, composed in 1831 and first
performed in New York in English in 1835.

Treatment of the sixth quadrille of this set, *Take Now
This Ring,* is characteristic of Johnson's approach to tran-
scriptions. The movement is based on the duet *Prendi:
l'anel ti dono* from Act I of *La Sonnambula.* Johnson alters
Bellini's 12/8 meter and tempo, marked *Andante sostenuto,*
to 3/4 meter and the tempo of a waltz. The melodic frag-
ments do not appear in the same order as the duet; further-
more, Johnson often changes phrase endings in order to omit
the cadenzas and to keep the strict phrase structure and
tempo of a dance movement. Bellini's melodies are chro-
matically elaborated and intervals are filled in, much as a
square dance fiddler embroiders repeated strains of dance
music.

Frank Johnson: *Quadrille, de contredanses suivi d'une valse
pour le piano forte composé & arrangé sur des motifs de
l'opéra de Bellini La Sonnambula.* No. 6: *The Sonnambula
Waltz, Take Now This Ring*

Evidently his efforts were successful, for a second set
of quadrilles based on *La Sonnambula* appeared with yet
another version of *Prendi: l'anel ti dono* as the untitled
second quadrille of the group. Set in 2/4 meter, this
version is a much shorter, more simple dance than the first
setting.

Frank Johnson: *Deux quadrilles de contredanses pour le
piano forte composés & arrangés sur des motifs de l'opéra
de Bellini, La Sonnambula.* 2d Set, No. 2

Valse à cinq temps, composed by A. J. R. Connor and published in 1847, is another example from the antebellum period. Although this is the only dance piece in the catalogue in 5/4 meter, it should be noted that the five-step waltz was in the social dance repertory of the day.(2)

A. J. R. Connor: *Valse à cinq temps*

By mid-century conceptions of piano music were changing. Reflecting the influence of visiting European virtuosi, writing was more idiomatic for the instrument. The melodic line in William Brady's *Empire State Quick Step,* for example, frequently moves in thirds and octaves, and there are occasional instructions to play a melody in a higher register. The right hand has broken-octave passages and full chords which demand rather athletic technique. Accompaniment figures made up of broken octaves and sextuplets with half notes held underneath take better advantage of the piano's potential for sound than many earlier compositions. Dynamic markings for fortissimo and pianissimo appear, and crescendi and decrescendi are indicated more frequently.

William Brady: *Empire State Quick Step*

Black composers were particularly successful in Southern and Midwestern cities such as New Orleans and St. Louis. Many compositions by J. W. Postlewaite (1837-1889) of St. Louis are listed in the *Complete Catalogue of Sheet Music and Musical Works, 1870.*(3) Most of these works are still in dance forms.

The Lambert brothers of New Orleans were gifted pianist-composers who studied and published works in Paris. Sydney (b. 1838) remained in Paris, while Lucien (b. 1828) later settled in Brazil. Compositions by Lucien exhibit particularly fine pianistic writing. His *Au Clair de la lune: Variations et final sur l'air,* Op. 30 features octaves, coloristic use of the soft pedal, and the layered approach to writing made popular first by Thalberg, then by Liszt. The melody is divided between the hands while a bass line and passage-work continue around it.

Lucien Lambert: *Au Clair de la lune: Variations et final sur l'air*, Op. 30

Lucien Lambert: *Au Clair de la lune: Variations et final sur l'air*, Op. 30

Also active in mid-century were Walter Craig (1854–1920), John Thomas Douglass (1847–1886), Frederick Elliot Lewis (1846–18?), and Jacob Sawyer (b. 1859?). Little is known about any of the four, and to date only one keyboard composition by each has been located. Both Douglass' *The Pilgrim: Grand Overture*(4) and Lewis' *Scenes of Youth: Fantasia for Piano*, Op. 3, resemble orchestral music transcribed or reduced for piano with coloristic use of scales, tremolos, and other figurations. These pieces may be a tantalizing suggestion that as yet undiscovered orchestral music exists from this period in the history of Afro-American music.

John Thomas Douglass: *The Pilgrim: Grand Overture*

Frederick Elliot Lewis: *Scenes of Youth: Fantasia for Piano*, Op. 3

The compositions of two remarkable composer-pianists, Thomas Greene "Blind Tom" Bethune (1849-1908) and John William "Blind" Boone (1864-1927), reveal late nineteenth-century developments in piano composition. Bethune's concert career lasted approximately thirty-five years. During this time he was both slave and freedman, touring in the United States and in Europe in the care of the Bethune family to whom he belonged before the Civil War. His importance may be questioned today, but many music critics and peers in the nineteenth century considered him a genius.

His compositions are surprisingly varied. Typical of his works are descriptive pieces, such as *The Battle of Manassas* and *Sewing Song: Imitation of the Sewing Machine*. His output also includes character pieces after European models, such as *Nocturne, Daylight: A Musical Expression for the Piano*; and *The Rainstorm*.

One of his earlist pieces was *Oliver Gallop*, composed when Tom was ten years old. It displays easy, natural writing for the keyboard, and it is clear from this example that he had considerable innate talent.

Thomas Greene Bethune: *Oliver Gallop*

The Rainstorm, Op. 6, was also written when Tom was very young, possibly as early as eleven. The banal opening tune does not reveal the drama of the music to come, but the subsequent use of texture, color, and pianistic effects contain the essential spirit of Romantic piano music. The piece requires virtuosic technique, not only in sheer digital ability but also in demands for tonal control and sophisticated pedaling. The sextuplet accompaniments, use of crescendi and descrescendi to mirror the wind, and chromatic scales representing the roll of thunder are reminiscent of Liszt's *Transcendental Etude*, No. 12. Although not of the same artistic stature as Liszt's etude, this piece should be noted for its descriptive use of the sound possibilities of the piano.

Thomas Greene Bethune: *The Rainstorm*, Op. 6

Rêve charmant is very similar to pieces written by other composers in America during this era. *Rêve charmant* is unusual in Bethune's works in that it combines melodic interest, harmonic motion, and sensitive use of texture to build a striking sense of climax at the close of the piece.

Thomas Greene Bethune: *Rêve charmant*

   The Battle of Manassas must be noted in any consideration of Bethune's career, not because the piece constitutes one of Bethune's greatest musical successes, but because it is one of the earliest pieces requiring the performer to make extra-musical sounds. The sounds include clusters played in a low register of the piano with the palm of the hand to represent cannon, train sounds (chu-chu-chu), and whistles representing the arrival of troops. The melodic material is comprised of a series of melodies such as *Dixie*, *The Girl I Left Behind Me*, *The Star-Spangled Banner*, and the *Marseillaise*.
   John William Boone (1864-1927) is another important

pianist and composer active at the end of the century.   He had a touring concert company, which enjoyed great financial success. He and the company toured the United States many times, and also traveled to Canada, Mexico, and Europe.   He had the unusual good fortune to have an excellent black manager, John Lange, with whom he shared a long and devoted friendship.   Unlike Blind Tom under the influence of the Bethune family, Boone avoided being advertised as a curiosity because of either blindness or extraordinary talent.   His slogan, "We travel on merit, not on sympathy," often was printed on his brochures and programs. He wrote many keyboard pieces--fantasias and variations--all of them virtuosic and brilliant.   He was concerned with color, texture, and the piano's ability to project a singing melody over a blanket of harmony.   Boone lived through the heyday of ragtime, and his works include rags as well as salon pieces, concert pieces, and some songs.

In Blind Boone's pieces, such as *Caprices de Concert*, Nos. 1 and 2; *Mélodies de nègres* (1893), and *Danse de nègres: Caprice de concert*, No. 3 (1902), we begin to see expressions of black identity as he uses titles and rhythms reflecting black themes.   The melody of the B section of *Caprice*, No. 2 is the same melody used by Louis Moreau Gottschalk in *Bamboula, Danse de nègres* (1844-1845), and later by Samuel Coleridge-Taylor in *The Bamboula (Negro Dance)* from *Twenty-four Negro Melodies* (1905).

A section of *Caprice*, No. 3 is entitled "Pickaninny's Dance," although the melody is not associated with a spiritual nor is it of African origin.   Coincidentally, Blind Boone's *Caprices* were written during the same period of time as Antonin Dvořák's *New World* Symphony. In 1895 he made his famous statement that a real American school of composition must be based on black spirituals, "for they are the folk songs of America, and your composers must turn to them."(5)

John William Boone: *Caprice de Concert*, No. 2: *Mélodies de nègres*

John William Boone: *Danse de nègres: Caprice de concert,*
No. 3

     The influences of their important predecessors,
Dvorak's well-known interest in Afro-American music, and
Coleridge-Taylor's use of Afro-American melodies inspired
later twentieth-century black composers to reach for their
musical legacy.   The successors to the nineteenth-century
pieces discussed here are the *Twenty-four Negro Melodies*
(1905) of Samuel Coleridge-Taylor (1875-1912) and the early
pieces of Nathaniel Dett (1882-1943); their historical
importance and availability are certain.   The pioneers who
blazed the trail in the nineteenth century created works of
lasting historical and musical worth.   Far too long
forgotten, this music is ripe for revival.

CATALOGUE OF EXTANT PUBLISHED KEYBOARD MUSIC BY

NINETEENTH-CENTURY AFRO-AMERICAN COMPOSERS

     This catalogue includes titles of compositions for
which complete published sheet music has been located.   The
sigla in parentheses at the end of each entry refer to
libraries where copies were located.   Complete information
about libraries may be found at the end of the catalogue.
The abbreviation "c." followed by a date refers to date of
copyright.

BARÈS, JEAN BASILE (1846-1902) (6)

Basile's galop pour piano, Op. 9.   New Orleans: A. E.
Blackmar, c. 1869.   (LSM, TU L)

*La Belle créole: Quadrille des lanciers américain pour le
piano.* New Orleans: A. Elie, c. 1866. (HNOC, TU L, TU M,
UNO L)

La Capriceuse: Valse de salon pour le piano, Op. 7. New
Orleans: A. E. Blackmar, 1869.   (HNOC, TU L, TU M, UNO A.
Reprinted in Trotter)

Les Cent gardes: Valse, Op. 22.   New Orleans: Louis
Grunewald, c. 1874.   (LSM, TU L)

La Coquette: Grand polka de salon pour le piano.   New
Orleans: A. Elie, c. 1866.   (TU L)

La Course: Galop brillante. New Orleans: A. E. Blackmar, c. 1866. (HNOC, LSM, UNO A)

La Creole: Polka mazurka. New Orleans: A. E. Blackmar, c. 1884. (TU M)

La Creole: Souvenir de la Louisiane, marche pour piano, Op. 10. New Orleans: A. E. Blackmar, c. 1869. (TU M)

Delphine: Grande valse brillante, Op. 11. New Orleans: Grunewald, c. 1870. (HNOC, TU L)

Les Folies du carnaval: Grande valse brillante. Galop du carnaval, Op. 24. New Orleans: A. E. Blackmar, c. 1866. (HNOC, TU L, TU M, UNO A)

Grande polka des chasseurs a pied de la Louisiane. c. 1860. (LSM, TU L)

La Louisianaise: Valse brillante. New Orleans: A. E. Blackmar, c. 1884. (LSM, TU L, UNO A)

Mamie: Waltz pour le piano, Op. 27. [New Orleans?]: Junius Hart, c. 1880. (HNOC, LSM, TU L, TU M, UNO A)

Merry Fifty Lanciers, Op. 21. New Orleans: Philip Werlein, c. 1873. (LSM, UNO A)

Minuit: Valse de salon composee pour piano, Op. 19. New Orleans: A. E. Blackmar, c. 1873. (HNOC)

Regina: Valse pour le piano, Op. 29. New Orleans: Louis Grunewald, c. 1881. (TU L, UNO A)

La Seduisante: Grand valse brillante. New Orleans: A. E. Blackmar, c. 1866. (LU, TU L, X)

Temple of Music: Polka Mazurka. New Orleans: A. E. Blackmar, c. 1871. (TU L)

Les Varietes du carnaval, Op. 23. New Orleans: Louis Grunewald, c. 1875. (HNOC, TU L, UNO A)

Les Violettes: Valse, Op. 25. New Orleans: Louis Grunewald, c. 1876. (TU J, UNO A. Reprinted in *Piano Music from New Orleans, 1851-1898,* compiled by John Baron. New York: Da Capo Press, 1980)

The Wedding: Heel and Toe Polka, Op. 26. New Orleans: Louis Grunewald, c. 1880. (HNOC, NOPL, TU L)

BETHUNE, THOMAS GREENE (1849-1908) "BLIND TOM"

The Battle of Manassas. Chicago: Root and Cady, c. 1866. (LC. Reprinted in *Piano Music in Nineteenth Century America,* Vol. 1, compiled and edited by Maurice Hinson. Chapel Hill, North Carolina: Hinshaw Music, 1975)

Blind Tom's March. New and rev. ed. by L. K. Boston: O. Ditson, 1888. (LC)

Blind Tom's Mazurka. J. C. Beckel, pseud. Rev. ed. by L. K. Boston: O. Ditson, c. 1888. (LC)

Blind Tom's Waltz, Op. 2. Philadelphia: J. Marsh, c. 1865. Rev. ed. by L. K. Boston: O. Ditson, c. 1888, 1892. (LC)

Columbus March. Rev. ed. L. K. Boston: O. Ditson, c. 1888. (LC)

Cyclone Galop. New York: William E. Ashnall, 1887. (NYPL)

Daylight: A Musical Expression for the Piano. Chicago: Root and Cady, c. 1866. (LC)

_____. Chicago: S. Brainard's Sons, 1866. Keck 616. (WU) (7)

Grand March Resurrection. Highlands, New Jersey: E. Bethune, c. 1901. (LC)

Improvisation: When This Cruel War is Over. Variations for piano. Rev. ed. by L. K. Boston: O. Ditson, 1888. (LC)

_____. Philadelphia: J. Marsh, 1865. Keck 627. (WU)

March Timpani. W. F. Raymond, pseud. New York: F. Blume, c. 1887. (LC)

Military Waltz. E. T. Messengale, pseud. Bucyrus, Ohio: Guckert Music Publishing Company, c. 1899. (LC)

Oliver Gallop. New York: H. Waters, c. 1860. Keck 628. (LC, WU)

The Rainstorm, Op. 6. Rev. ed. L. K. Boston: O. Ditson, c. 1888. (LC)

_____. New York: J. L. Peters, 1865. Keck 629. (WU)

_____. Philadelphia: J. Marsh, 1865. Keck 630. (WU)

Rêve charmant: Nocturne for Piano. J. G. Bethune, c. 1881. (LC)

Sewing Song: Imitation of the Sewing Machine. New York: W. A. Pond, c. 1888. (LC)

Virginia Polka. New York: H. Waters, c. 1860. (LC)

Water in the Moonlight. Chicago: S. Brainard's Sons, c. 1866. (LC)

Wellenklänge: Concert Waltz für das Pianoforte von François Sexalise. New York: J. G. Bethune, 1882. New York: Spear and Dehnhott, 1887. (LC)

BOONE, JOHN WILLIAM (1864-1927)   "BLIND BOONE"

Aurora Waltz. Columbia, Missouri: Allen Music Co., 1907.
(LC)

Caprice de concert, No. 1: *Mélodies de nègres.* St. Louis:
Kunkel Brothers, 1893. (LC)

Caprice de concert, No. 2: *Mélodies de nègres.* St. Louis:
Kunkel Brothers, 1893. (LC)

Danse de negres: Caprice de concert, No. 3. St. Louis:
Kunkel Brothers, 1902. (LC)

Grand valse de concert, Op. 13. Kansas City, Missouri: J.
W. Jenkins' Sons, 1893. (LC. Fuell) (8)

The Hummingbird: Morceau de salon. Boston: O. Ditson,
1886. (LC)

Josephine Polka. Cincinnati, Ohio: The John Church
Company, 1891. (NYPL)

Last Dream: Waltz. Columbia, Missouri: W. B. Allen,
1909. (LC, BPL)

Love Feast: Waltz. Arr. Dave Peyton. Columbia, Missouri:
W. B. Allen, 1913. (LC)

Old Folks at Home: Grand Concert Fantaisie. St. Louis:
Kunkel Brothers, 1894. (LC. Fuell)

Serenade: Song without Words. Boston: O. Ditson, 1887.
(LC)

Southern Rag Medley, No. 1: *Strains from the Alleys.*
Columbia, Missouri: Allen Music Co., 1908. (LC)

Southern Rag Medley, No. 2: *Strains from the Flat Branch.*
Columbia, Missouri: Allen Music Co., 1909. (LC)

Sparks: Grand galop de concert. St. Louis: Kunkel
Brothers, 1894. (LC)

Sparks: Grand galop de concert. Piano duet. St. Louis:
Kunkel Brothers, 1894. (Private collection)

The Spring: Reverie for Piano. Boston: O. Ditson, 1885.
(LC)

Whippoorwill: Romance for Pianoforte. Boston: White-Smith
Publishing Co., 1891. (LC)

Woodland Murmurs: A Spinning Song. Boston: O. Ditson,
1888. (LC)

BRADY, WILLIAM (d. 1854)

Carnaval Waltz. New York: Atwill, 1845. (AAS. Reprinted in the *Black Perspective in Music*, Vol. 4, p. 245)

Empire State Quick Step. New York: Atwill, 1845. (LC)

CONNOR, AARON J. R. (d. 1850)

Chestnut Street Promenade Quadrilles. Philadelphia: Edward L. Walker, 1850. (Private collection)

Connor's Third Sett of Polka Quadrilles. Philadelphia: Edward L. Walker, 1850. (LC)

The Evergreen Polka. Philadelphia: A. Fiot, 1847. Keck 1054. (LC, WU)

Fashionable London Polka Waltz. (Private collection)

General Taylor's Gallop. Philadelphia: Osbourn's Music Saloon, 1846. (Private collection)

I. O. O. F. Quadrilles. Philadelphia: T. J. Williams, 1846. (Private collection)

The Mallet or Stop Waltz. Philadelphia: Lee & Walker, 1846. (Private collection)

New York Polka Waltz. Philadelphia: A. Fiot, 1846. (LC)

Remedy Against Sleep: A Waltz Selected from Strauss. Philadelphia: Lee & Walker. (AAS)

Valse à cinq temps. Philadelphia: A Fiot, 1847. (LC)

CRAIG, WALTER F. (1854-1920)

Rays of Hope March, Op. 1. (Trotter)

DOUGLASS, JOHN THOMAS (1847-1886)

The Pilgrim: Grand Overture. (Trotter)

DUBUCLET, LAWRENCE (1866-1909)

The Belle of the Carnival: March Two Step. New Orleans: Louis Grunewald, c. 1897. (HNOC, TU L)

Bettina Waltz. New Orleans, c. 1886. (TU L)

National Defense March. New Orleans, c. 1899. (HNOC)

World's Fair March, Op. 7. New Orleans, c. 1893. (TU L)

Les Yeux deux: Mazurka de salon. New Orleans, c. 1886.
(HNOC, TU L)

GOTAY, FRANCES (SISTER MARIE SERAPHINE)

La Puertorriquena: Rêverie. [New Orleans?]: Junius Hart,
c. 1896. (UNO)

HAZZARD, ISAAC (1804-1864)

The Alarm Gun Quadrille. 1842. (AAS. Reprinted in the
Black Perspective in Music, Vol. 4, p. 250)

Croton Waltz. Philadelphia: Osbourn's Music Saloon, 1846.
(Private collection)

Davis' Quick Step. Philadelphia: Osbourn's Music Saloon,
1843. (AAS)

Hazzard Favorite Waltz. Arr. J. G. Osbourn. Philadelphia:
Geo. Willig. (AAS)

Miss Lucy Neal Quadrille. Philadelphia: George Willig,
1841. Keck 2083. (WU)

The Terpsichore; a New Sett of Quadrilles. Philadelphia,
1837. 1. *Washington.* 2. *Caroline.* 3. *Elisabeth.*
4. *Susana.* 5. *Henrietta.* 6. *Martha (Waltz).* 7. *Amanda
(Galopade).* (LC)

HEMMENWAY, JAMES (1800-1849)

Cupid's Frolic. Philadelphia, 1818? With *Miss Billings'
Waltz.* Wolfe 3655. (JBU) (9)

General LaFayette's Trumpet March and Quickstep.
Philadelphia: G. Willig, 1824. Wolfe 3656. (LC)

Lt. Charles S. Smith's Bugle Quick Step. Philadelphia:
George Bacon. (Private collection)

Miss Billing's Waltz. Philadelphia: Bacon & Co, 1819?
Wolfe 3657. (JBU)

The Philadelphia Hop Waltz. Boston: Bradlee;
Philadelphia: Willig, Keck 2110; New York: Firth, Pond &
Co, Keck 2111. (AAS, WU. Reprinted in the *Black Perspective in Music,* Vol. 4, p. 423)

The Second Set of Quadrilles. Philadelphia: G. Willig,
1825. Wolfe 3659. 1. *Independence.* 2. *The Arcade.*
3. *Washington Hall.* 4. *Boliver.* 5. *The Patriot.* (AAS)

A Set of New Cottillions for the Year 1825. Philadelphia:
G. Willig, 1825. Wolfe 3658. 1. *Eliza.* 2. *Maria.* 3. *Emma.*

4. *James.* 5. *William.* (AAS)

The Sixth Sett of Quadrilles. Philadelphia: G. Willig.
1. *Tancredi.* 2. *La Dame Blanche.* 3. *Elizabeth.* 4. *Tancredi.*
5. *Napoleon.* (AAS)

The Third Set of Quadrilles. Philadelphia: G. Willig,
1827. 1. *Charles.* 2. *Dashing White Sergeant.* 3. *Lysander.*
4. *Rachel.* 5. *Colonel Riter's Spanish Dance.* (Private
collection)

JOHNSON, FRANCIS (FRANK) (1792-1844)

Bingham's Cotillion. Philadelphia: George Willig, c. 1820.
Wolfe 4642. (JBU. Reprinted in the *Black Perspective in
Music*, Vol. 8, p. 178)

Boone Infantry Quick Step. Philadelphia: Osbourn's Music
Saloon, 184-. (Private collection)

Buffalo City Guards Quickstep. Philadelphia: Osbourn's
Music Saloon. (Private collection)

Butchers and Drovers Grand March. Philadelphia: J. G.
Osbourn. (Private collection)

Cape May Gallopade. Philadelphia: George Willig. (AAS)

Captain I. G. Watmough's Slow March. Philadelphia: published for the author, c. 1820. Wolfe 4643. (LC. Reprinted
in the *Black Perspective in Music*, Vol. 8, p. 180)

Captain Page Kent Bugle Quick Step. n. p., c. 1819. (AAS)

A Choice Collection of New Cottillions. Philadelphia: G.
E. Blake. 1. *Paddy O'Rafferty* 2. *The Patriot.* 3. *Tho'
'Tis All but a Dream.* 4. *Even as the Sun.* 5. *The Dashing
White Sergeant.* 6. *Retour de Windsor.* (Private collection)

The Citizen's Quadrilles. Philadelphia: Fiot, Meignen &
Co., 1837. (Private collection)

A Collection of New Cotillions. 1st & 2nd sett.
Philadelphia: G. Willig, 1818. Wolfe 4647. 1. *The Cym-
bals.* 2. *Maria Caroline.* 3. *Augustus.* 4. *Caroline.*
5. *William.* 6. *Johnson's Jig Cotillion.* 7. *Ford.*
8. *Lewis.* 9. *Francis.* 10. *Fort Erie.* 11. *The Arrival.*
12. *Castilian.* (AAS)

A Collection of New Cotillions. 5th & 6th sett.
Philadelphia: Geo. Willig, 182? Wolfe 4648. 1. *Marian.*
2. *March in Macbeth.* 3. *Ellen.* 4. *Matilda.* 5. *The Moor.*
6. *Dorothea.* 7. *Aurora.* 8. *Susan.* 9. *Rosalthe.* 10. *Ann.*
11. *James.* 12. *The Triumph.* (AAS)

A Collection of New Cotillions. 7th & 8th sett. Philadelphia: Geo. Willig, 182? Wolfe 4648. 1. *Is There a Heavy Heart.* 2. *The Ladies Choice.* 3. *Deidamia.* 4. *March in Rob Roy.* 5. *Knight Errant.* 6. *Hurrah! Hurrah!* 7. *Major Beckus.* 8. *Johnsons New Deceiver.* 9. *Congress Hall.* 10. *Roy's Wife.* 11. *Antoinetta.* 12. *The Stag Brisk.* (AAS)

Choice Collection of New Cottillions. 1st sett. Philadelphia: G. E. Blake, 1824? Wolfe 4649. 1. *The General.* 2. *Monmouth.* 3. *German Town.* 4. *Brandy Wine.* 5. *York Town.* 6. *The Cadmus.* 7. *Lafayette's Welcome (Country Dance).* (JBU)

A Choice Collection of New Cottillions. 6th sett. Philadelphia: G. E. Blake. Wolfe 4649. 1. *The New Theatre.* 2. *The Spanish Seguadille.* 3. *Milton.* 4. *The Sun Flower.* 5. *Dorothea.* 6. *The Bride.* 7. *Johnson's Favorite Virginia Reel.* (AAS)

Colonel C. G. Childs' Parade March. Philadelphia: G. Willig, 1826. (Reprinted in the *Black Perspective in Music,* Vol. 4, p. 247)

Colonel Geo. D. B. Kelm's March and Quick Step. Philadelphia: G. Willig. (AAS)

Dream Waltz. Philadelphia: Fiot, Meignen & Co. (AAS)

Deux quadrilles de contredanses pour le piano forte composés & arrangés sur des motifs de l'opéra de Bellini, La Sonnambula. 2d set. Philadelphia: Fiot, Meignen & Co. (AAS)

Favorite Quick March. Philadelphia: G. E. Blake. (AAS)

General Cadwalader's March. Philadelphia: Geo. Willig, 1819-20. Wolfe 4651. (AAS) Wolfe 4651A. (JBU)

Honor to the Brave. Genl. LaFayette's Grand March. Philadelphia: printed for the author, 1824. Wolfe 4654. (Reprinted in *Anthology of Early American Keyboard Music, 1787-1830,* Pt. II, edited by J. Bunker Clark. Madison, Wisconsin: A-R Editions, 1977)

The Irish Volunteers' Parade March and Quick-Step. (AAS)

Kent Bugle Quick Step. Philadelphia: G. E. Blake, 1825-26. Wolfe 4658. (JBU)

Lieut. Harrison's Kent Bugle Quick March. (Reprinted in the *Black Perspective in Music,* Vol. 8, p. 182)

Lafayette Waltz. Philadelphia. No. 7 of *Taw's Musical Miscellany.* (AAS)

Major R. Campbell Slow March and Quick Step. Philadelphia: G. Willig, 1823? Wolfe 4660. (JBU)

March in the Catarct [sic] of the Ganges. Philadelphia:
Geo. Willig. (AAS)

Miss Lucy Long, arranged as a Cotillion. Philadelphia:
George Willig, 1842. Keck 3229. (WU)

Monongehela Waltz. Philadelphia: Osbourn's Music Saloon,
1815. (Private collection)

Mrs. Camac's March, Waltz, and Cotillion. Philadelphia: G.
E. Blake, 1829. (AAS)

New Bird Waltz. Philadelphia: Osbourn's Music Saloon.
(Private collection)

New Cotillions and March with the National Airs.
Philadelphia: printed for the author, 1824. Wolfe 4657,
No. 2.   1. *Tom and Jerry*. 2. *Anna*.   3. *Alice*.
4. *Ballston*. 5. *Love in a Village*. 6. *Saratoga*. (AAS)

New Cotillions and March with the National Airs.
Philadelphia: printed for the author, 1824. Wolfe 4657,
No. 3.   1. *La Fayette*. 2. *Washington*. 3. *The Morris*.
4. *The National Guest*. 5. *Cadwallader*. 6. *J. C. Taws*.
(LC.   Nos. 1, 2, and 4 reprinted in *Anthology of Early
American Keyboard Music, 1787-1830*, Pt, II, edited by J.
Bunker Clark. Madison, Wisconsin: A-R Editions, 1977)

A New Spanish Dance. Philadelphia: G. Willig, 1824-27.
Wolfe 4663. (JBU)

Philadelphia Grays Quick Step. Philadelphia: Fiot,
Meignen & Co. (Private collection)

*Quadrille, de contredanses suivi d'une valse pour le piano
forte compose & arrange sur des motifs de l'opera de
Bellini La Sonnambula*. Philadelphia: Fiot, Meignen, &
Co. 1. *Do Not Mingle, One Human Feeling*. 2. *Oh! Love
For Me Thy Power*. 3. *As I View These Scenes So Charming*.
4. *Still So Gently O'er Me Stealing.* 5. *Sounds So Joyful*.
6. *The Sonnambula Waltz, Take Now This Ring*. (AAS)

Recognition March of the Independence of Hayti.
Philadelphia: G. Willig, 1825? Wolfe 4662. (Reprinted in
the *Black Perspective in Music*, Vol. 4, p. 240)

St. Louis Grand March. New York: Firth, Pond, & Co.,
1848-1855. Keck 2418. (WU)

The Star Spangled Banner: a New Set of Cotillons.
Philadelphia: Fiot, Meignen, & Co., 1828. 1. *Edward*.
2. *Margaretta*. 3. *Eliza*. 4. *Charlotte*. 5. *The Promenade*.
(Private collection)

Victoria Gallop. Philadelphia: Osbourn's Music Saloon,
1839. Keck 2420. (AAS, WU)

LAMBERT, LUCIEN (b. 1828)

Au clair de la lune: Variations et final sur l'air, Op. 30. (A portion of the piece is reprinted in Trotter.)

Warbling Birds. Boston: O. Ditson. (AAS)

LEWIS, FREDERICK ELLIOT (1846-18?)

Scenes of Youth: Fantasia for Piano, Op. 3. (Trotter)

MACARTY, EUGENE VICTOR (1821-1881)

Fleurs de salon: 2 Favorite Polkas. New Orleans, c. 1854. 1. *L'azalea.* 2. *La Caprifolia.* (TU L, UNO A)

MARTIN, THOMAS J. (fl. 1850-1860)

The Creole Waltz. New Orleans: William T. Mayo, c. 1848. (SM, TU L)

Free Mason's Grand March. New Orleans: Werlein, c. 1854. (HNOC, NOPL, TU L, TU M, UNO A)

Genl. Persifor F. Smith the Hero of Contreras' March. Baltimore: F. D. Benteen, c. 1848. New Orleans: William T. Mayo. (LSM, TU L, UNO A)

Oratorial Grand March to the Memory of Henry Clay. New Orleans: F. Hartel, c. 1860. (HNOC, LSM)

NICKERSON, WILLIAM J.

The New Era March. New Orleans: Louis Grunewald, c. 1900. (HNOC)

POSTLEWAITE, JOSEPH WILLIAM (1837-1889) (10)

Almira Waltz. St. Louis: Balmer & Weber, 1849. (FLP)

Annie Polka Mazurka. St. Louis: Henry P. Sherburne, 1854. (MHS)

Aurora Schottisch. St. Louis: G. Brainard. (UVC)

Bessie Waltz. St. Louis: J. Ballhouse, 1855. (MHS)

Dew Drop Schottisch. St. Louis: Balmer & Weber, 1851. (MHS)

Dramatic Schottisch. St. Louis: H. Pilcher & Sons, 1856. (LC, MHS)

Evangeline Waltz. (FLP)

Galena Waltz. St. Louis: Balmer & Weber, 1850. (MHS)

Geraldine's Dream. St. Louis: Balmer & Weber, 1854? (FLP)

Iola Waltz. St. Louis: Balmer & Weber, 1850. (MHS)

Kasky Waltz. St. Louis: Balmer & Weber, c. 1850. Keck 3658. (WU)

Lillie Polka Mazurka. St. Louis: Compton & Doan, 1867. (MHS)

Love's Dream Waltz. St. Louis: Balmer & Weber, 1874. (MHS)

Pleyade Schottisch. St. Louis: Balmer and Weber, 1859. (MHS)

Recreation Schottisch. St. Louis: Henry P. Sherburne, 1854. (MHS)

Red Petticoat Mazurka. St. Louis: J. W. Postlewaite, 1858. (MHS)

Ruth Polka. St. Louis: R. J. Compton, c. 1866. Keck 3659. (WU)

Schottisch Quadrille. St. Louis: Balmer & Weber, 1853. (MHS)

St. Louis Greys Quick Step. St. Louis: Balmer & Weber. Keck 3660. (WU, tenth edition, c. 1852. Reprinted in the *Black Perspective in Music*, Vol. 8, p. 191)

ROLAND, EDWARD (1803-1894)

Ladies Polka Quadrilles. Philadelphia: Lee & Walker, 1849. (JBU. Reprinted in the *Black Perspective in Music*, Vol. 8, p. 183)

SAWYER, JACOB (b. c1859)

Welcome to the Era March. John F. Perry, 1877. (Trotter)

WILLIAMS, HENRY F. (1813-1903)

Chitarra Polka. Boston: O. Ditson, 1853. (HHU)

Croton Waltz. Philadelphia: A. Fiot, 1844. (AAS)

Gov. Fairfield's Quick Step. Boston: Bradlee. (AAS)

Maysville March. Philadelphia: John F. Nunns. (AAS)

Rose Schottische.   Boston: O. Ditson, 1852. (Private collection)

Sunny Side Polka. Boston: O. Ditson, 1852. (AAS. Reprinted in the *Black Perspective in Music*, Vol. 4, p. 219)

SIGLA FOR LIBRARIES CONTAINING SHEET MUSIC

AAS   American Antiquarian Society, Worcester, Massachusetts
BPL   Boston Public Library, Boston, Massachusetts
FLP   Free Library of Philadelphia, Pennsylvania
WU   Gaylord Music Library, Washington University, St. Louis, Missouri
HNOC   Historic New Orleans Collection, New Orleans, Louisiana
HHU   Houghton Library, Harvard University, Cambridge, Massachusetts
JBU   John Hay Library Special Collections, Brown University, Providence, Rhode Island
LC   Library of Congress, Washington, D.C.
LSM   Louisiana State Museum, Old United States Mint, Louisiana Historical Center, New Orleans, Louisiana
LU   Loyola University, Department of Archives and Special Collections, New Orleans, Louisiana
MHS   Missouri Historical Society, St. Louis, Missouri
NOPL   New Orleans Public Library, Main Branch, Louisiana Division, New Orleans, Louisiana
NYPL   New York Public Library, New York, New York
TU J   Tulane University, Howard-Tilton Memorial Library, William Ransom Hogan Jazz Archive, New Orleans, Louisiana
TU L   Tulane University, Howard-Tilton Memorial Library, Louisiana Collection, Sheet Music Collection, New Orleans, Louisiana
TU M   Tulane University, Howard-Tilton Memorial Library, Manuscripts, Blackmar Collection, New Orleans, Louisiana
UNO A   University of New Orleans, Earl K. Long Library, Archives and Special Collections, Marcus Bruce Christian Papers, New Orleans, Louisiana
UNO L   University of New Orleans, Earl K. Long Library, Louisiana Collection, Sheet Music Collection, New Orleans, Louisiana
UVC   University of Virginia Library, Charlottesville, Virginia
X   Xavier University of Lousiana, Library, Basile Jean Barès Collection, New Orleans, Lousiana

NOTES

    1. For biographical information and historical background concerning nineteenth-century composers see Eileen

Southern, *Biographical Dictionary of Afro-American and African Musicians* (Westport, Conn.: Greenwood Press, 1982); *Music of Black Americans: A History*, 2d ed. (New York: Norton, 1983), 97-261.

2. Samuel A. Floyd and Marsha J. Reisser, "Social Dance Music of Black Composers in the Nineteenth Century and the Emergence of Classic Ragtime," *Black Perspective in Music*, 6 (1978): 161-193. Note the reprint of a dance program including Connor's *Valse à cinq temps* on page 164.

3. *Complete Catalogue of Sheet Music and Musical Works, 1870* (Published by Board of Music Trade of the United States of America, 1870. Reprint with introduction by Dena Epstein. New York: Da Capo, 1973).

4. See James Monroe Trotter, *Music and Some Highly Musical People* (1878. Reprint. New York: Johnson Publishing Company, 1968), 30-43. Although not all the keyboard pieces in the volume are complete, more compositions are available here than in any other single volume.

5. This quotation originally appeared in the *New York Herald*, May 25, 1893); it has been reprinted in Gilbert Chase's *America's Music*, 2d ed. rev. (New York: 1966), 391, and in Eileen Southern's *The Music of Black Americans*, 265.

6. Lester Sullivan, "Composers of Color in Nineteenth-century New Orleans: The History Behind the Music." Unpublished paper presented at the Center for Black Music Research in New Orleans, Louisiana, on October 16, 1987. Information about the music of New Orleans composers Barès, Dubuclet, Gotay, Macarty, Martin, and Richard was graciously shared by Mr. Sullivan, Archivist, Amistad Research Center, Tulane University, New Orleans.

7. George Keck, *Pre-1875 American Imprint Sheet Music in the Ernst C. Krohn Special Collections, Gaylord Music Library, Washington University, St. Louis, Missouri: A Catalogue and Descriptive Study* (Ph.D. Dissertation, University of Iowa, 1982). Keck numbers in the appendix refer to the catalogue portion of this dissertation, which includes a catalogue of approximately five thousand pieces of sheet music, many of which are not available elsewhere.

8. Melissa Fuell, *Blind Boone: His Early Life and His Achievements*. (Kansas City, Missouri: Burton Publishing Company, 1915), 218-228.

9. Richard J. Wolfe, *Secular Music in America, 1801-1825: A Bibliography* (New York: New York Public Library, 1964). Wolfe numbers in this article refer to the catalogue numbers in this three-volume bibliography, which has become a standard numbering and identification system in many libraries.

10. Samuel A. Floyd, "J. W. Postlewaite of St. Louis: A Search for His Identity." *Black Perspective in Music*. 8 (1980): 151-167. Compositions located at the Missouri Historical Society are listed in this article. For a more complete works lists see Samuel A. Floyd, Jr., "A Black Composer in Nineteenth-Century St. Louis," *Nineteenth Century Music* 4 (1980).

REFERENCES

Brown, Ernest James. *An Annotated Bibliography of Selected Solo Music Written for the Piano by Black Composers.* D.M.A. Dissertation, University of Maryland, 1976.

Desdunes, Rudolphe Lucien. *Nos hommes et notre histoire.* 1911. Translated by Dorothea Olga McCants as *Our People and Our History.* Baton Rouge: Louisiana State University Press, 1973.

Dichter, Harry, and Elliott Shapiro. *Handbook of Early American Sheet Music, 1768-1889.* New York: Dover Publications, 1977.

Fuell, Melissa. *Blind Boone: His Early Life and His Achievements.* Kansas City, Missouri: Burton Publishing Company, 1915.

Gillespie, John, and Anna Gillespie. *A Bibliography of Nineteenth-Century American Piano Music.* Westport, Conn.: Greenwood Press, 1984.

Gillespie, John, ed. *Nineteenth-Century American Piano Music.* New York: Dover Publications, 1978.

Hare, Maude Cuney. *Negro Musicians and Their Music.* Washington, D.C.: Associated Music Publishers, 1936.

Kmen, Henry. *Music in New Orleans: The Formative Years, 1791-1841.* Baton Rouge: Louisisana State University Press, 1966.

Phillips, Linda Nell. *Piano Music by Black Composers: A Computer-Based Bibliography.* D.M.A. Dissertation, Ohio State University, 1977.

Spillane, David. *History of the American Pianoforte.* 1890. Reprint. New York: Da Capo Press, 1969.

Southall, Geneva A. "Blind Tom: A Misrepresented and Neglected Composer-Pianist," *Black Perspective in Music,* 3 (May 1975): 141-59.

_____. *Blind Tom: The Post-Civil War Enslavement of a Black Musical Genius,* Book I. Minneapolis: Challenge Productions, Inc., 1979; *The Continuing Enslavement of Blind Tom, the Black Pianist-Composer (1865-1887),* Book II. Minneapolis: Challenge Productions, 1983.

Trotter, James Monroe. *Music and Some Highly Musical People.* 1878. Reprint. New York: Johnson Publishing Company, 1968.

Promoting Black Music in Nineteenth-Century America: Some Aspects of Concert Management in New York and Boston

George R. Keck

A large number of outstanding black performers on the concert stage in nineteenth-century America were able to achieve notable and successful careers. Many aspects of concert life have been examined by scholars, especially the professional careers of those who achieved fame. However, the questions of how these artists reached the stage and sustained careers over a period of time have not yet been addressed.

Among the difficulties facing concert artists in all periods of music history are the problems of finding opportunities for performances and of attracting financial support. These problems were especially real in the nineteenth century, a period when audiences with a lack of cultural self-confidence preferred performances by touring European artists.

Artists active before the Civil War achieved their success mainly through promoting their own careers and through their good fortune in attracting patrons who were willing to help them. It was not until after the war that entrepreneurs established modern professional management, seeking actively to promote and to guide concert artists in developing their careers. Beginning with the earliest attempts to manage concert artists immediately after the Civil War, the profession evolved by 1900 into that which is typical today. The formative period is particularly interesting because of the different approaches of managers to dealing with the difficulties of concert life. The questions of how black artists were related to this development and why managers sought to promote blacks during this formative period are important ones in the history of black music.

This chapter examines the relationships between managers, both white and black, and the black concert artists whose careers they promoted during the last three decades of the nineteenth century. The examination will consider the questions of why the managers were interested in promoting black performers, how the managers promoted their clients, who the performers were, what the financial arrangements were, what kinds of concerts were given and where, and what problems existed between managers and artists. Study is confined to managers in Boston and New York, because these were the important centers for activity during this period. Those who made significant contributions or whose careers illustrate important aspects of the developing management field were considered. These white managers include James Redpath, James B. Pond, and James G. Bergen, and black managers William H. Dupree and James Trotter.

James Redpath was perhaps the most influential manager in nineteenth-century America. Founding the Redpath Lyceum Bureau in Boston in 1868, Redpath and his partner, George L. Fall, were pioneers in the field of concert management and established many of the practices that have lasted until the present.

An examination of Redpath's life and professional career clearly reveals why he was interested in promoting black artists. He was born in Berwick-on-Tweed, Scotland, August 24, 1833.(1) His family emigrated to America in 1848 and settled on a farm in Michigan. He learned the printing trade in Kalamazoo, Michigan, then he went to Detroit where his newspaper articles attracted the attention of Horace Greeley, who offered him a position on the staff of the New York *Tribune* in 1852. Redpath continued his association with this newspaper intermittently for the next thirty years.(2)

From 1854 to 1860 Redpath, while a correspondent for the *Tribune*, devoted himself to the abolitionist cause. Beginning in 1854, he traveled widely throughout the South in order to witness for himself the conditions of slavery. James Pond stated that "during all this long journey he talked with the slaves, slept in their cabins, ate of their humble fare, and listened to their distressing revelations."(3)

In 1855-56 Redpath was in Kansas, taking an active part in the difficult and bitter politics of the Free State movement and acting as a correspondent for several newspapers. Redpath was also a correspondent during the Civil War. After the fall of Charleston he was appointed superintendent of education in that city. He completely reorganized the educational institutions of the city. He organized day schools, established night schools for adults, opened a library for the recently freed slaves, recruited the first black militia companies in the city, and founded an asylum for black orphans. On his return to the North, Redpath lived in Boston and wrote for Boston and New York newspapers until 1868.

In 1867 Redpath conceived the idea of booking lecturers for the small-town lecture circuit based on the idea of the lyceums which had been popular before the war. The lyceum, founded in 1826 to encourage adult education in the United States, stressed lectures, debates, and readings, and promoted improvement in the public schools and establishment of libraries. Many of America's most talented and highly educated thinkers appeared on the lyceum lecture platform. Before the Redpath Lyceum Bureau was established, lecture committees made up from the leading citizens in each town contacted lecturers directly. Fees were generally small,

covering expenses and a small honorarium. Performers of
music had not been included, as music was usually considered popular entertainment.

   After the war those men and women whose patriotism and
abilities had made their names famous were in great demand
as lecturers.   Through his abolitionist activities Redpath
had become friends with many of these men and women--
Wendell Phillips, William Lloyd Garrison, John Greenleaf
Whittier, Harriet Beecher Stowe, and Henry Ward Beecher.
All of these became Redpath clients.

   Redpath founded his management business in 1868 under
the name The Boston Lyceum Bureau. His partner, George L.
Fall, acted as business manager for the firm.   The first
season for the new company was 1868-1869, but no information about the activities for that season has yet been
uncovered.   Beginning in May 1869, however, the Lyceum
Bureau sent out annually the *Lyceum Magazine*, a publication
for lyceum committees describing the lecturers, musicians,
and entertainments available.(4)   The issue dated May 1869,
a four-page circular, advertised an "Evening of Sacred
Song" performed by Philip Phillips (1834-1895), evangelis-
tic singer, composer of gospel hymns, and compiler of
hymnbooks. The Band of the Institution for the Blind was
also listed.

   The *Lyceum Magazine* of January 1871 included a notice
that the Lyceum Bureau had engaged as clients all the best
vocalists and instrumentalists in Boston, and that concerts
could be booked for a minimum of $75 plus expenses.   The
notice also explained that expenses for musical people
meant "the carriage-hire at both ends,--for the ladies, at
least,--the hotel bills, and the rail-road-fare to and from
their residences."(5)   Fees for concerts were paid in advance to the Bureau, but expenses were paid to the artists
at the time of the concert.

   By July 1873 the concert management portion of the
business had grown to a sufficient level to justify hiring
Edward S. Payson as manager for concerts alone.   In an
article announcing Payson's appointment it was pointed out
that "he will devote his whole time to this work," an
indication of the volume of musical business handled by the
bureau.(6)   In 1873 the name of the business was changed
from the Boston Lyceum Bureau to the Redpath Lyceum
Bureau.(7)

   According to James Pond, there was a lessening of
interest in lecturers during the 1874-75 season.   Pond
stated that one of the reasons for this was that large
numbers of people who had never attended musical performances before were going to hear Gilbert and Sullivan
operettas.(8)   In July 1874 the bureau advertised that the
Redpath English Opera Company had been organized and was
available to present the opera, *Martha*, in the English
language.   The fee to engage the opera company was $250, or
less if the performance was given in a simple setting
without costumes. Pond related that *Martha* was the "most
delightful hit of the season," and he reported that the
bureau made over eighteen thousand dollars on the company
the first season.(9)   That first effort was such a great
success that the next year, 1875, in addition to *Martha*,

Flotow's *The Spectre* was added to the company's repertory.
     In addition, in 1875 a truly new attraction appeared--
the Hyers Sisters Concert Company. Consisting of Anna
Hyers, soprano; Emma Hyers, contralto; John Luca, baritone;
and A. C. Taylor, pianist; the company was advertised as:

> a quartet of colored vocalists, and the best that has
> ever been organized. The Sisters are the most wonder-
> ful vocalists that the colored race in this country has
> thus far produced. The Company will try and bring out
> an original Operetta for next season, illustrative of
> the progress of the colored race.(10)

The operetta was entitled *Out of Bondage*.
     The drama, interspersed with songs, opened on a
Southern plantation before the Civil War and traced the
coming of the Union army, the emancipation of the slaves,
and their subsequent lives in freedom in the North. As is
often the case with this type of drama, the fourth act
concluded the entertainment with a "grand concert" consisting of selections from the operas *Il Trovatore* and *Ernani*.
This type of ending gave the singers the opportunity to
show their abilities in performing the serious repertory of
the concert stage.
     In this opera company the Redpath Bureau introduced to
lyceum audiences some of the finest black concert artists
of the last quarter of the nineteenth century: the Hyers
Sisters, Sam Lucas, John Luca, Wallace King, A. C. Taylor,
Dora King, Billy Kersands, William Edward Lew and the Lew
Male Quartet, and Flora Batson.
     The next season *Out of Bondage* was advertised in
glowing terms as available for another year. The author of
the article praised the production:

> The success of this dramatic and musical novelty last
> season was almost unprecedented in the annals of any
> managerial experience. It was, in the first place, so
> entirely distinct from any entertainment which has ever
> been given before by any company of artists, and in the
> second place, it was so pleasing to all classes of
> amusement seekers.(11)

The article was continued with a quote from a letter of
Mark Twain, a personal friend of Redpath as well as a
lecturer for the Bureau, to an acquaintance in Boston:

> I went a mile and a half in the most furious tempest of
> wind and snow that I have seen for five years, to see
> the plantation sketches of the Hyers Troupe and hear
> their exquisite music, and I would go three miles
> through just such a tempest to have that pleasant and
> satisfactory experience again.(12)

Based on the evidence of newspaper reviews, *Out of
Bondage* was performed all over the East coast and Midwest.
Reviews appeared as far West as Muscatine and Keokuk, Iowa,
as well as in New York, Pennsylvania, Maine, Massachusetts,
Rhode Island, Indiana, and Illinois. The play was such a

favorite that it was retained in the repertory even after a new play, *Urlina; or, the African Princess*, was added in the season of 1878-79.

In 1878 the company was called the Hyers Sisters Combination. *Urlina* was announced as a "Grand Oriental Opera Bouffe in Three Acts and Several Tableaux." Urlina, sung by Madah Hyers, was the unfortunate Princess, who, robbed of her throne, was banished to a desert island by a usurper and tyrant. Louise Hyers sang the role of a man, Prince Zurleska, "son of the usurper and prospective heir to the throne--a Prince who prints his name in large type typically speaking."(13) The cast reportedly included characters representing an American traveler, a witch, an Irish missionary, a "Christian Chinaman," and the king's jester. Such an assemblage offered opportunities for almost any situation to occur on stage.

It is not possible to identify exactly how long the Hyers Sisters remained with the Redpath Lyceum Bureau, because issues of the *Lyceum Magazine* for 1879 through 1882 have not yet been located. Other sources do not mention the Bureau, and the Hyers were not included in the 1882 issue.

In October 1875 Redpath sold the Lyceum Bureau to Major James B. Pond and George H. Hathaway and moved to New York City. Redpath had known Pond as a reporter in Kansas and had hired him to work for the Bureau in 1874. Hathaway had managed the Chicago office for several years. Pond and Hathaway ran the business together until 1879, when Pond sold out to Hathaway and moved to New York to open his own office. The Redpath Lyceum Bureau continued operations in Boston until 1969, the last year in which the company is listed in the *Boston City Directory*. The Chicago branch also continued well into the twentieth century, forming the parent for the Chautauqua Circuit, so important to the cultural and intellectual development of the Midwest.

Pond's contributions to the promotion of black musicians were very different from those of Redpath, as were the experiences that prepared him for that career. He was born in Cuba, New York, in 1838.(14) Pond grew up in Wisconsin, learned the printing trade, and worked for several different newspapers in the Midwest before the Civil War.

Pond served in the Union army during the Civil War. Afterwards he was involved in several different mercantile businesses in the Midwest. While in Salt Lake City he made the acquaintance of Ann Eliza Young, the nineteenth wife of Brigham Young, who had recently left Young's household and renounced the Mormon faith. Pond persuaded her to lecture about her experiences and managed her tour. When Pond went to Boston in 1874, Redpath hired him to work for his bureau, where he was responsible primarily for promoting the tours of foreign lecturers. It appears that Pond was not directly involved in managing the musical attractions for the Redpath Lyceum Bureau. In 1879 Pond sold his interest to George Hathaway and went to New York City, where he opened a new office.(15)

The only important black concert artist managed by Pond after he left Boston for New York was Sissieretta Jones.

Pond signed a contract with her for one year in June 1892. According to the terms of the contract, Jones was to receive $150 per week, traveling expenses, and all her accommodations.(16)

The relationship between Pond and his artist, however, was not entirely satisfactory. In the spring of 1893 Pond sued Jones, who wanted to arrange for concerts outside Pond's management, and he sought a court injunction to prevent her doing so. In addition, there was disagreement over a clause in the contract that gave Pond the option of re-engaging Jones for an additional two years under the same terms as the original contract. The court granted Pond's motion and admonished Jones in these terms:

> She feels now as if she could get along without her benefactor, and she has thrown down the ladder on which she ascended to the position she now enjoys. Every sense of gratitude requires her to be loyal to the manager who furnished her with the opportunity for greatness.(17)

This did not address all the issues, however, because Jones had been singing in public with great success since 1889, three years before she signed with Pond. If the number of concerts in which Jones was advertised to appear during the 1893-94 season is any indication, as well as the fact that Pond pursued a court injunction in order to retain sole management, Jones must have been earning for her manager far more than her $150 salary.(18)

Further relevant information may be found in *Women of Distinction* by L. A. Scruggs. Pond, in a contract agreement with Ednorah Nahar, allowed Jones to sing four concerts for Nahar in February and March 1893 for a total of $600, an indication of the amount Jones could draw per concert.(19) Soon after the court case ended, Jones left Pond's management. In July it was announced that Ednorah Nahar was her manager,(20) and in October she signed a contract with the Walter Damrosch Orchestra Company for a three-year tour of Mexico and Europe for a reported salary of $35,000 per year.(21) Pond continued in the management business in New York until his death on June 21, 1903.

A completely novel approach to management was taken by James G. Bergen. From 1883 until his death in 1897 Bergen organized concerts featuring prominent black concert artists, promoted the concerts through advertising and P. T. Barnum style showmanship, and achieved a degree of financial success unattained by any other manager of black concert artists in the nineteenth century. Although he was white, Bergen built his career on the promotion of black artists in benefit concerts for black churches and other black institutions, and on his successful management of the career of Flora Batson, one of the outstanding black singers of the period.

The first advertisement for a star concert that I have located appeared in the *New York Globe*, October 13, 1883. The concert was planned to take place on October 31 at 8:00 P.M. at the Music Hall, Brooklyn, as a benefit performance for Prince Street Presbyterian Church of Brooklyn.   In addition to several local performers, stars appearing on the program included Nellie Brown Mitchell, Emma Fisher, and Adelaide G. Smith, with Mrs. Gassaway and Virginia Montgomery as accompanists.   All of these artists had established reputations in the East by this time and were expected to attract an audience.   Tickets were twenty-five cents and were available from Bergen or the church pastor.

This type of concert in which several well-known artists appeared supported by local talent was not a new idea, nor was the idea of benefit concerts to raise money for local churches and social institutions.   Black churches had sponsored concerts since the 1820s.   But Bergen was successful from the beginning, because he achieved a reputation for thorough organization and for financial success, and he secured the support of the black community. In addition, he had the original idea of giving prizes to those willing to sell tickets.   The advertisement for the October 31 concert stated that prizes would be presented. Twenty-five dollars in gold would be awarded to the person selling the most tickets; second would receive $15; third $10; and fourth $5.   This scheme promoted the sale of tickets by church members who worked to raise money for their churches and a cash prize for themselves.

The 1883-84 season was a great success for Bergen and his artists.   Almost immediately Bergen doubled the value of the original prizes for selling tickets.   Reviewers of concerts stated that audiences ranged in size from approximately one thousand to three thousand and that individual tickets were fifty cents with an additional twenty-five cent charge for a reserved seat.   One reviewer mentioned that the benefit church received $300 after all expenses were paid.(22)

Other managers were quick to realize that Bergen had good and profitable ideas.   H. F. Downing of New York City advertised a "Grand Musical and Literary Festival" in January 1884.   He, too, featured Nellie Brown Mitchell, Adelaide Smith, a group called the Magnolia Quartette, and several others.   He also offered prizes for selling tickets but only charged twenty-five cents per ticket.(23)

The concert was, however, not a success, and the following letter-to-the-editor appeared in the *Globe:*

To the editor of the Globe: In consequence of many erroneous statements in relation to the concert given at Cooper Union, January 31, 1884, I give below a tabulated statement of the enterprise.   I also wish to state that Cooper Union seats 1700 people, and the hall was three-fourths full.   I trust that the public will treat me with justice.(24)

A list of expenses and receipts followed showing that $333.50 was taken in ticket sales and that $343.55 was paid out, leaving a deficit of $10.05.   The list of expenses revealed that Nellie Brown Mitchell was paid $51.50, Smith $37.25, and Mrs. Gassaway, the accompanist, $12.   Rent for

the Cooper Union was $50, and for the piano rent was $6.
The letter was signed H. F. Downing, Manager. No further
mention of any managerial activity by the unfortunate Mr.
Downing has come to light.

Several articles appearing in the *New York Freeman*
during 1884-85 reveal the extent of Bergen's success as a
concert manager and reasons for continued competition aside
from financial ones. In an article on November 22 the
editor stated:

> Mr. J. G. Bergen's concerts are always artistic
> successes. Mr. Bergen understands the rare art of
> bringing the people together, and of satisfying them
> when they do come. The artists are always paid
> promptly, and the prizes, often very valuable and
> handsome, are always distributed at the close of the
> entertainments without any unnecessary red tape.(25)

The following week an article appeared in the same
newspaper that disclosed the dissatisfaction of some members of the New York black community with Bergen. The
writer pointed out that there had been a great deal of
adverse criticism against Bergen coming from "New York
gentlemen who have not themselves made much success in the
concert line."(26) The writer continued by relating that
Bergen gave most of his concerts in conjunction with black
churches. Included was a list of those churches for whose
benefit concerts were presented and the amount each had
made. The list included twenty-seven concerts with total
earnings of $10,107.47.

The unidentified author of the letter also stated that
one of the most severe criticisms was that Bergen cleared
more than the churches. But the writer defended Bergen's
profits, because he gave his time, money, and experience.
This person believed Bergen should make a decent living,
because "Mr. Bergen has been more successful than anyone
in drawing out colored talent. Artists affirm that terms
with them are liberal and always strictly complied with."
In reply another anonymous writer stated, "Mr. Bergen is
white. The race should patronize colored concert givers
instead of a white one!"(27) The challenges to Bergen's
supremacy as a concert manager were based on jealousy of
his success and resentment towards a white man who, it was
felt by some, was exploiting black artists and the black
community.

A reviewer of a star concert in June stated how much
Bergen made from the benefit concerts. The writer noted
that the packed house resulted in total receipts of $775
with $325 expenses and a net gain of $450. This amount was
divided evenly between the benefit church and Bergen, so
that each received $225.(28) Later articles and reviewers
also mentioned this equal division of the profits after
expenses were paid.

The season of 1885-86 was an important one for Bergen
because of his discovery of Flora Batson. That season he
opened his programs in Newport, Rhode Island, near Batson's
city of residence, Providence. The star of that concert

was Sam Lucas. Lucas appeared again in Providence, sharing the stage with Flora Batson, who was appearing on a Bergen concert for the first time.(29) From this time Batson appeared on Bergen Star Concerts, as well as in other performances, under the management of James Bergen, who was listed as her manager in all advertisements and usually mentioned in reviews of her concerts as well. In 1887 an advertisement appeared in which it was announced "Miss Batson being under permanent contract with the undersigned, all applications for her services will hereafter be addressed to J. G. Bergen, Manager."(30)

During the 1886-87 season, Bergen took his star on a tour of the Midwest and South. By the following season her reputation was so great that Bergen could sell admission tickets for fifty cents, but demand $1 for a reserved seat and still sell 7,532 tickets for one performance. The proceeds for that concert were $1400 above expenses.(31)

At a concert in Philadelphia in December 1887 Batson was presented with a "crown of solid gold set with precious stones," proclaiming Batson "Queen of Song," a title she used from that point in her career.(32) Not to be outdone in honoring Batson, the citizens of New York presented her a "solid gold diamond cut bead necklace with a gold plate: Presented to Mrs. Flora Batson-Bergen, Queen of Song, By the Citizens of New York City, At Steinway Hall, January 31, 1888."(33)

The plaque was inscribed to Mrs. Flora Batson-Bergen, because Manager Bergen and Batson were married on December 13, 1887, in New York City.(34) The engagement had been announced in November.(35) The announcement carried extensive biographical information about Bergen and Batson.

According to information in the article Bergen was forty-one at the time of his engagement and had been in business for twelve years. He must, therefore, have been born about 1846 and have begun his management career in 1875, although no information about his activities before 1883 is known. The article also carried the information that Bergen was born in Petersburg, Illinois, and was related to the Bergens of Bergen, New Jersey. Bergen was a widower, his first wife having died November 6, 1886,(36) and he was the father of a twelve-year-old son.

Following Batson's triumphs in Philadelphia and New York and her marriage, the Bergens departed for an extended tour of the West which was apparently successful. Later their annual tours were expanded to include the South as well. An advertisement that appeared in 1888 reveals much information about Bergen's managerial practices:

> To churches and Societies: Do you need money! If so secure Miss Batson for one, two or three concerts, supporting her with your "best local talent." Distribute carefully a large number of neatly printed circulars giving the above press notices, [which appeared in the advertisement along with a portrait of Batson] and under favorable business management, there is no church or Music Hall in America large enough to hold the multitude that will flock to hear her.(37)

The fees for performances were also listed. Batson could be engaged for one night for $50 and expenses, two successive nights for $80 and expenses, and three successive nights for $100 and expenses. The expenses were to include board, hack hire, and railroad fare for Batson and her manager.

In July 1889 the *New York Age* published a report on the success Batson was achieving on her tour. The paper reported that the concert company had traveled over five thousand miles and had performed in all the leading cities of the South and West in white and colored churches--both Catholic and Protestant. The article mentioned that Batson would continue her tour all the way to San Francisco, and "the name of Flora Batson shall have become a household word from the Atlantic to the Pacific."(38)

By December 1890 Bergen was advertising Batson's return to the East coast. On December 13 he noted that after an absence of over two years she would return home early in January and would be singing in Philadelphia, New York, Boston, Washington, and other cities. The next advertisement appeared on January 10, proclaiming Batson "The Greatest Colored Singer in the World." On January 17 the advertisement stated:

> The South Conquered
> The Middle States Captured
> California Surrenders
> The Queen of Song completes 15,000 mile tour of the continent and will appear in concert at Association Hall, Brooklyn, February 2, 1891.(39)

After the Brooklyn performance one reviewer declared the concert a complete success. The writer also included a closing paragraph, giving what is probably the earliest indication that the marriage of the Bergens was a troubled one:

> At the close of the program Mr. Bergen came before the footlights and said that the marriage bells that began to ring in New York three years ago had continued to ring merrily and happily straight across the continent and were ringing still, regardless of rumors to the contrary.(40)

Sometime before the beginning of the 1891-92 season Bergen undertook the management of Sissieretta Jones, who had sung on his star concerts in the late 1880s.(41) Bergen began to advertise that Batson and Jones could be engaged for concerts separately or together. On September 19 of that year a joint appearance on a Bergen Star Concert was announced.(42) It was not until October 12, 1896, at Carnegie Hall that Jones, Batson, and Marie Selika, the three leading female black singers of the period, sang together.(43)

At this point Bergen had arrived at the height of his career as a manager. He had achieved a successful itinerary for his group of artists, so that they performed in the East during the winter season and traveled West or

South for the spring and summer. He continued to introduce
artists of the next generation, promoting such performers
as Harry T. Burleigh and Joseph Douglass.(44)

By 1896 the marriage of Batson and her manager was at
an end. She announced her separation from Bergen on stage
at a concert on December 3. Newspapers reported the separation and explained it as a misunderstanding between them.
Batson continued to perform through the spring, but the
advertisements for her concerts do not mention the name of
her former manager and husband.

Bergen continued his career, also. He organized a
Bergen Star Concert without Batson as an artist on May 13,
1897, in New York City.(45) Five days later Bergen was
dead. He died suddenly on Monday afternoon May 18, 1897,
of a heart attack. The obituaries stressed Bergen's
successful concert management career and the excellence of
the concerts he organized.(46)

A statement was made in an article in the *New York Age*
after Batson's death implying that Bergen did not provide
for the financial future of Batson. It was stated in the
article: "Then Bergen died, and his wife was left without
inheritance and she had to depend upon her own resources."(47)

Bergen made significant achievements as a concert
manager in promoting benefit concerts, encouraging local
talent, and managing the career of Flora Batson. He was
also an opportunist--taking full advantage of the newspapers for free, as well as paid advertisements, promoting
the "star" system, and ultimately marrying his star
performer. But perhaps the final summary of his career
should be that which was printed in an article in the *New
York Freeman* January 2, 1886:

> No manager of colored concerts has reaped his measure
> of success. We have yet to hear of a financial or
> artistic failure. . . . From interviews we have had
> with Mr. Bergen we are led to believe he takes an
> honest pride in bringing forward the artistic talent of
> the race. . . . And what manager would not feel grati-
> fied at his ability to command the time and talents of
> such artists.

Thus far consideration has been given to the careers of
white managers who managed black concert artists, but there
were a number of black managers who were also successful in
promoting black artists during the nineteenth century.
Foremost among these were James M. Trotter and William H.
Dupree. Trotter and Dupree were at first partners, and
later Dupree managed on his own. Trotter and Dupree were
acquainted from at least the period of the Civil War, as
both served in the Fifty-fifth Massachusetts Regiment.(48)
Both rose through the ranks of noncommissioned officers and
were eventually commissioned as officers. In addition,
Dupree was manager of the regimental band.

After the war both served in the Boston post office,
and both were members of the Wendell Phillips Club, a club
formed in 1876 for political and intellectual stimulation
and for social enjoyment of its members. In 1883 Trotter

resigned from his position at the post office and turned
his attention to the management business.

The first indication that Trotter was interested in the
musical world occurred in 1883 in an article in the *New
York Globe*.(49)   The article appeared with a dateline,
"Boston, Feb. 26," and was signed James M. Trotter.   It was
noted in the article that Marie Selika and her husband,
Sampson Williams, were having a brilliant success on a
concert tour of Europe.   There was no mention in the
article of a manager.

In July 1883 Trotter began actively to manage the
career of Henrietta Vinton Davis, a dramatic reader who
appeared on programs accompanied by Adelaide G. Smith, and
with pianist, Samuel W. Jamieson.(50)   By this time Trotter
had formed a partnership with Dupree, and Trotter's address
in Hyde Park was given as the business address.   Throughout
the season of 1883-84 Trotter and Dupree managed the concerts of Davis, Smith, and Jamieson, as they appeared
together in cities along the East coast.

This was Trotter's only activity in the management
field, while Dupree continued to act on his own as manager
for several artists.   Beginning in the spring 1885, newspapers carried advertisements announcing the availability of
Marie Selika and S. W. Williams   for   concerts through
William H. Dupree, Manager.   From   September 1885 through
March 1886 the notices also included the name of Carrie
Melvin from Providence, Rhode Island, performer on the
violin, cornet, mandolin, and glockenspiel.   After August
1886 Dupree is no longer listed as manager for any of these
artists.

By June 1886 Carrie Melvin placed her own advertisements, which did not mention a manager but indicated that
all correspondence should be addressed to Melvin at 10
Howard Place, Providence, Rhode Island.   Advertisements in
the *Freeman* during the first three weeks of August 1886
mention Dupree as agent and business manager for Selika and
Williams, but all   advertisements   after   August 28   stated
that for terms and business engagements all letters should
be addressed to Marie Selika.

Trotter and Dupree were not active over a long period
of time, but they managed two of the most important black
concert artists of the period: Selika and Williams.   Both
of these managers had other careers, turned to management
at a difficult period in their lives, and quickly moved on
to other enterprises after a short time in the field.

In the last three decades of the nineteenth century
there was a great deal of activity in an attempt to promote
black artists on the concert stage.   Through various means,
with varying degrees of success, and for different reasons,
both black and white managers sought to give black artists
a forum for public performances.   Those who were most
successful, James Redpath and James Bergen,   established a
reputation early in their careers for successful concerts
and secure financial foundations, and both had original
ideas for creating opportunities for the artists they
managed.

In spite of all this activity in promoting black
concert artists, black performers found it difficult to

sustain a professional career in performance for an artistic lifetime. However, black concert artists achieved a great deal under the prevailing conditions of the time: several attained reputations enviable even by today's standards and many were well paid for their performances and reached a high level of income.

Managers were able to promote black stars in the newspapers and journals of black and white America. The managers promoted artists outside the black churches in commercial recital halls in concerts attended by both blacks and whites. As difficult as it was to find suitable managers and to maintain careers, black artists and managers were able to find avenues of success and to achieve professional careers.

NOTES

1. Biographical information about James Redpath can be found in three principal sources: Charles F. Horner, *The Life of James Redpath* (New York: Barse & Hopkins, 1926); James Burton Pond, *Eccentricities of Genius* (New York: G. W. Dillingham, 1900); and Alvin F. Harlow, "James Redpath," *Dictionary of American Biography* (New York: Scribner's Sons, 1943), 15:443.

2. *Dictionary of American Biography*, 15:444.

3. Pond, 534.

4. *Lyceum Magazine* (title varies); the 1869-71 and 1873-76 seasons may be found in the Department of Rare Books and Manuscripts, Boston Public Library; the 1877-79 and 1882-84 seasons are in Gutman Library, Harvard University; 1882-83 season is also in the Boston Athanaeum. An issue without number, dated May 1869, is in the Massachusetts Historical Society.

5. *Lyceum Magazine*, January 1871, 2.

6. *Lyceum Magazine*, July 1873, 9.

7. *Lyceum Magazine*, July 1873, 2.

8. Pond, 543.

9. Pond, 547. Pond stated that the Redpath English Opera Company was formed in 1875. *Lyceum Magazine*, July, 1874, p. 3, however, advertised this attraction for the 1874-75 season. The dates in Pond are unreliable throughout.

10. *Lyceum Magazine*, August 1875, 6.

11. *Lyceum Magazine*, season of 1877-78, 71.

12. Ibid.

13. *Lyceum Magazine*, season of 1878-79, 70.

14. Biographical information can be found in the *New York Times*, June 22, 1903, p. 1; William Bristol Shaw, "James Burton Pond," *Dictionary of American Biography* (New York: Scribner's Sons, 1943), 15:60-61; and Pond, *Eccentricities of Genius*.

15. *Dictionary of American Biography*, 15:60.

16. *New York Times*, June 27, 1893, 8.

17. Ibid.

18. See advertisements in issues of *New York Age*, *Indianapolis Freeman*, and *Cleveland Gazette* for 1883-94.

19. L. A. Scruggs, *Women of Distinction* (Raleigh, N. C.: L. A. Scruggs, 1893), 183.
20. See the *Indianapolis Freeman*, July 28, 1894.
21. *Indianapolis Freeman*, October 27, 1894. The reported salary of $35,000 per year seems unbelievably high. Surely, the amount was $35,000 for the three years of the contract.
22. *New York Globe*, January 12, 1884, 3.
23. *New York Globe*, January 5, 1884, 3.
24. *New York Globe*, February 9, 1884, 3.
25. *New York Freeman*, November 22, 1884, 3.
26. *New York Freeman*, November 29, 1884, 2.
27. *New York Freeman*, December 20, 1884, 2.
28. *New York Freeman*, June 13, 1885, 3.
29. *New York Freeman*, October 24, 1885, 2.
30. *New York Freeman*, August 27, 1887, 3.
31. *New York Freeman*, January 7, 1888, 3.
32. *New York Freeman*, January 28, 1888, 3.
33. *New York Freeman*, February 4, 1888, 3.
34. Monroe Alphus Majors, *Noted Negro Women* (Chicago: Donahue & Henneberry, 1893), 92.
35. See *New York World*, November 13, 1887, and *New York Age*, December 3, 1887, 1.
36. *Indianapolis Freeman*, May 29, 1897, 7.
37. *New York Age*, August 11, 1888, 3.
38. *New York Age*, July 13, 1889, 1.
39. See issues of *New York Age*, December 13, 1890, 3; January 10, 1891, 3; and January 17, 1891, 3.
40. *New York Age*, February 7, 1891, 1.
41. *New York Age*, August 22, 1891, 3.
42. *New York Age*, September 19, 1891, 3.
43. *Indianapolis Freeman*, October 10, 1896, 6.
44. *Indianapolis Freeman*, December 12, 1896, 6.
45. *Indianapolis Freeman*, May 8, 1897, 5.
46. *Indianapolis Freeman*, May 29, 1897, 7; and the New York *Daily Tribune*, May 18, 1897, 4.
47. *New York Age*, December 27, 1906, 1.
48. Further biographical information about Trotter can be found in William J. Simmons, *Men of Mark* (Cleveland, Oh.: Geo. M. Russell, 1887); issues of *New York Age* (see especially February 24, March 5, and March 12, 1887); and issues of the *Cleveland Gazette* (see especially March 12, 1887). Further biographical information about Dupree can be found in the *Cleveland Gazette*, April 11, 1885.
49. *New York Globe*, March 3, 1883, 1.
50. *New York Globe*, July 7, 1883, 3.

REFERENCES

Harlow, Alvin F. "James Redpath," *Dictionary of American Biography*. New York: Scribner's Sons, 1943, 15:443.
Horner, Charles F. *The Life of James Redpath*. New York: Barse & Hopkins, 1926.
Majors, Monroe Alphus. *Noted Negro Women*. Chicago: Donahue & Henneberry, 1893.

Pond, James Burton.   *Eccentricities of Genius*. New York:
      G. W. Dillingham, 1900.
The Redpath Lyceum Bureau. *Lyceum Magazine*. 1869-1883.
Scruggs, L. A. *Women   of   Distinction*. Raleigh, N.C.: L.
      A. Scruggs, 1893.
Shaw, William Bristol. "James Burton Pond," *Dictionary of
      American Biography*. New York: Scribner's Sons, 1943,
      15:60-61.
Simmons, William J. *Men of Mark*. Cleveland, Oh.: Geo. M.
      Russell, 1887.

Newspapers

Cleveland Gazette
Indianapolis Freeman
New York Age
New York Daily Tribune
New York Times

Nineteenth-Century Afro-American Music: A Bibliographical Guide to Sources for Research

GEORGE R. KECK AND SHERRILL V. MARTIN

This bibliographical guide surveys and assesses the most important sources for research on major topics in nineteenth-century Afro-American music and musicians. The essay is devoted to a consideration of primary sources, although many secondary sources are listed along with several recent indexes.

A wealth of primary sources exists from the second half of the nineteenth century. Secondary sources based on this material are more limited. There are virtually no indexes providing access to this valuable information, and facts must be gathered through painstaking searches of the surviving records. There are, however, two works that seek to address this lack of access: James de T. Abajian, comp., *Blacks in Selected Newspapers, Censuses and Other Sources: An Index to Names and Subjects*, 3 vols. (Boston: G. K. Hall, 1977); and Mary Mace Spradling, ed., *In Black and White: Afro-Americans in Print: A Guide to Magazine Articles, Newspaper Articles, and Books Concerning More than 15,000 Black Individuals and Groups*, 1971, 3rd ed. Detroit: Gale Research Co., 1980).

In addition, there are several bibliographies and bio-graphical works that provide initial help in research in this field. Eileen Southern's pioneering work, *The Music of Black Americans: A History*, 2d ed. (New York: Norton, 1983), not only provides a thorough overview of the history of black music, but also reveals the social context in which the music was created. In addition, the book includes an extensive bibliography of primary and secondary sources divided according to historical periods. Maude Cuney Hare's *Negro Musicians and Their Music* (1936. Reprint. New York: Da Capo Press, 1974) also contains much valuable information. Hare's effort was one of the earliest attempts to compile a history of Afro-American music, and the reader should be aware that the work contains many factual errors.

Newspapers are the most useful primary sources for research in Afro-American music in the nineteenth century; especially important are those published by blacks for the black community. Many of these newspapers include

advertisements, reviews of concerts, news stories about
famous and important performers, gossip columns, personal
columns, and reprints of interesting items from other newspapers throughout the country. The most important
newspapers with their dates of publication include:

> *Washington Bee*, 1882–1922
> *Cleveland Gazette*, 1883–1945
> *New York Age*, 1883–1900; 1905–1960. (The name of this
>   newspaper was changed from *New York Globe* to
>   *New York Freeman* in 1884, and to *New York Age*
>   in 1887.)
> *Indianapolis Freeman*, 1886–1916

Other important and useful newspapers of the period are:

> *Freedom's Journal*, New York City, 1827–1829
> *Colored American*, New York City, 1837–1842
> *North Star*, Rochester, New York, 1847–1851
> *Frederick Douglass' Paper*, Rochester, New York,
>   1851–1860
> *Douglass' Monthly*, 1859–1863
> *Weekly Anglo-African*, New York City, 1859–1860
> *L'Union*, New Orleans, 1862–1864
> *New Orleans Tribune*, 1864–1869
> *Weekly Louisianian*, New Orleans, 1870–1882
> *St. Paul Appeal*, 1889–1923
> *Richmond (Virginia) Planet*, 1890–1894; 1899–1938
> *Baltimore Afro-American*, 1893––
> *Chicago Broad Ax*, 1895–1927

All of the newspapers listed are available on microfilm.
    Two nineteenth-century periodicals, the New York
Clipper and *Folio*, contain a wealth of information about
Afro-American musicians. The *Clipper*, published 1853–1924,
included a weekly column devoted to black as well as white
performers in minstrel shows and vaudeville. This periodical, a forerunner of *Billboard* and *Variety Magazine*, contains much information about the popular musical stage.
Published 1870–1888, *Folio* was a Boston journal including
items of gossip about stars of the stage, notices of public
performances, reviews, and articles about performers.
    There are two contemporary periodicals devoted to black
music: *Black Perspective in Music*, begun in 1971, and *Black
Music Research Journal*, begun in 1980. Both of these
contain articles covering a broad spectrum of topics, many
on nineteenth-century Afro-American music and musicians. A
ten-year index is available covering the period 1973–1982
for *Black Perspective in Music*.
    Two biographical dictionaries that include information
about blacks are: Eileen Southern, *Biographical Dictionary
of Afro-American and African Musicians* (Westport, Conn.:
Greenwood Press, 1982), and Edward T. James and Janet
Wilson, *Notable American Women 1607–1950: A Biographical
Dictionary*, 5 vols. (Cambridge, Mass.: Belnap Press,
1971). Southern's dictionary contains entries for
more than 1400 individuals and groups and includes all
areas of musical activity. The work by James and Wilson

includes entries for a limited number of important black women.

Several works published in the nineteenth century include biographical information about important black musicians of the period. The most helpful information about those active before the Civil War can be found in Martin Robison Delany, *The Condition, Elevation, Emigration, and Destiny of the Colored People of the United States* (Philadelphia: Published by the author, 1852. Reprint. New York, 1968). Important female musicians active in the last two decades of the century are covered in M. A. Majors, *Noted Negro Women* (Chicago: Donohue & Henneberry Printers, 1893) and Lawson Scruggs, *Women of Distinction* (Raleigh, N. C.: Published by the author, 1893). Biographical sketches of notable black men of the late nineteenth century, including musicians, are found in William Simmons, *Men of Mark: Eminent, Progressive and Rising* (Cleveland: G. M. Russell, 1887. Reprint. Chicago, 1970). The best source for material on both male and female black musicians of the nineteenth century is James M. Trotter, *Music and Some Highly Musical People; with Sketches of the Lives of Remarkable Musicians of the Colored Race: with Portraits, and an Appendix Containing Copies of Music Composed by Colored Men* (1878. Reprint. New York: Johnson Publishing Co., 1968). The book is well written, filled with information on many different aspects of the careers of those covered, and the information is, apparently, accurate. In addition, this is one of the few contemporary sources that includes scores of some of the compositions discussed in the text.

A number of anthologies of black folk music and books dealing with this repertory survive from the nineteenth century. The earliest extant published collection is that of William Wells Brown, *The Anti-Slavery Harp: A Collection of Songs for Anti-Slavery Meetings* (Boston: B. Marsh, 1849), containing texts only for the songs, but with suggestions for appropriate tunes. Immediately following the Civil War a number of anthologies appeared that included commentaries. Among these are William Francis Allen, Charles Pickard Ware, and Lucy McKim Garrison, eds., *Slave Songs of the United States* (New York: A. Simpson, 1867); Theodore F. Seward, *Jubilee Songs: As Sung by the Jubilee Singers of Fisk University* (New York: Biglow & Main, 1872. Several editions appeared between 1872 and 1903); Gustavus D. Pike, *The Jubilee Singers and Their Campaign for Twenty-Thousand Dollars* (Boston: Lee and Shepard, 1873); and *The Singing Campaign for Ten-Thousand Pounds: The Jubilee Singers in Great Britain* (New York: American Missionary Association, 1875); Mary Alice Ford Armstrong and Helen W. Ludlow, *Hampton and Its Students, by Two of Its Teachers . . . With Fifty Cabin and Plantation Songs, Arranged by Thomas P. Fenner* (New York: G. P. Putnam's Sons, 1874, 1875, and 1878). The books dealing with the singing tours of the Jubilee Singers and the Hampton students contain information about the singing tours of these groups, who helped to spread knowledge about and appreciation of black folk music, in addition to the music and texts of the songs.

Another useful collection is that compiled by Marshall
W. Taylor entitled *A Collection of Revival Hymns and Plantation Melodies* (Cincinnati: Marshall W. Taylor and W. C.
Echols, 1882 and later editions). The first edition contained the words and music for 150 songs and the words only
for an additional seven songs.

Many details about the music of Afro-Americans at the
time of the war and emancipation can be gathered from books
detailing personal experiences in working with these freedmen during and immediately following the Civil War.
Elizabeth Hyde Botume's *First Days amongst the Contrabands*
(1893. Reprint. New York: Arno Press, 1968) reports on
this teacher's experiences with the ex-slaves in the 1860s.
Two additional works of this type include those by Linda
Warfel Slaughter, *The Freedmen of the South* (Cincinnati:
Elm Street Printing Co., 1869. Reprint. New York: Kraus
Reprint Co., 1969) and Maria Waterbury, *Seven Years among
the Freemen*, 2d ed., revised and expanded (Chicago: T. B.
Arnold, 1891). A reminiscence by Charlotte Forten, *The
Journal of Charlotte L. Forten*, edited by Ray Allen
Billington (New York: Dryden Press, 1953), includes
descriptions of the singing during this era by ex-slaves
from the Sea Islands, South Carolina.

There are a number of primary sources chronicling the
roles of blacks during the Civil War that include information about music. One of the earliest of these was written
by a black man, William Wells Brown, the compiler of *The
Anti-Slavery Harp*. Brown wrote *The Negro in the American
Rebellion* (Boston, 1867), relying on newspaper articles,
interviews, and his memory of the war. The work includes
texts of spirituals. Another important memoir by a black
participant in the Civil War is Susie King Taylor's
Reminiscences of My Life in Camp (Boston, 1902). Taylor
was an escaped slave who became a laundress, murse, and
teacher in Higginson's First South Carolina Volunteers, the
first slave regiment mustered into the service of the
United States. Thomas Wentworth Higginson also wrote about
his experiences with the blacks during the war. *Army Life
in a Black Regiment* (Boston: Fields, Osgood, 1870) and
Negro Songs (Harvard University, Houghton Library ms. Am
1162.7) include information about Higginson's personal
observations of black music making.

Black and abolitionist newspapers are the most
important sources for information on the black man's role
in the Civil War. Especially important was the *Liberator*,
the most significant newspaper edited by a white man, which
reported on the activities of blacks in New England. The
National Anti-Slavery Standard, the official journal of the
American Anti-Slavery Society, included reports on many
different aspects of the activities of blacks during the
war. In addition, many of the newspapers previously mentioned, which were published during the 1860s, include
valuable information about war activities of Afro-Americans
and their music during this time.

A number of scholars have written about the roles of
Afro-American musicians in the development of the theater.
Important works that illuminate specific aspects of the
careers of blacks include those by Langston Hughes and

Milton Meltzer, *Black Magic: A Pictorial History of the Negro in American Entertainment* (Englewood Cliffs, N.J.: Prentice-Hall, 1967); James Weldon Johnson, *Black Manhattan* (New York: Alfred A. Knopf, 1940. Reprint. New York: Arno Press and the *New York Times*, 1968); Lindsay Patterson, *Anthology of the American Negro in the Theatre* (New York: Publisher's Co., 1967); and Sam Lucas, *Sam Lucas Plantation Songster* (Boston: White, Smith, n.d.).

Studies that record the activities of a single performer, but containing valuable information about many performers active during the same period, include works by Tom Fletcher, *100 Years of the Negro in Show Business* (New York: Burdge, 1954); Ike Simond, *Old Slack's Reminiscence and Pocket History of the Colored Profession from 1865 to 1891* (1891. Reprint with preface by Francis Lee Utley and introduction by Robert C. Toll. Bowling Green, Oh.: Bowling Green University Popular Press, 1974); and W. C. Handy, *Father of the Blues: An Autobiography*, edited by Arna Bontemps, with a foreword by Abble Niles (1941. Reprint. London: Sedgwick & Jackson, 1957).

Two works not specifically concerned with black entertainers in the American theater but which relate contributions to the profession are those by Harry Birdoff, *The World's Greatest Hit: Uncle Tom's Cabin* (New York: S. F. Varni, 1947) and Gerald Bordman, *American Musical Theatre: A Chronicle* (New York: Oxford University Press, 1978). Probably the most indispensable work for research on this topic is the fifteen-volume compilation by George Odell, *Annals of the New York Stage* (New York: Columbia University Press, 1927-1949). Odell recorded daily and year-by-year the names of those appearing on the stages of New York, along with as much information about each appearance as he could gather. The work is essential for dating the activities and the roles and repertory performed by minor, as well as major figures in the American theater, including Afro-Americans.

Many of the musicians who performed on the American stage were also involved in the early history of ragtime, blues, and jazz. Afro-American musicians who were active as instrumentalists are often covered in works dealing with stage personalities. The previously cited *100 Years of the Negro in Show Business*, by Tom Fletcher, and W. C. Handy's *Father of the Blues: An Autobiography*, are especially useful. Additional facts about early instrumentalists are found in works by Imamu Amiri Baraka, *Blues People* (New York: William Morrow, 1963); Albert McCarthy, *Big Band Jazz* (London: G. P. Putnam's Sons, 1974); and Giles Oakley, *The Devil's Music: A History of the Blues* (New York: Taplinger, 1977).

Many Afro-American musicians began their careers performing in circus bands. Information about these musicians may be found in several important sources, including John and Alice Durant, *Pictorial History of the American Circus* (New York: A. S. Barnes, 1957); Charles Phillip Fox and Tom Parkinson, *The Circus in America* (Waukesha, Wis.: Country Beautiful, 1969); and Gene

178 KECK AND MARTIN

Plowden, *Those Amazing Ringlings and Their Circus* (Caldwell, Idaho: Coston, 1967).

The Circus Scrapbook, published in Jersey City, New Jersey, from 1929 to 1932, includes many articles with information about Afro-American musicians. For information about women performers, consult D. Antoinette Handy, *Black Women in American Bands and Orchestras* (Metuchen, N.J.: Scarecrow Press, 1981).

Finally, scholars in this field should be aware of the Negro Collection in The Trevor-Arnett Library at Atlanta University. The collection consists of over ten thousand items relating to the history and development of black culture. Over six thousand items are readily accessible through an index compiled by Atlanta University and Bell & Howell entitled *Bell & Howell Black Culture Collection Catalog*, 3 vols. (Wooster, Oh.: Bell & Howell, 1974). Authors are listed in volume 1, titles in volume 2, and subjects in volume 3. Items included in this index are selected from primary sources dealing with the development of black culture in the United States.

Index

About the Contributors

RONALD HENRY HIGH is Assistant Professor of Music at South Carolina State College in Orangeburg. He has contributed articles to the *National Association of Teachers of Singing Journal* and wrote the biography of avant-garde writer, Russell Atkins, for volume 41 of the *Dictionary of Literary Biography of Afro-American Writers*.

ELLISTINE PERKINS HOLLY is Assistant Professor of Music at Jackson State University in Jackson, Mississippi. Her research has centered around nineteenth- and twentieth-century black music and musicians in Chicago. She has published articles in the *Black Music Research Newsletter*, a publication of the Center for Black Music Research, Columbia College, Chicago.

ROBIN HOUGH is Assistant Professor of Religion at Central Michigan University. His research interests include Reverend Marshall W. Taylor, The Cleveland Colored Quintette, and the interaction between black religious music traditions and the evangelical religious tradition in America.

CAROLYNE LAMAR JORDAN serves as assistant to the president of Suffolk University in Boston. Her recent research interests include female singers and nineteenth-century women's studies. She has published a chapter, "The Music of World Cultures," in *Exploring Music*.

GEORGE R. KECK is Professor of Music at Ouachita Baptist University in Arkadelphia, Arkansas. For four years he was editor of the *Arkansas State Music Teacher* and is the author of *Francis Poulenc: A Bio-Bibliography*, published by Greenwood Press. His research interests include nineteenth-century American music and music of the twentieth century.

SHERRILL V. MARTIN is Associate Professor of Music at the University of North Carolina in Wilmington. She has served as National Musicology Chairman and National American Music Chairman for the Music Teachers National Association, as well as National Musicology Editor for the *American Music Teacher*. She received the National Federation of Music Clubs Merit Award in 1979 for her lecture recitals in American music. Her research interests include women in music and the music of Afro-Americans.

ORAL L. MOSES is Assistant Professor of Voice and Music Literature at Kennesaw College in Marietta, Georgia. He held a Thomas J. Watson Fellowship for study and performance in Europe. He continues to pursue a career as a recitalist while engaged in research on black American spirituals and gospel music.

ANN SEARS is Associate Professor of Music and Director of Performance at Wheaton College, Norton, Massachusetts. Her research interests include women composers, Afro-American keyboard composers, and twentieth-century American music. She is an active performer in New England, well-known for performances of chamber music, music by women composers, and American music.

LOUIS D. SILVERI is Professor of History at Assumption College in Worcester, Massachusetts. His research interest is the American South and Oral History, and he has published numerous articles on both subjects. He is the co-founder of the New England Oral History Association. Under a grant from the Hillsdale Fund of Greensboro, North Carolina, he established at the University of North Carolina at Asheville an oral history collection about the mountain people of Western North Carolina.

CLIFFORD EDWARD WATKINS is Professor of Music and Chair of the Music Department at the North Carolina Agricultural and Technical State University at Greensboro. He is a former military bandsman and high school and university band director whose research interest is Afro-American pioneers of the modern show and military bands. His publications include several original compositions and biographical studies of Fetaque Sanders and Chick Chavis.